IMAGES
of America

WAKULLA COUNTY

Eddie Page

ARCADIA
PUBLISHING

ISBN 978-0-7385-1371-3

Published by Arcadia Publishing
Charleston, South Carolina

Printed in the United States of America

Library of Congress Catalog Card Number: 2001090616

For all general information contact Arcadia Publishing at:
Telephone 843-853-2070
Fax 843-853-0044
E-mail sales@arcadiapublishing.com
For customer service and orders:
Toll-Free 1-888-313-2665

Visit us on the Internet at www.arcadiapublishing.com

This book is dedicated with love to Edward and Peggy Page.

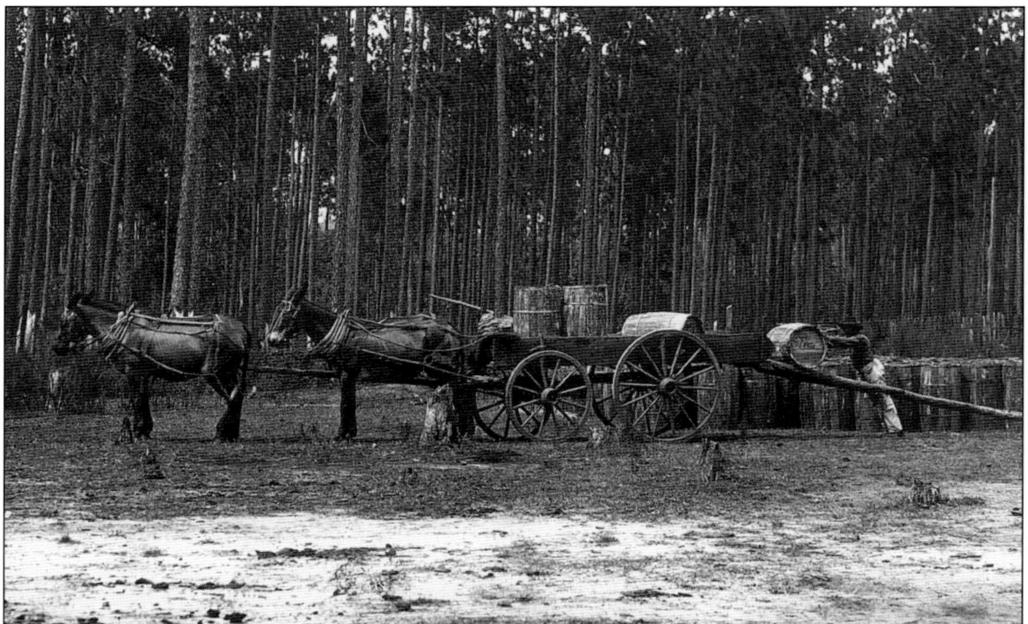

Turpentine barrels are loaded onto a wagon in the 1920s. (Courtesy Florida Photographic Collection.)

IMAGES
of America

WAKULLA COUNTY

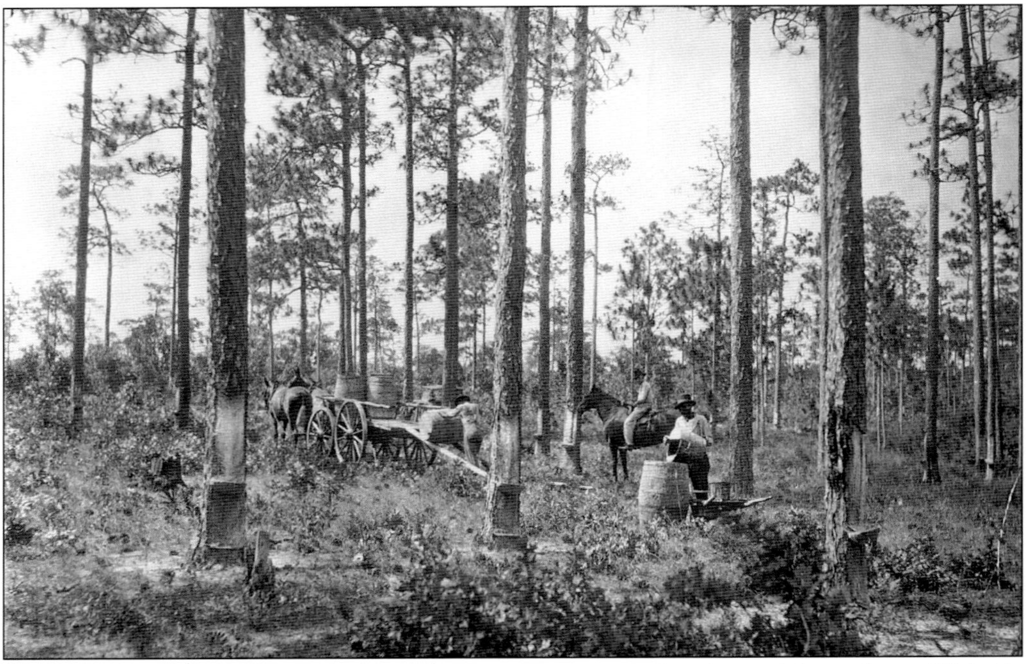

Dense forests producing timber, saw logs, turpentine, and pulpwood have been Wakulla County's greatest economic resource for decades. Sawmills and turpentine camps, in addition to providing employment, also brought large numbers of people to the county. Workers in these two photographs are collecting turpentine in the 1920s. (Both photos courtesy Florida Photographic Collection.)

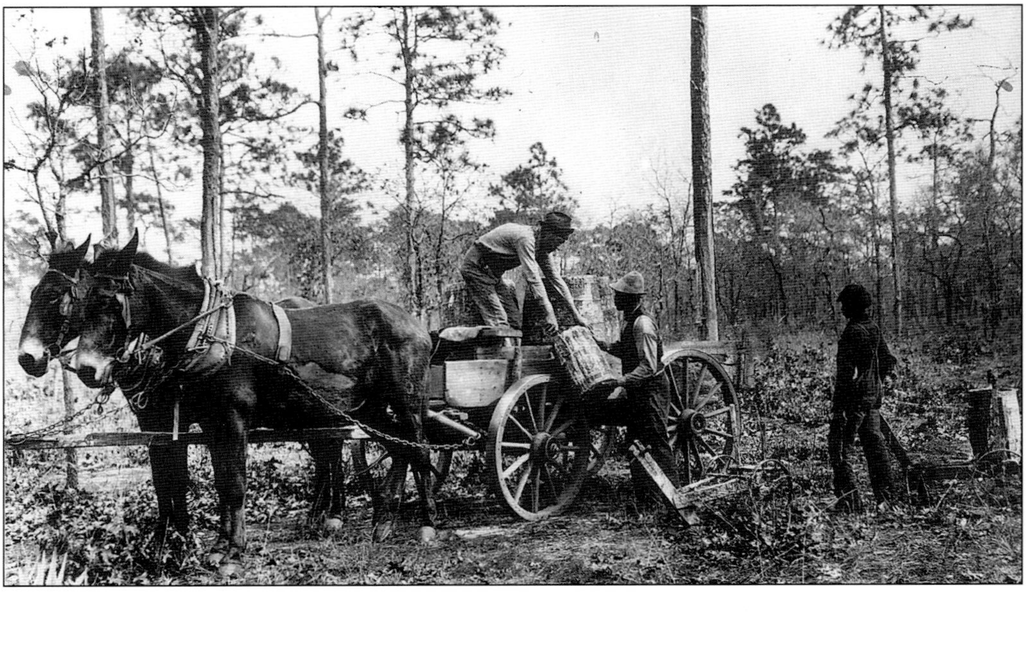

Contents

ACKNOWLEDGMENTS

I would like to thank the following people who generously shared their time, information, and photographs. Without their help this work could not have been possible. They are Ivary Adams, Carol Allbritton, Fred "Booker T." Allen, Freeman Ashmore, Lizzie Barwick, Mike Begley, Virginia Branch, Malcolm Brett, Jon Bridges, Monette Brooks, Joy Brown, Donna Jo Card, Marylou Carter, George Childress, Ernie Cox, Genie Cox, Melvin Cozart, Audrey Crum, Donnie Crum, Eloise Crum, Glynwood Crum, Rosa Lee Crum, Kathryn DeShirlia, Janalyn Dowden, Jenny Druda, John Ferrell, Johnny Ferrell, Dr. John Foster, Marjorie Ann Freeman, Joyce Fryson, Vera Geddy, Don Gavin, Betty Green, Inez Gresham, Andrew Hargrett Jr., Cliff Harper, Naomi Harper Buchan, John D. Harvey, Guinn Haskins, Dr. Jeff Howard, Jerelene Howard, Mott Howard, Florence Jackson, Mary Triplett Jackson, Thelma Jernigan, Terri Johnson, Doug Jones, Lily Jean Jordan, Arlo Kelly, Fred Kinsey, George Kochaniec Jr., Newell Ladd, Edna Lambert, Patrick and Patsy Langston, Tommie Lee and Frenchie Lewis, Barbara Ann Linton (deceased), Ann Little, Eva Linda Lobdill, Garrett Lockley, William Lynn, Betty Lyons, John Massey, Inez Maxey, Johnnie McCallister, Emily Merritt, Herman Metcalf, Dr. James Miller, Chip Morrison, H.D. and Mildred Musgrove, Fred and Rachel Oliver, Buddy Page, Edward and Peggy Page, Dr. Luther Pararo Jr., Daisy Petty, Earlene Pigott, Don and Jean Piplack, Othan and Lila Porter, Robert Porter, Callie Quigg, Maurice Raker, Betty Reeves, Clarence Rehwinkel, James Revell, Mable Roberts, Mary Beth Roberts, Dr. and Mrs. W.F. Robison Jr., David Roddenberry, Dr. William Rogers, Sara Ruryk, Alton Russ, Shirley Ann Sanders, Myrtle Shields, Josephus and Jessie Shingles, Lee and Barbara Spears, George and Eloise Strickland Sr., Tony Strickland, Lavon and Patsy Tadlock, Clarice Taff, Houston Taff, Ron and Linda Thompson, Brent Thurmond, Anita Townsend, Roscoe Triplett, Wakulla County Historical Society, William May Walker Jr., Tony Bill Ward, Vivian Weaver, Ron Weiss, Elder Emmett and Celia Whaley, Anne Williams, Mae Williams, Ruth Williams, Vilena Williams, Alberta Williamson, and Ava Culbreath Wilson. Special thanks are given to Joan Morris and her staff at the Florida State Archive Photo Collection for patiently and courteously making available many of the photos in this collection.

INTRODUCTION

That the name Wakulla is of Native-American origin is beyond dispute. What it actually means, however, is open to interpretation. When Wakulla County was established on March 11, 1843, it took the name of the large spring that had attracted visitors from as early as the Paleoindian period (12,000–9,500 BC). According to James Clarence Simpson in the 1956 publication *A Provisional Gazetteer of Florida Place-Names of Indian Derivation*, the name Wakulla comes from the Spanish spelling of an unknown Timucuan word. The Spanish spelling of "Guacara" became modified in pronunciation by the Indians resulting in Wakulla. In *Florida Place-Names of Indian Origins* (1934), William Read points out that Wakulla may derive from the Creek Indian word for a loon, "wahkola." Most modern sources, however, interpret Wakulla to mean "mystery" although no factual evidence exists to support it.

Blessed with abundant resources such as rivers, dense forests, and miles of coastline along the Gulf of Mexico, generations of Wakulla County residents have been afforded a means of economic survival amid its natural beauty. Wakulla also contains four springs (the highest number in the state) designated as first-magnitude, meaning that their average flow exceeds 100 cubic feet of water per second. A significant portion of the county retains its pristine condition as over three-quarters of the county's total acreage (388,300 acres) is contained within the Apalachicola National Forest, the Aucilla Wildlife Management Area, and the St. Marks National Wildlife Refuge, which protect tens of thousands of acres of timber, marsh, and coastal estuaries.

The men, women, and children who appear in this book represent only a tiny fraction of the many individuals who have contributed to a history that dates from well before the Spanish conquest. It is hoped that this work will serve as a small reminder of the thousands whose individual contributions helped create and sustain Wakulla County. As one of the fastest growing counties in the state, Wakulla's future promises to be every bit as exciting as its past.

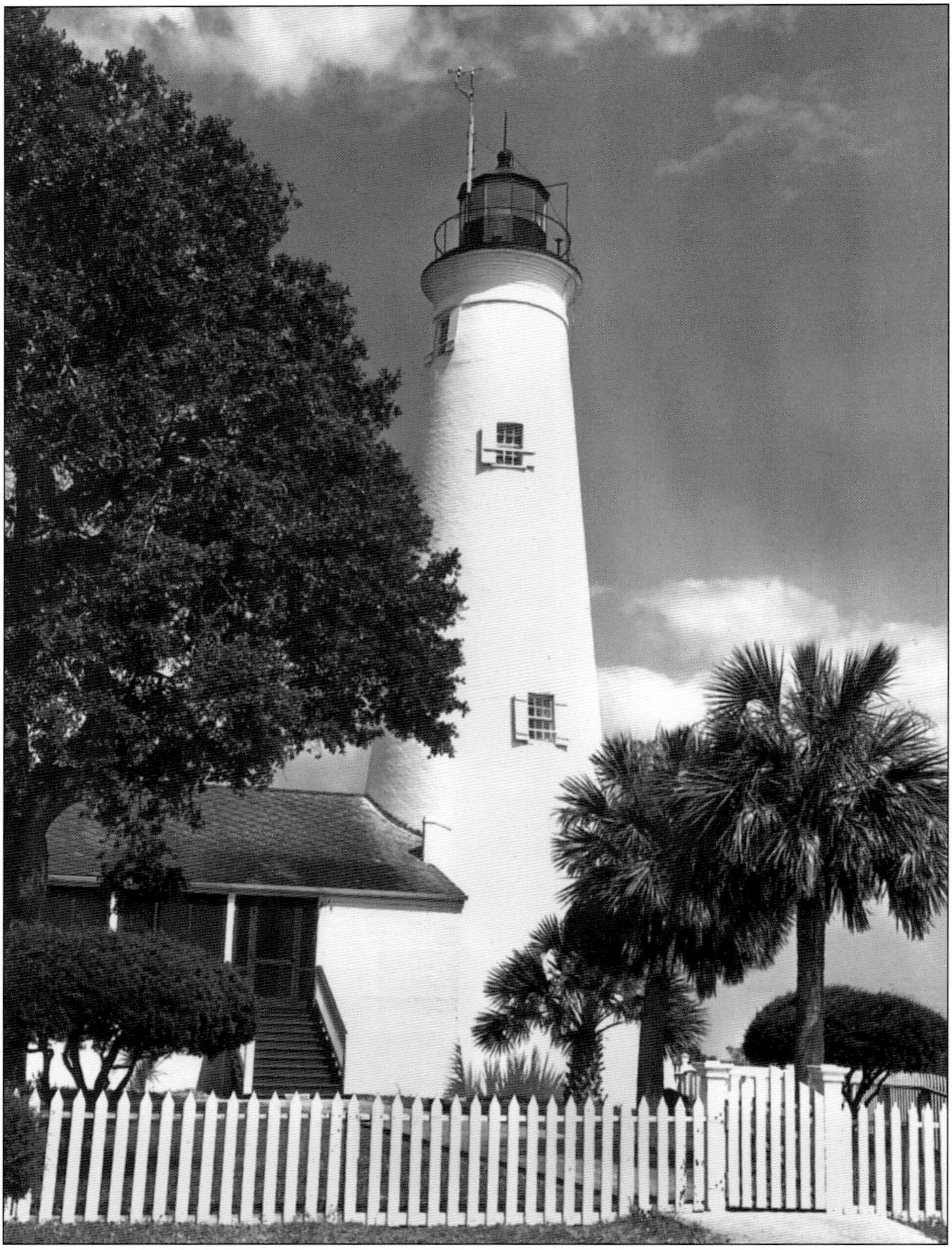

The St. Marks lighthouse is seen here as it appeared in the 1960s. (Courtesy Florida Photographic Collection.)

One

St. Marks

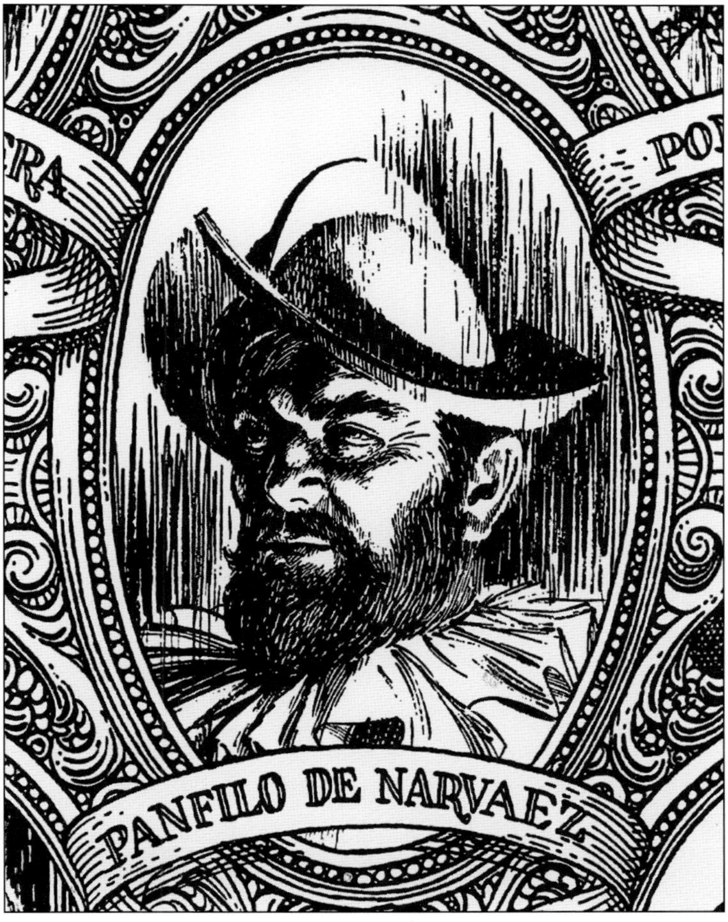

The first European to explore the interior of Florida was Panfilo de Narvaez (c. 1478–1528). In July of 1528, Narvaez entered the Apalachee Indian village of Aute near the mouth of the St. Marks River. Struck by illness and abandoning its search for gold, members of the ill-fated expedition were forced to escape the hostile Indians aboard five make-shift boats. (Courtesy Florida Photographic Collection.)

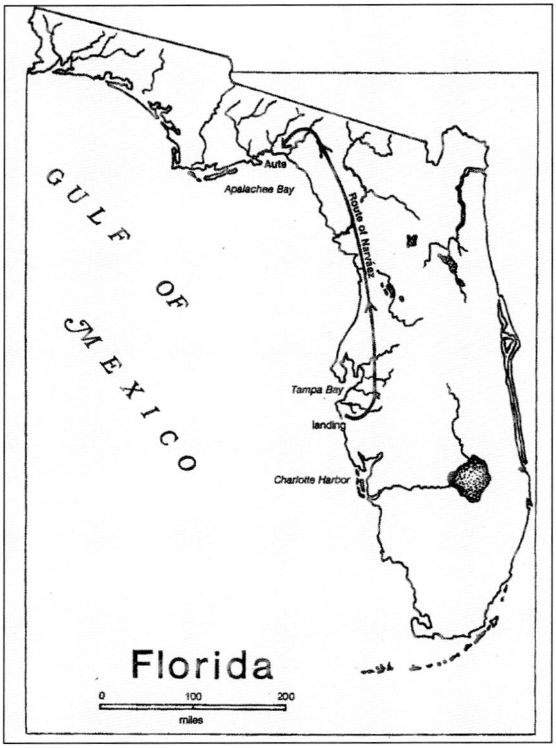

Landing in the Tampa Bay area in April of 1528, Narvaez and a force of 300 men spent several weeks in the St. Marks area preparing for escape. Constructing a simple forge and using all the materials at their disposal, the party assembled five crude boats and set sail out into Apalachee Bay. Narvaez and the majority of his men were lost at sea. (Reprinted courtesy of the University Press of Florida.)

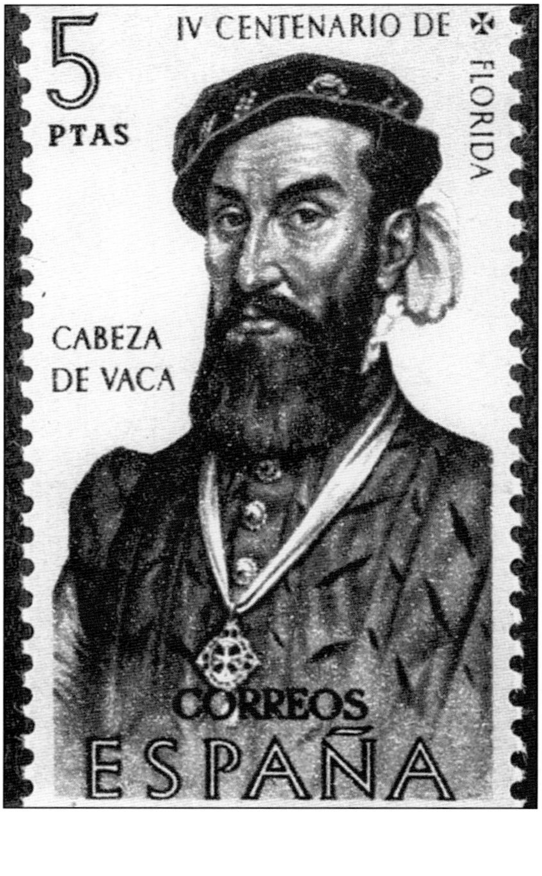

Accompanying Narvaez on his journey was Alvar Nuñez Cabeza de Vaca (*c.* 1490–1560). One of only four survivors, De Vaca washed ashore near Pensacola where he wandered westward for over seven years before being found and returned to Spain. His narrative account of the Narvaez expedition provides one of the earliest descriptions of the area's Apalachee Indian tribe and culture. (Courtesy Florida Photographic Collection.)

In 1539, Hernando de Soto (*c.* 1500–1542) led a successful expedition into the Florida interior. In September, de Soto moved into the St. Marks region, discovering the area where the doomed Narvaez party had prepared for its escape 11 years earlier. In late October, a Spanish ship sailed into Apalachee Bay for the first time bringing supplies to de Soto who would continue his journey north. (Courtesy Florida Photographic Collection.)

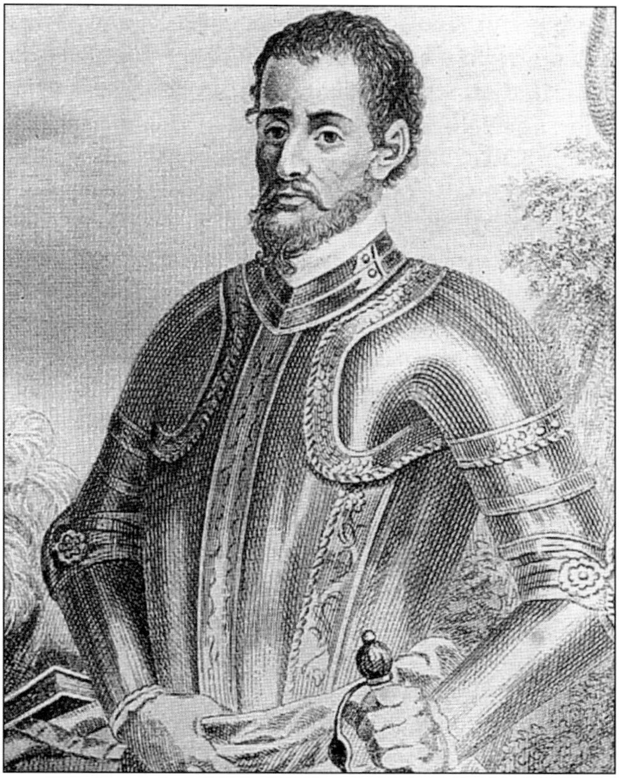

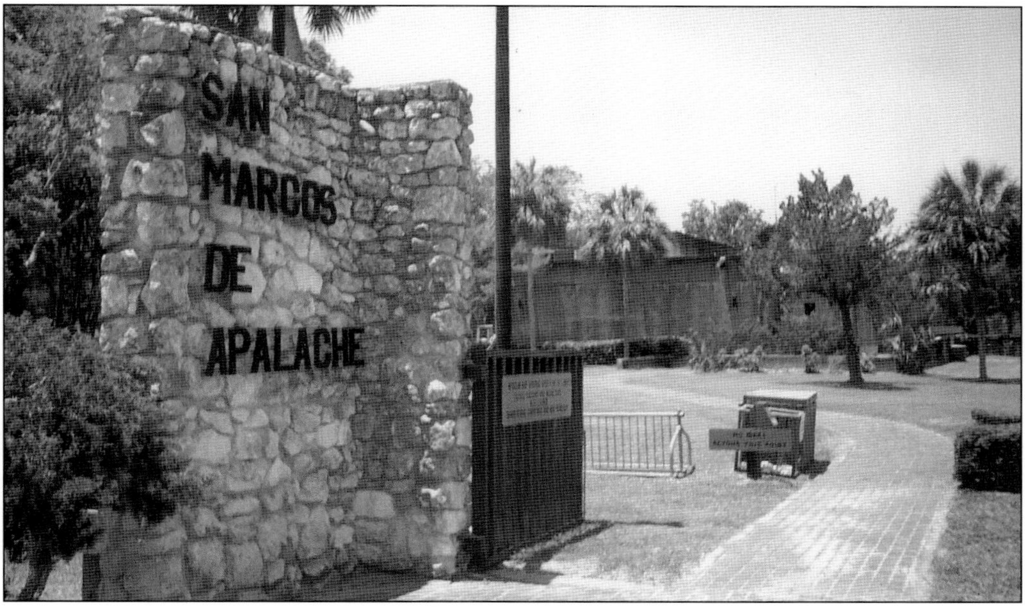

Central to the history of St. Marks is Fort San Marcos de Apalachee, "one of the few relics of the Spanish colonial period remaining in Florida." The point at the confluence of the St. Marks and Wakulla Rivers has been host to a series of forts occupied by Spanish, British, and American forces since 1679. In 1861 the site was refortified by Confederates and named Fort Ward. In 1963, the site was purchased by the state and designated as the San Marcos de Apalachee Historic State Park. (Courtesy Peggy Page.)

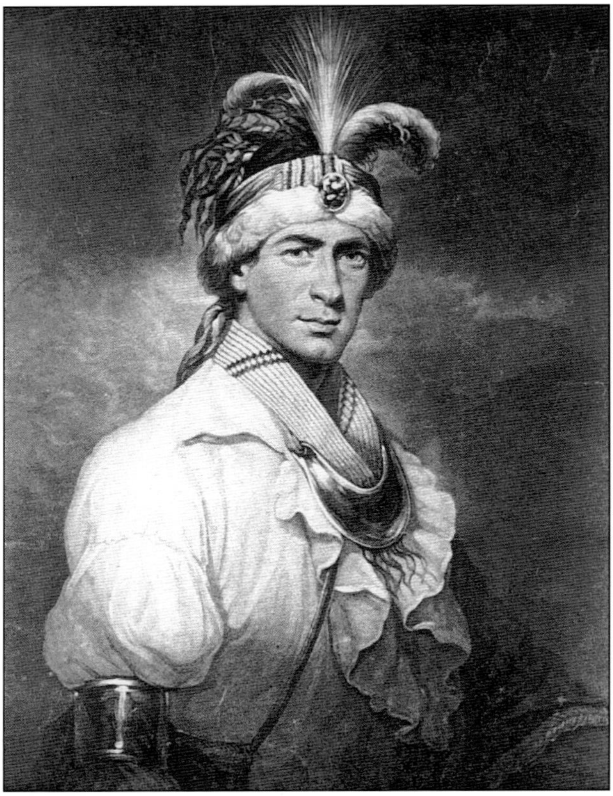

In May of 1800, English adventurer William Augustus Bowles (1763–1805) and followers captured the Panton, Leslie, and Company trading post located upriver from Fort San Marcos to end the firm's trading monopoly among the Native Americans. Declaring himself director general of the Creek Nation and establishing the Nation of Muskogee, Bowles and his Indian band also declared war on Spain, forcing the fort's commandant to surrender. Holding the fort for several weeks, Bowles was ultimately driven out and captured. He died in a Havana prison. (Courtesy Florida Photographic Collection.)

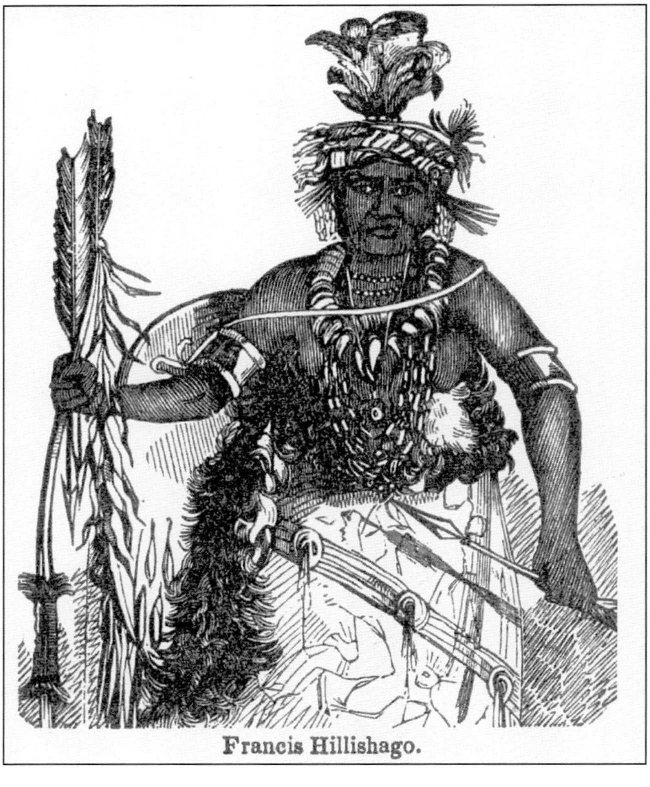

Francis Hillishago.

As the result of the 1813–1814 campaign against the Creek Indians in Florida by Andrew Jackson, the colorful Creek chief Hillis Hadjo, also known as the Prophet Francis, was driven into Spanish Florida, settling near Fort San Marcos. Sympathetic to the British cause in Florida, Francis was unfortunate in seeking refuge in Fort San Marcos as it was seized by Jackson in 1818. Charged with inciting hostilities among the Indian people, he was hanged at the fort on April 7, 1818. (Courtesy Florida Photographic Collection.)

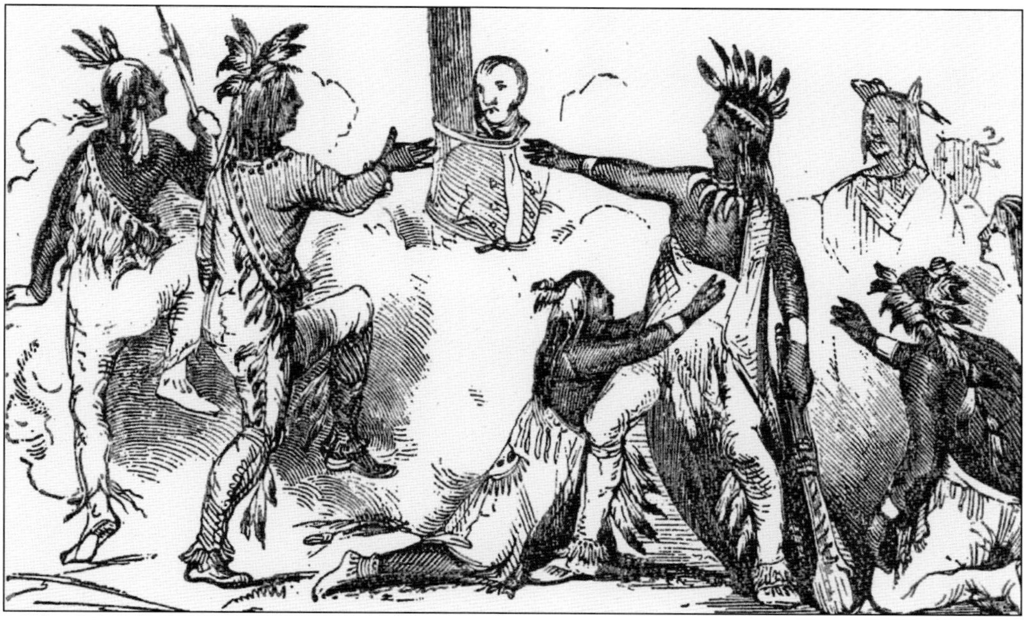

In March of 1818, during Jackson's march to Fort San Marcos, Pvt. Duncan McKrimmon was captured by Indians and taken to the town of the Prophet Francis on the Wakulla River where it was ordered that he be shot. Learning of the impending execution, Francis's 15-year-old daughter Millie successfully fought for his release. After her father was executed by Jackson, Millie left the area and moved west. In 1844, in appreciation for her act of humanity, an act was passed in Congress providing Millie with a pension of $96. The act also called for a medal to be struck in her honor. Unfortunately by the time the pension and medal reached the "Florida Pocahontas," as she was then called, she lay dying of tuberculosis. She died May 19, 1848, at the age of approximately 45. (Courtesy Florida Photographic Collection.)

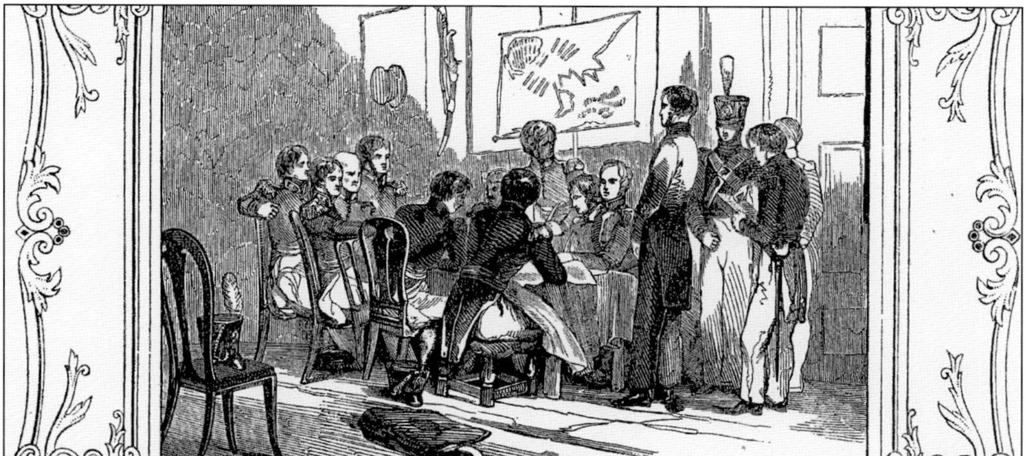

In April of 1818, Andrew Jackson led a force into St. Marks for the purpose of capturing two British subjects accused of "inciting the Indians to hostilities." Seizing Fort San Marcos from the Spanish, Jackson had Robert Ambrister and Alexander Arbuthnot arrested and court-martialed. Arbuthnot was hanged and Armbrister shot on the morning of April 29th. Control of the fort was returned to the Spanish and Jackson departed. Reaction to the executions was severe among the Spanish, British, and American governments but soon subsided. Seen here is the trial of Ambrister. (Courtesy Florida Photographic Collection.)

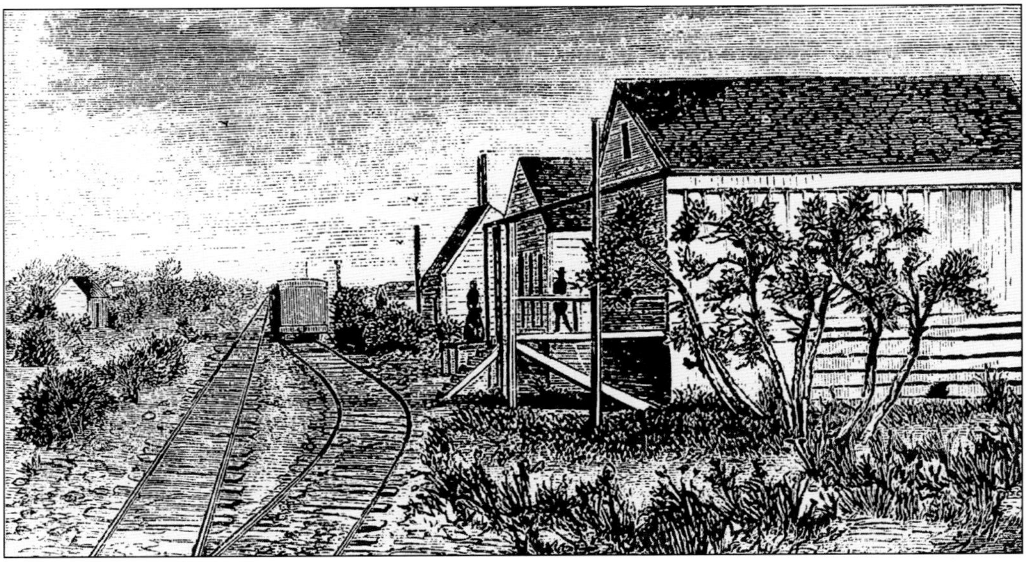

Completed in 1837 to allow Middle Florida cotton planters a more direct route in delivering their crops to the shipping port at St. Marks, the Tallahassee-St. Marks Railroad was the second railroad to have been built in Florida. Two years later the road was extended to the new town of Port Leon where tens of thousands of bales of cotton were shipped until the town's destruction by hurricane in 1843. The road to St. Marks remained in operation for 147 years (the oldest in the state) when in 1984 it became the Tallahassee-St. Marks Historic Railroad State Trail. St. Marks is seen here in an 1870s engraving. (Courtesy Florida Photographic Collection.)

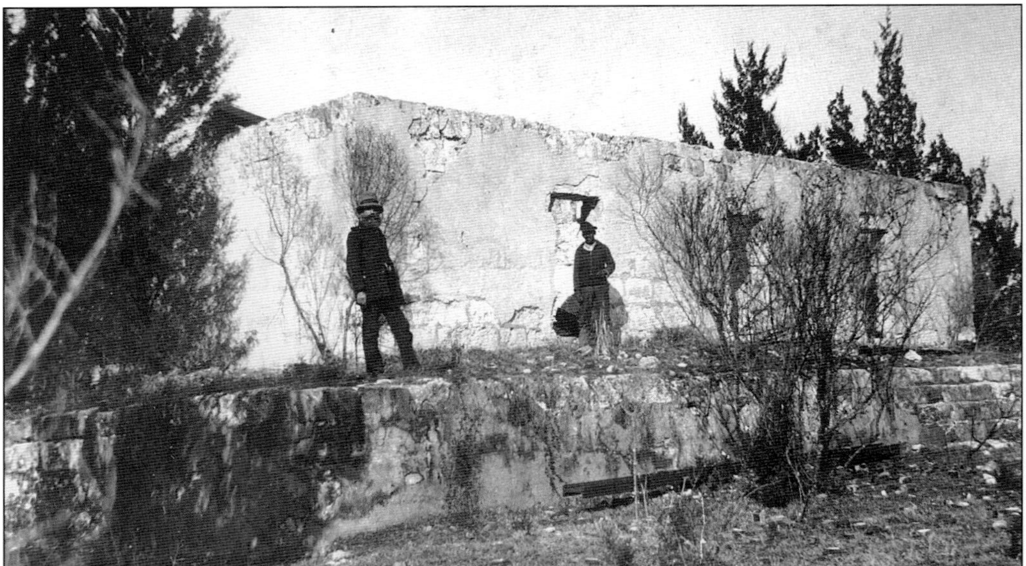

In this 1920s photograph are the remains of the Marine Hospital, which was built by the federal government in 1857. As St. Marks was a thriving port at the time, the hospital was constructed as a place to care for seamen who had contracted yellow fever. Resting on a foundation of stones salvaged from the remains of the 18th-century Spanish Fort San Marcos, the multi-storied hospital was abandoned at the onset of the Civil War and later destroyed by a hurricane. Today the San Marcos de Apalachee State Historic Site visitor center rests upon this foundation. (Courtesy Florida Photographic Collection.)

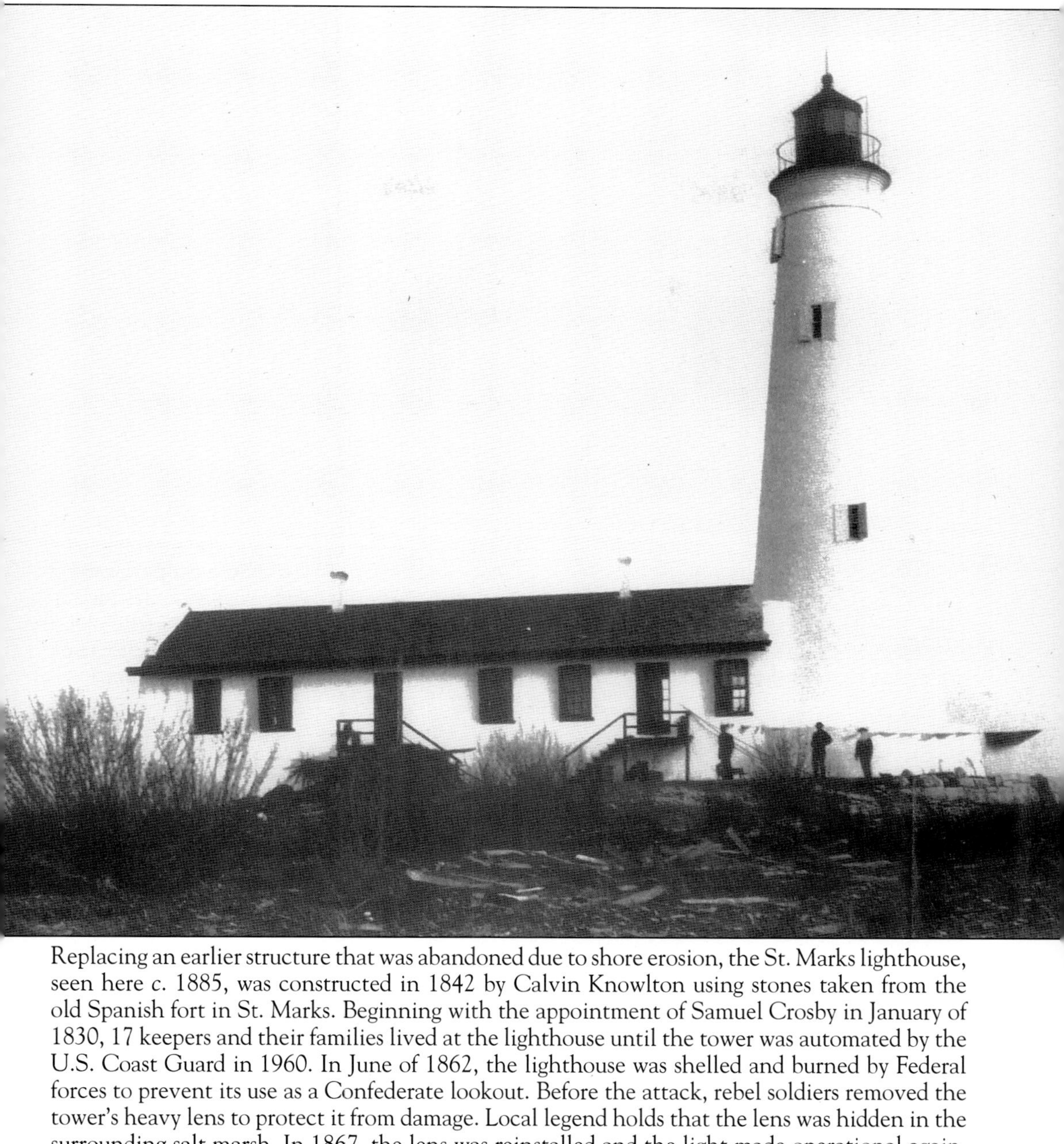

Replacing an earlier structure that was abandoned due to shore erosion, the St. Marks lighthouse, seen here c. 1885, was constructed in 1842 by Calvin Knowlton using stones taken from the old Spanish fort in St. Marks. Beginning with the appointment of Samuel Crosby in January of 1830, 17 keepers and their families lived at the lighthouse until the tower was automated by the U.S. Coast Guard in 1960. In June of 1862, the lighthouse was shelled and burned by Federal forces to prevent its use as a Confederate lookout. Before the attack, rebel soldiers removed the tower's heavy lens to protect it from damage. Local legend holds that the lens was hidden in the surrounding salt marsh. In 1867, the lens was reinstalled and the light made operational again. (Courtesy John Hairr.)

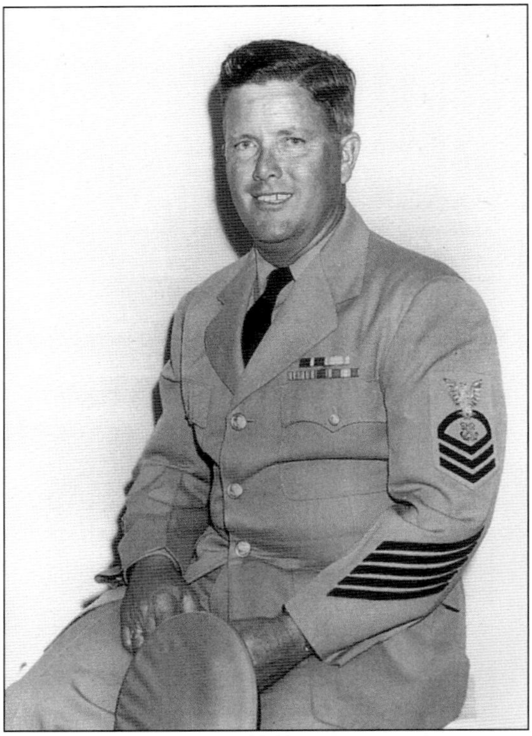

In 1916, John Young Gresham Sr. (1888–1957) became the last full-time keeper of the St. Marks lighthouse, living there with his wife, Lela Fine Gresham, and their eight children. Lela Gresham's parents, Charles and Sarah Fine, had themselves tended the lighthouse for 32 years until failing health forced his retirement. In 1957, Gresham's son Alton T. Gresham Sr. (1912–1999), a member of the U.S. Coast Guard (seen at left in a 1950 photo), secured a transfer to St. Marks and maintained the lighthouse until it was automated in 1960. (Courtesy Inez Gresham.)

This aerial photo from the 1950s shows the lighthouse complex at the time it was maintained by Alton T. Gresham Sr., the last keeper of the tower. The long dock and boathouse seen in the top of the photo was built by Gresham's father, John, who preceded him as keeper. (Courtesy Myrtle Shields.)

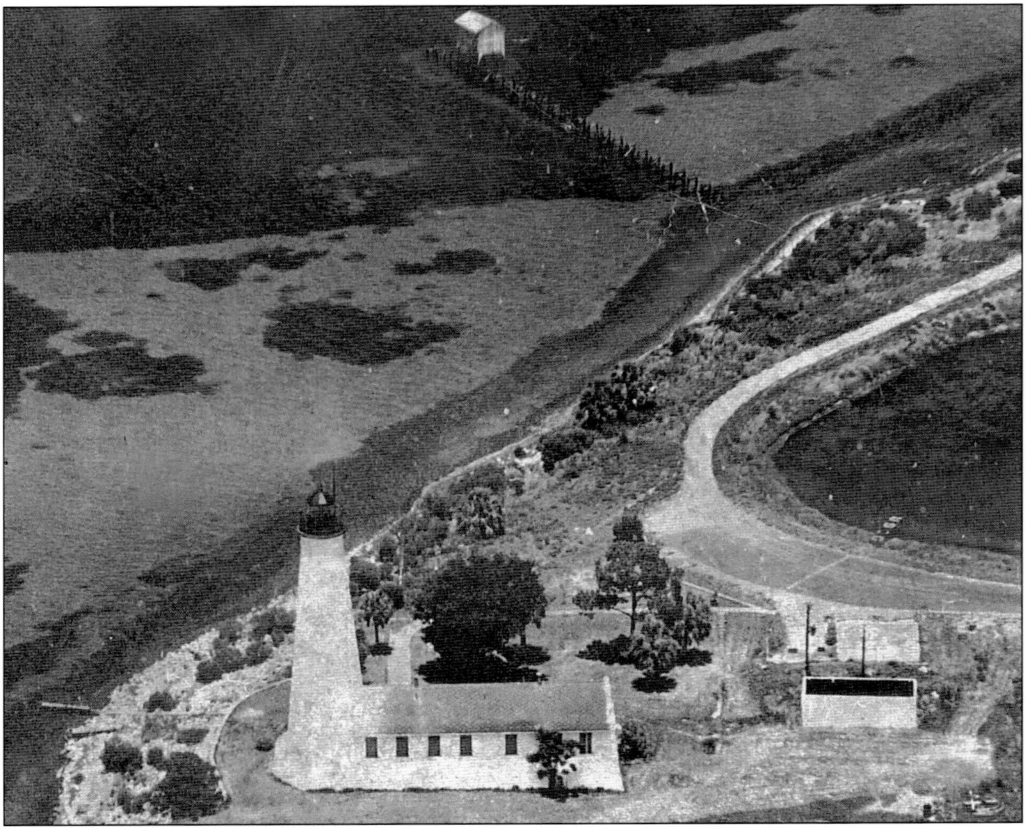

O.P. Shields (1893–1960) was for many years a successful businessman and booster of St. Marks. Moving to the area in 1928, Shields opened a hardware business, in addition to operating several for-hire fishing party boats, and promoted St. Marks as a tourist destination during the 1930s. He was also postmaster from 1936 to 1960. (Courtesy Myrtle Shields.)

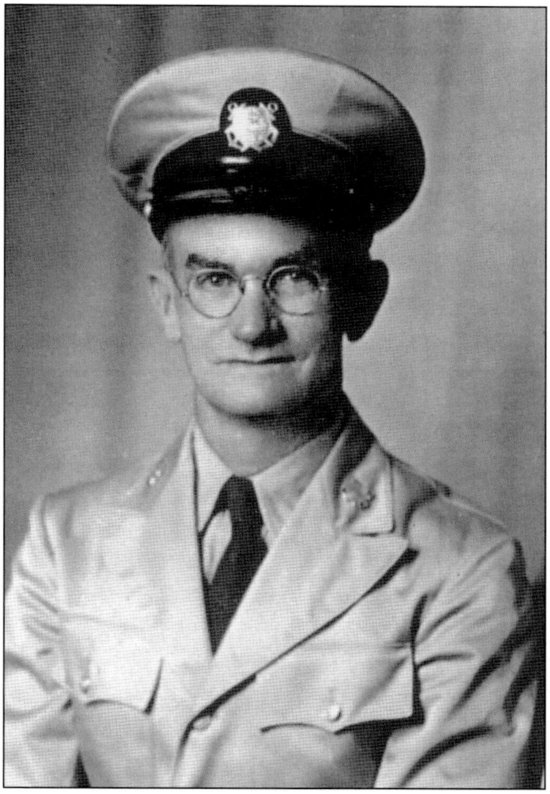

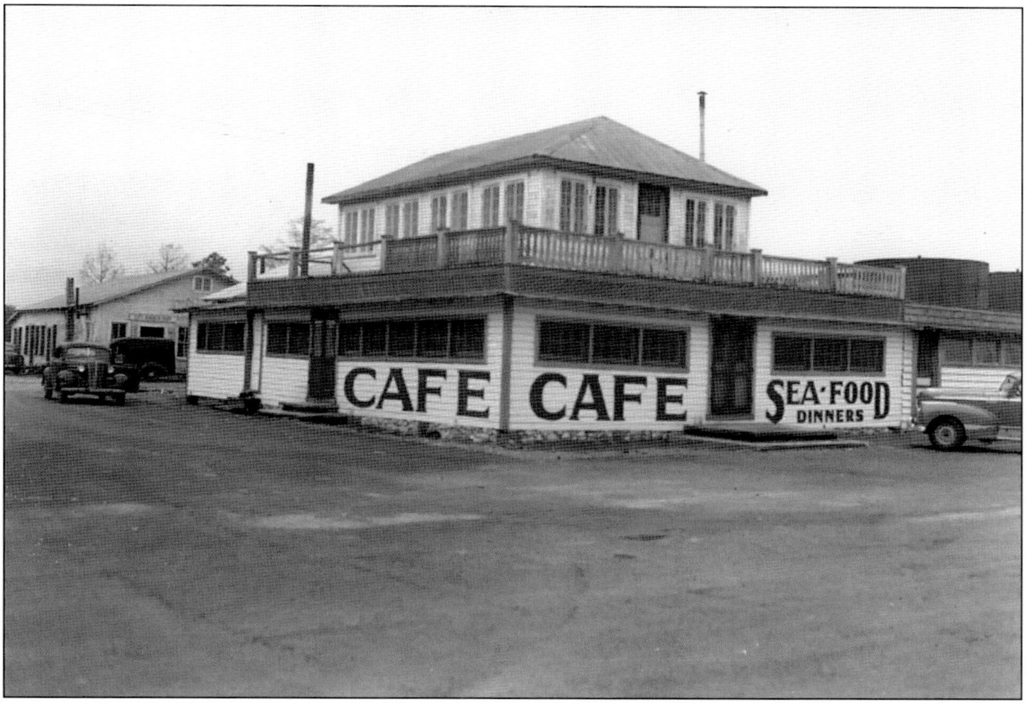

Opened in 1935 by O.P. Shields, the Shields Cafe, seen here in 1947, was one of the county's most popular seafood restaurants for many years. (Courtesy Florida Photographic Collection.)

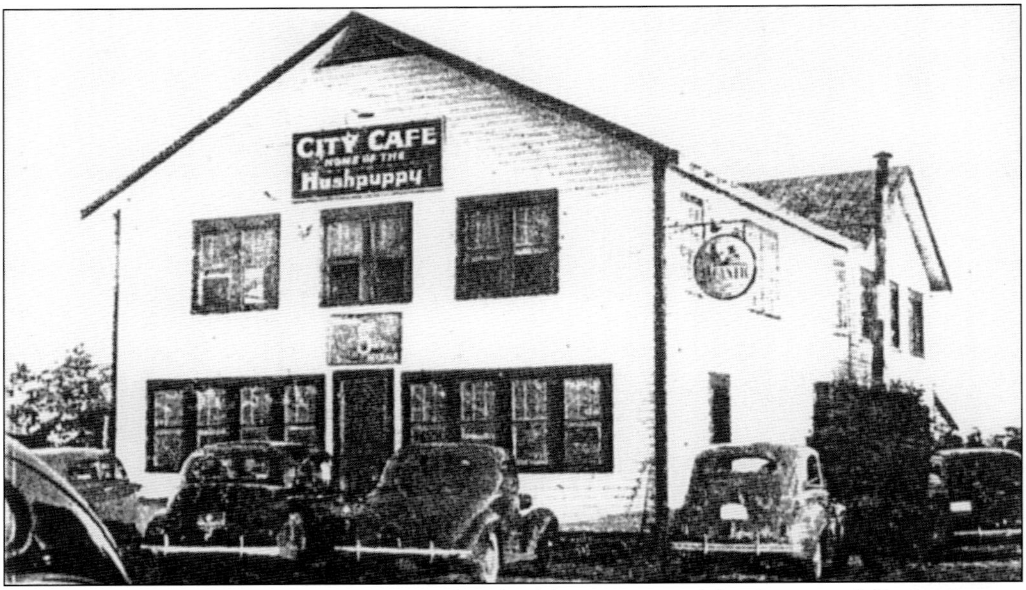

In 1929, replacing a smaller restaurant that had been operated by Steve and Birdie Linton Coggins, T.J. Posey opened the City Cafe in St. Marks. Billing itself as the "Home of the Hushpuppy," the cafe quickly grew from a tiny tin building with three tables to the two-storied structure pictured here in 1942, complete with an upstairs banquet room. Posey, who for many years served as St. Marks mayor and city commissioner, closed the cafe at the end of World War II and reopened it in the early 1950s as Posey's Oyster Bar. (Courtesy author.)

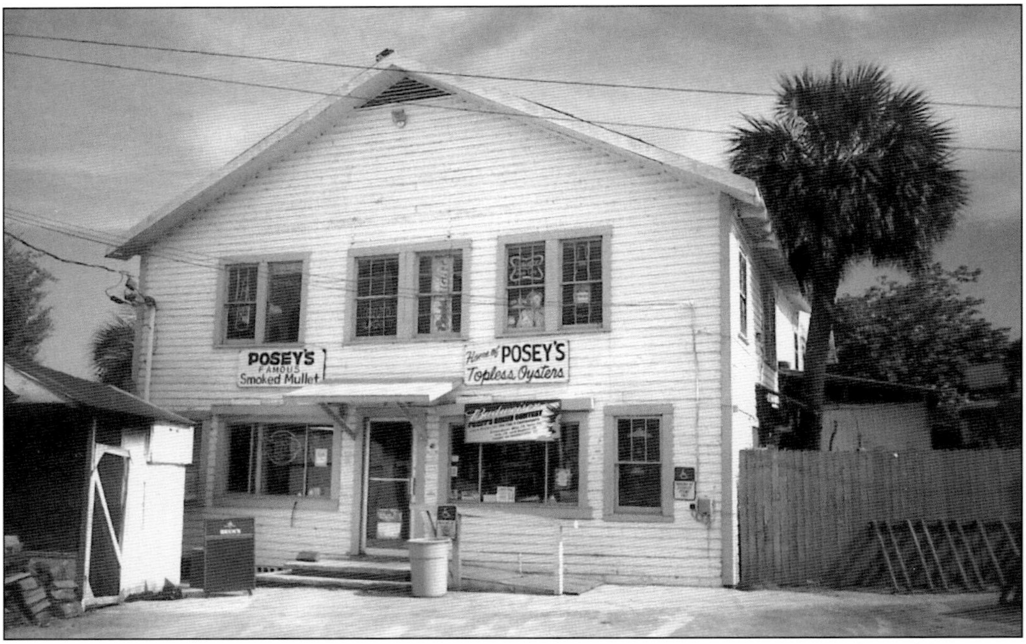

Posey's Oyster Bar remains one of the county's most popular tourist stops. Purchased from T.J. Posey in 1972, it was operated by Bill Helson under the name Posey's Topless Oysters for close to 20 years before Helson sold it to restaurateur Walter Beckham in 1989. Through the years Posey's has become a landmark attracting visitors from around the United States. (Courtesy Peggy Page.)

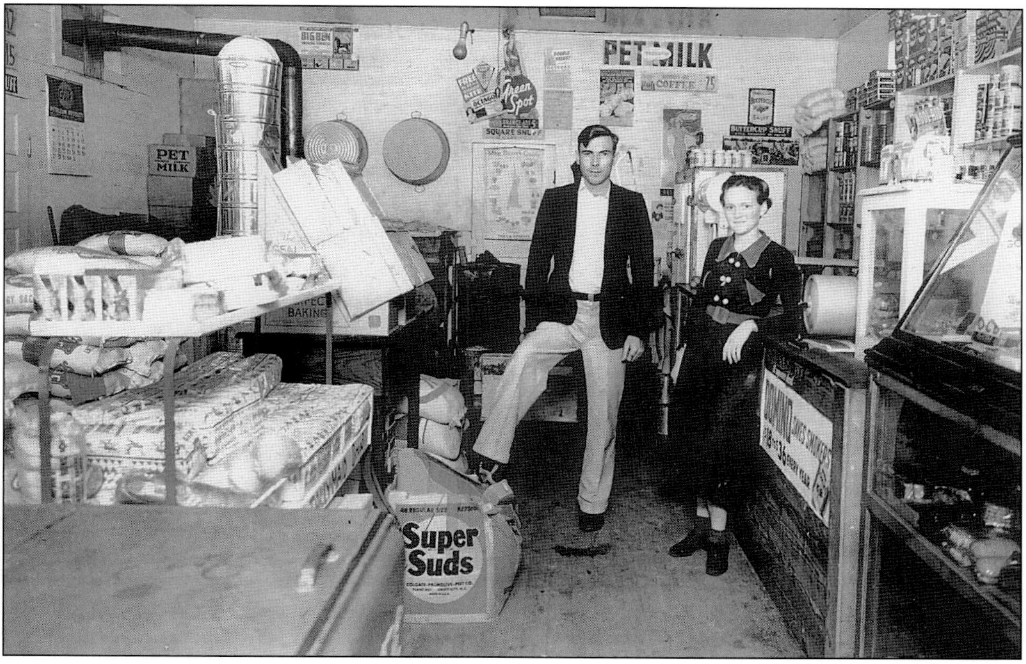

J.T. "Bo" Lynn (1909–1957) is seen here inside his store in 1936 with clerk Louise Bragg. Opened in the early 1930s, the business was operated by Lynn until his accidental drowning in 1957. His wife, Lillian "Lea" Lynn (1913–1994), ran the store until 1965 when it was purchased by Joy Brown of Dublin, Georgia. Ms. Joy continues to operate the store in St. Marks. (Courtesy Joy Brown.)

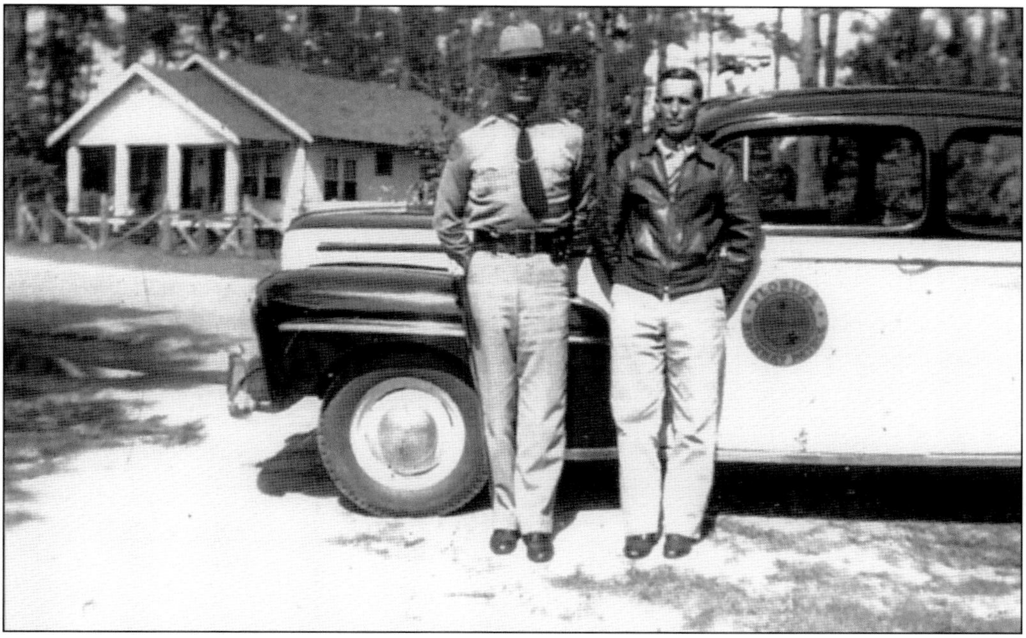

Serving as St. Marks constable in the 1920s and 1930s, Fred Oliver Sr. (1906–1988), on the right, is seen here with an unidentified Florida state trooper shortly after his appointment as a sheriff's deputy in the early 1940s. At his retirement in 1977, Oliver was the county's chief deputy and bailiff. (Courtesy Rachel Oliver.)

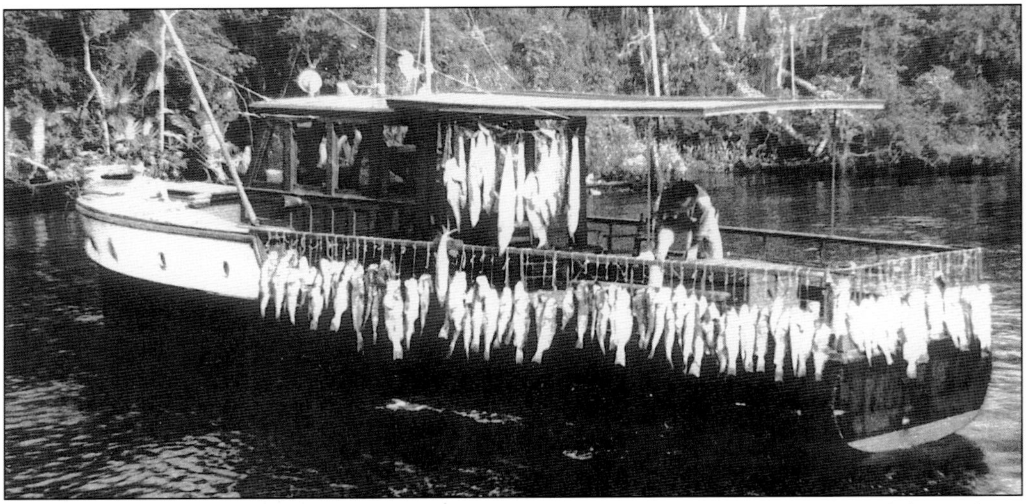

Moving to St. Marks in 1932, William "Heck" Lynn served as an engineer aboard the tugboat *Lapwing* for 14 years before becoming captain of a number of fishing-party boats. This picture from 1956 shows the number of grouper and king mackerel that could be caught on a good day. (Courtesy William Lynn.)

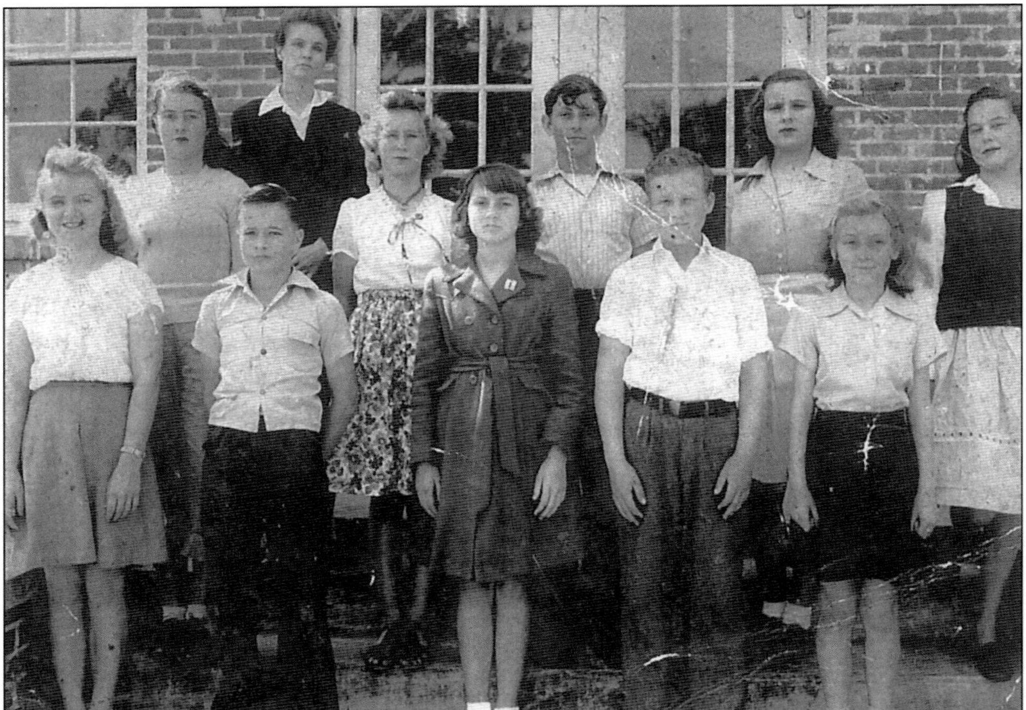

Members of the 1945–1946 seventh-grade class pose outside of the St. Marks school. From left to right are (front row) unidentified, Dave Laque Raker, Bertha Benton, Grover Whaley, and Elna Ward; (back row) June Ouzts, Frances Ladd, Edward Ward, Judy Bishop, and Sarah Tooke; (rear) Teacher Mary Brooks. Replacing an old wooden structure, the St. Marks school was built in 1938 for grades one through eight under the direction of Alberta Glover Williamson, who served as the new school's principal in its first year. From 1951 to 1967, when the school closed, it served grades one through six. (Courtesy Tony Bill Ward.)

Seen here are members of the last eighth grade class to graduate from the St. Marks school in 1950. They are, from left to right, (seated) Genevieve Whaley and Nell Roberts; (standing) Marion Ouzts, Shirley Strickland, and Anita Shields. (Courtesy Myrtle Shields.)

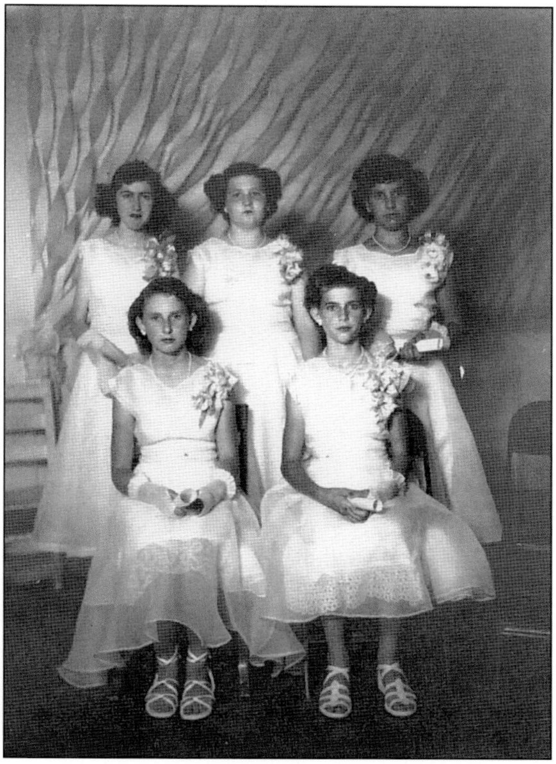

Moving to St. Marks in 1918, Jesse Thomas "Jack" Ward (1896–1979) was a lifelong commercial fisherman. Ward served as St. Marks' first mayor under the city's new incorporation charter. (Courtesy Tony Bill Ward.)

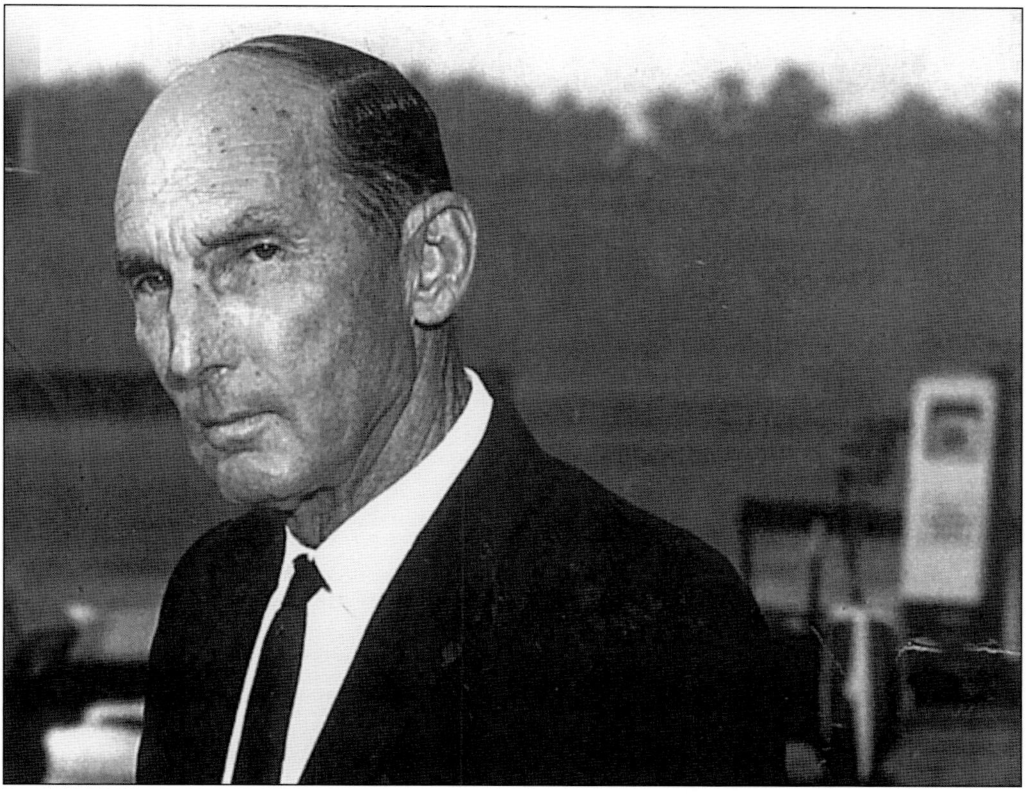

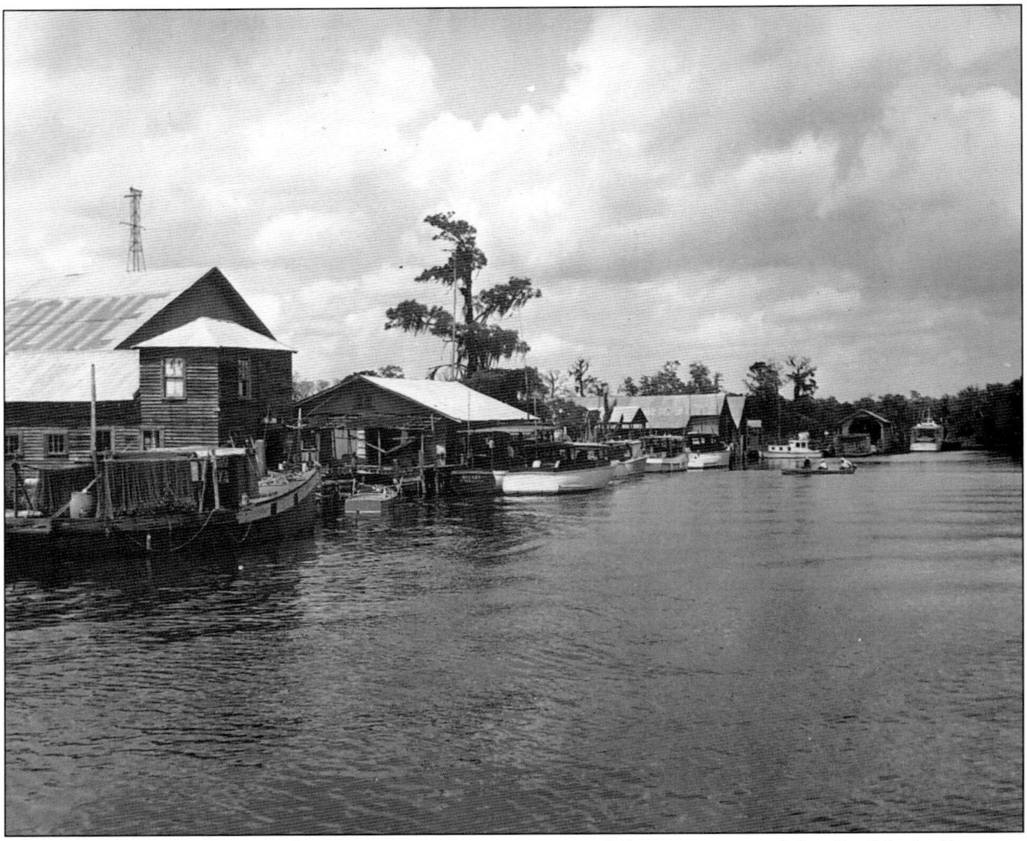

This is a view of the St. Marks River as it appeared in the 1950s. (Courtesy Florida Photographic Collection.)

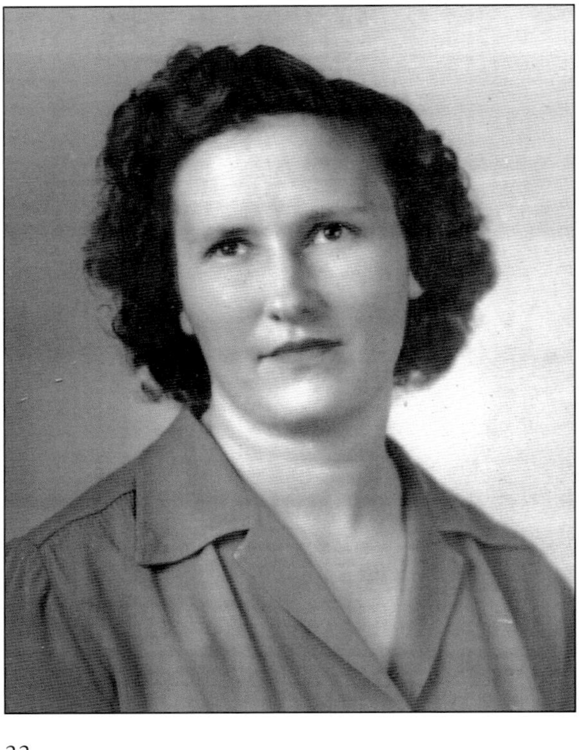

Myrtle Smith Shields is one of the community's most well-known citizens. After the death of her husband, Curtis Shields (1916–1985), who served as mayor for several years, she began painting as a hobby at the age of 67. Her works depict scenes familiar to older area residents in addition to land and seascapes and are displayed in homes and businesses throughout the country. (Courtesy Myrtle Shields.)

Two

Magnolia and Newport

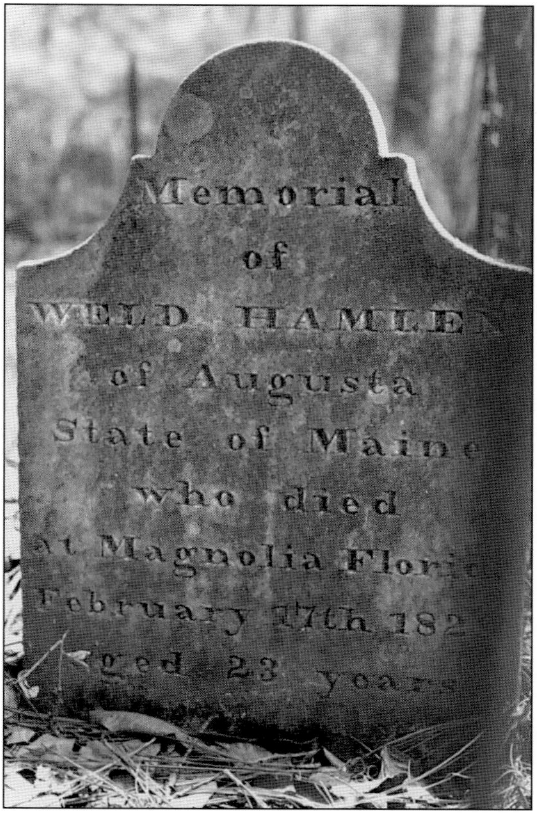

In 1825 John, George, Weld, and Nathaniel Hamlin, four brothers from Augusta, Maine, moved into the Apalachee Bay area approximately eight miles above St. Marks. Purchasing land from the U.S. government they established the port town of Magnolia in hopes of taking advantage of the fast-growing Middle Florida cotton trade. The brothers advertised lots for sale, and the new port town grew quickly in competition with St. Marks. By 1833, it contained four warehouses, a cotton press, three stores, two boarding houses, a saw and grist mill, a post office, and a bank. By 1838, only two brothers, John and Nathaniel, remained in Magnolia and were forced to sell their holdings due to accumulated debt. The town died. The headstone of Weld Hamlin (1805–1829), the oldest in Wakulla County, is all that remains of this once thriving port. (Courtesy Terri Johnson.)

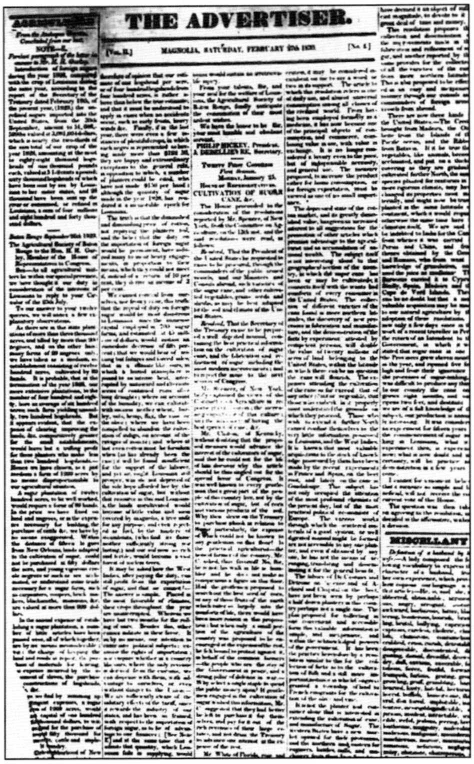

THE ADVERTISER.

MAGNOLIA, SATURDAY, FEBRUARY 27th 1830.

Established in 1828 by Augustus Steele, *The Magnolia Advertiser* served as the town's newspaper during its heyday before ceasing publication two years later. In this issue dated February 27, 1830, the paper relayed agricultural news, an assessment of the current cotton market, and minutes from the 21st Congress. (Courtesy Florida Photographic Collection.)

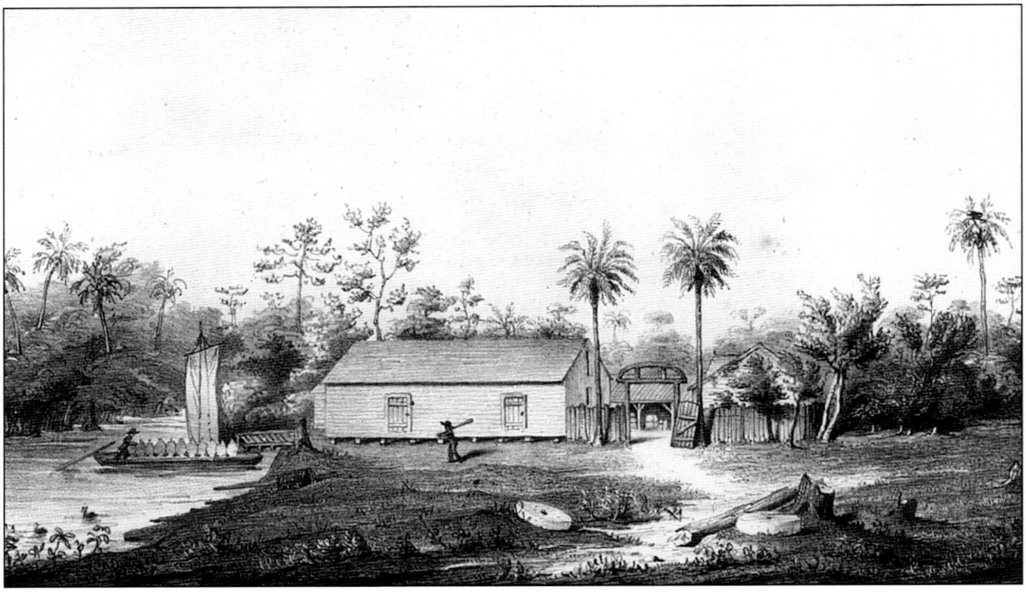

Francis de la Porte, Comte de Castelnau (1812–1880) led a French scientific expedition through Canada, the United States, and Mexico between 1837 and 1841. Between November of 1837 and March of 1838, Castelnau traveled through the Tallahassee-Wakulla area, making a brief stop in Magnolia where this sketch was made. The accompanying caption reads, "Nothing is now left of the town of Magnolia, once a place of some importance on the St. Marks river in Wakulla County, but already in decline when this picture was made." (Courtesy Florida Photographic Collection.)

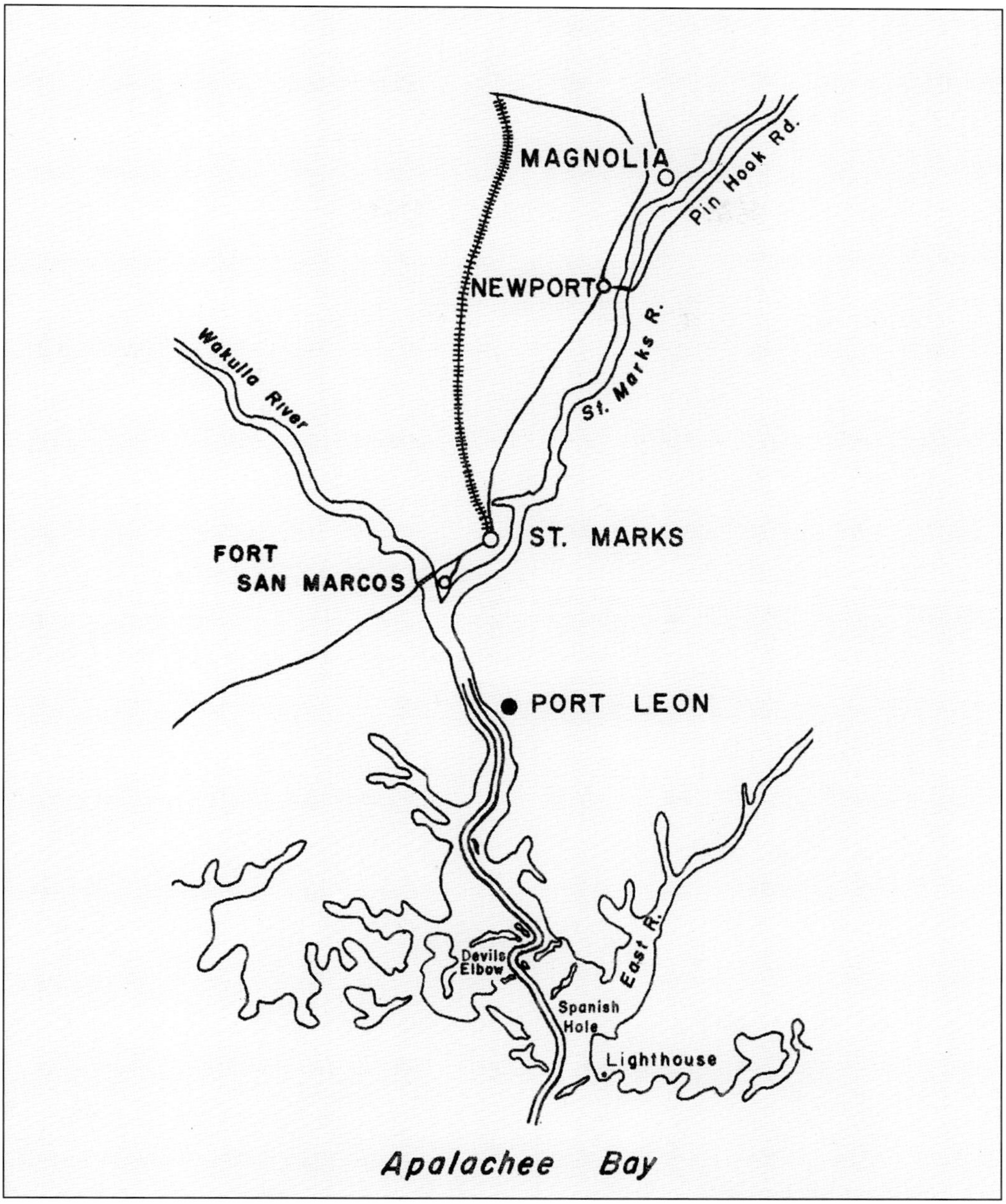

With the demise of Magnolia, Richard Keith Call, along with the Tallahassee-St. Marks Railroad Company, promoted the creation of Port Leon as Middle Florida's new deep-water port. Situated approximately three miles downriver from the crowded harbor at St. Marks, the new town began to be developed in 1838, with the rail line being extended from St. Marks in 1839. By 1843, Port Leon contained warehouses, general merchandise stores, two taverns, and the Port Leon City Hotel. On March 11, 1843, six months after having become the county seat of the newly created Wakulla County, Port Leon was destroyed by a hurricane and abandoned. (Map work done by James N. Reese, FSU Department of Geography, and by Charles Shofner. Reprinted courtesy University Press of Florida.)

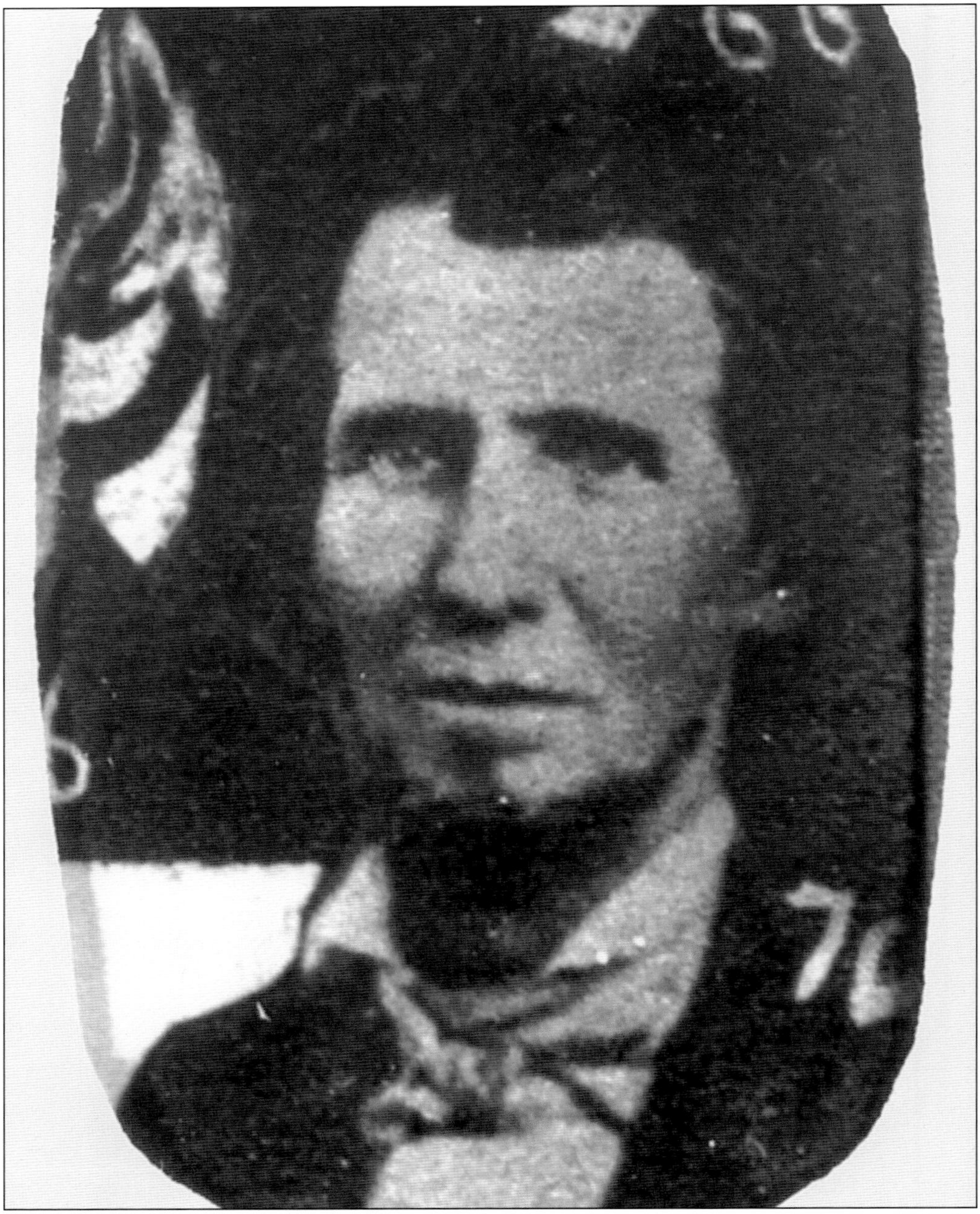

Daniel Ladd (1817–1872) moved to Magnolia from Augusta, Maine in 1833 to work for his uncles, the Hamlin brothers, and he quickly became the area's leading merchant and entrepreneur. After the demise of Magnolia and the destruction of Port Leon in 1843, Ladd was instrumental in establishing the town of Newport and in a few short years was responsible for making it the economic center of the Middle Florida economy. Ladd owned and operated many businesses including warehouses, general merchandise stores, a saw mill, and the Wakulla Iron Works. In 1844, Newport became the county seat and, by 1860, had grown to include a dozen stores, a turpentine still, a saloon, and two hotels. Seriously damaged during the Civil War and bypassed as a trade route after the war, Newport had been nearly abandoned at the time of Ladd's death. (Courtesy Florida Photographic Collection.)

In June of 1843, Albert R. Alexander established the Port Leon *Commercial Gazette*. After the town's destruction Alexander relocated to Newport and began publishing the *Newport Patriot*. Replacing the *Patriot* was the *Newport Gazette* edited by J.B. Carlisle. In this issue dated December 22, 1846, readers were treated to news from Washington, D.C. of a speech made by President James K. Polk, a small bit of poetry, and the restorative powers of sweetened rice water. (Courtesy Florida Photographic Collection.)

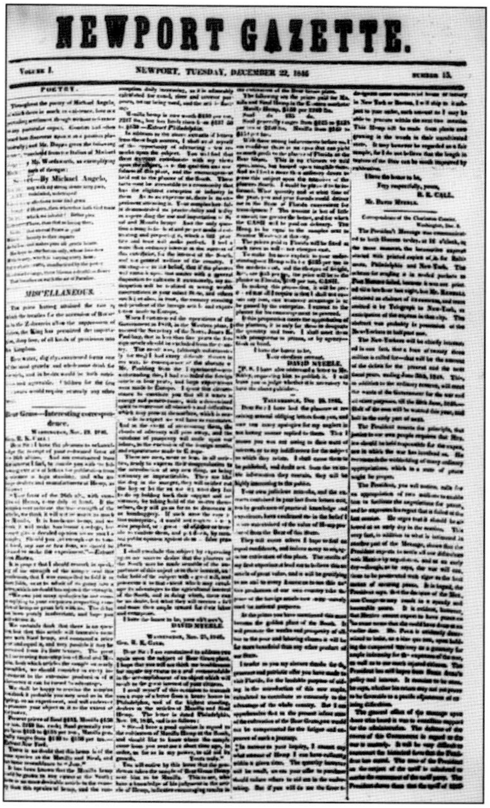
NEWPORT GAZETTE.

NEWPORT, TUESDAY, DECEMBER 22, 1846

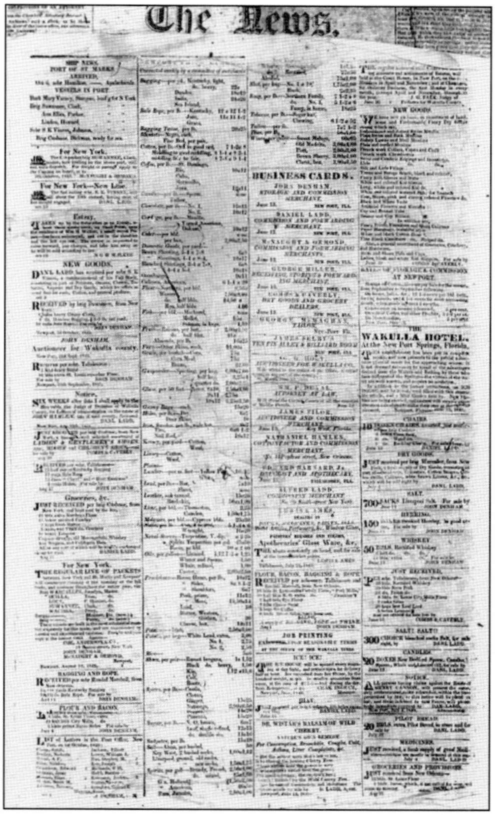
The News.

In this issue of the *The News*, published in Newport in June of 1849, one is able to get an idea of the town's commercial activities at the time. Daniel Ladd reported the availability of hay, candles, assorted candies, and Dr. Wistar's Balsam of Wild Cherry next to ads for George McMaghan, tailor, and James Selby's Ten Pin Alley and Billiard Room. The Wakulla Hotel boasted of the sulfur springs swimming pool located nearby. By October *The News* was replaced by the *Wakulla Times*, which was published up until the Civil War. (Courtesy Florida Photographic Collection.)

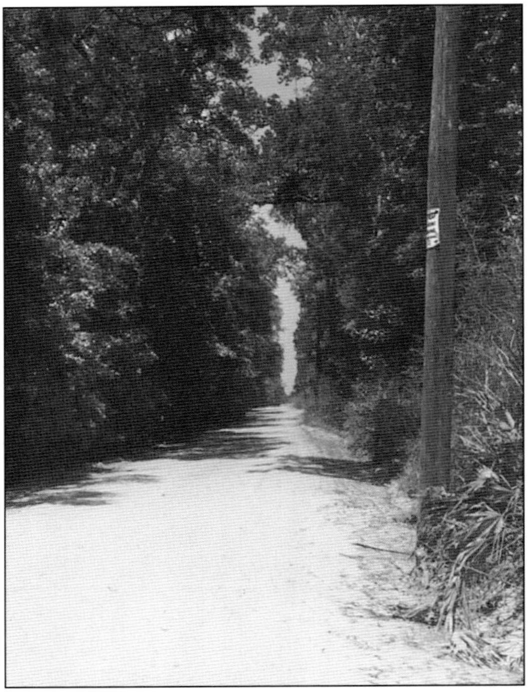

In order to improve conditions for Middle Florida and South Georgia planters in getting their cotton to his shipping port in Newport, Daniel Ladd, along with members of the Chaires family in neighboring Leon County, received a charter in 1851 creating the Georgia and Florida Plank Road Company. By 1852, the road, seen here, was built from Newport up into Leon County. While the road was never extended to the Georgia line it did serve its purpose for a short while. (Courtesy Terri Johnson.)

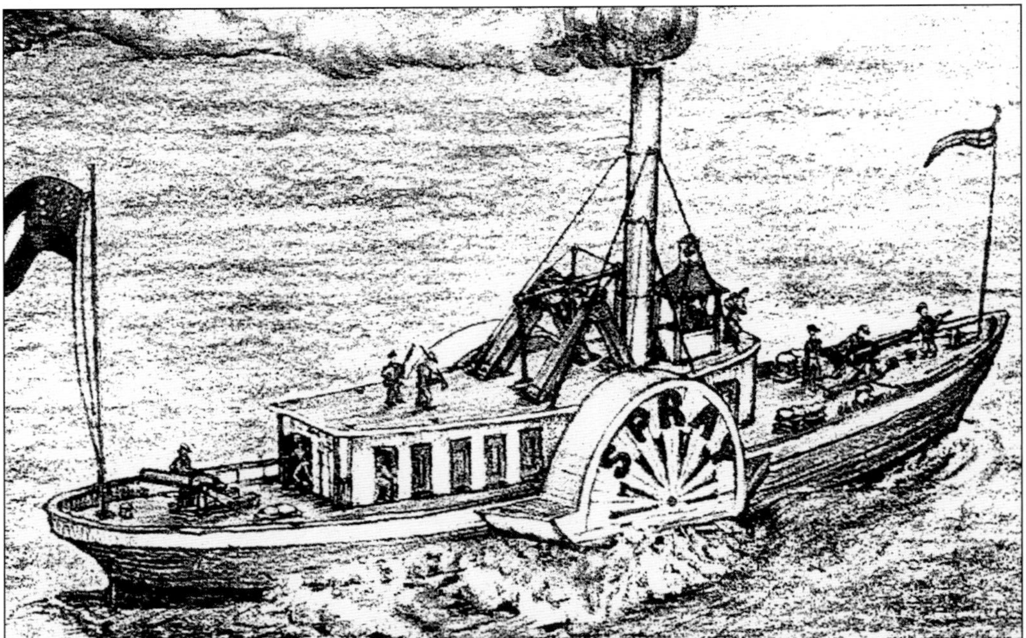

In 1850, Daniel Ladd purchased a 118-ton side-wheel steamer called the *Spray*, which he used as a tow boat and lighter hauling passengers and cargo from deep-water ships to and from Newport. In addition to creating a passenger line between Tallahassee and New Orleans the *Spray* also carried mail. When St. Marks was blockaded by Federal forces during the Civil War, the *Spray* was converted into a Confederate gunboat. Hauling men and equipment, the *Spray* was central to the St. Marks harbor defense throughout the war. The *Spray* is seen here in a painting by the late Dr. Frank Howard. (Courtesy Dr. Frank Howard.)

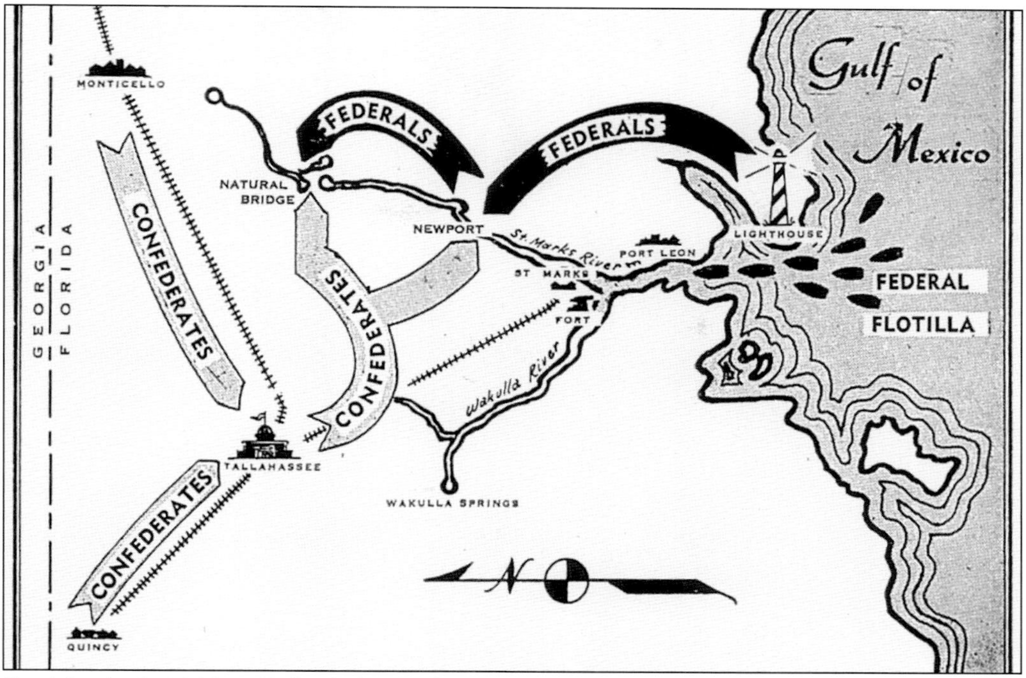

On March 5, 1865, a Federal force of 500 men came ashore at the St. Marks lighthouse to destroy Daniel Ladd's iron works. Alerted to the attack, Confederate forces set fire to the iron works and the bridge over the Newport River forcing the Federals to march around Newport towards their next objective, capturing the state's capital. Eight miles to the north in Leon County Federal troops were engaged at the Battle of Natural Bridge. Unable to break through Confederate defenses the Federals retreated back to the coast. (Courtesy Florida Photographic Collection.)

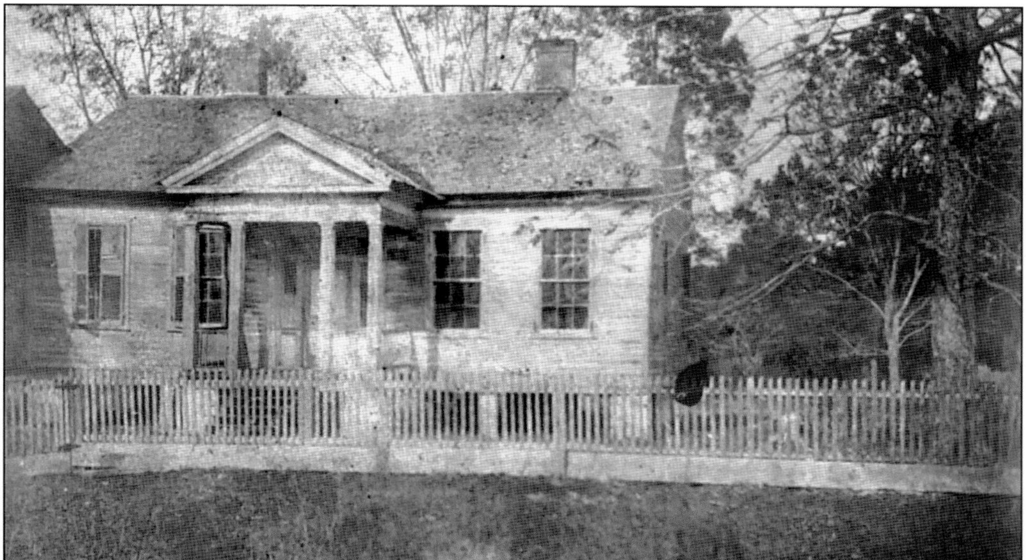

Gen. William Miller, who led Confederate defense forces at Newport and later at the Battle of Natural Bridge, is reported to have used this Newport residence as his headquarters prior to the invasion. (Courtesy Florida Photographic Collection.)

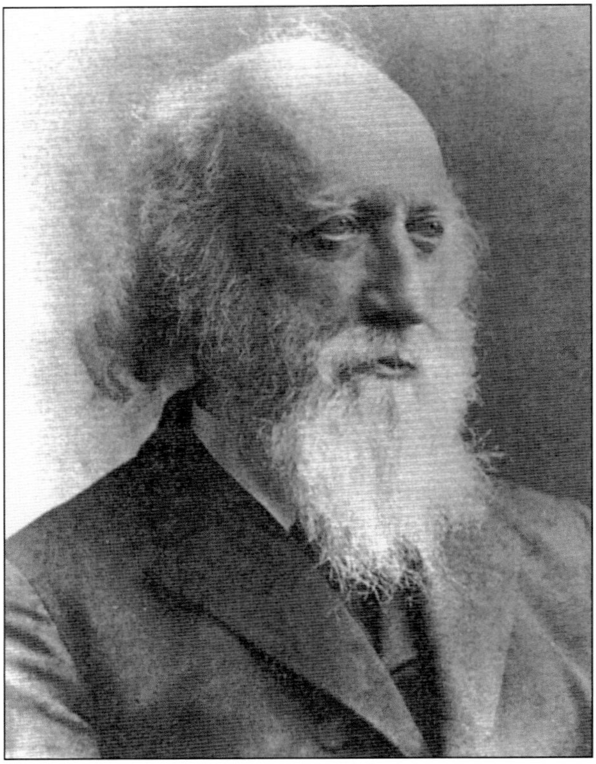

In 1867, Charles Beecher (1815–1900), the brother of Harriet Beecher Stowe (the author of *Uncle Tom's Cabin)*, moved to Newport for health-related reasons and lived there for 15 years. He was appointed as Florida's superintendent of public instruction in 1871, serving for almost two years. In 1879, his sister-in-law Eunice Bullard Beecher published *Letters from Florida* containing information gathered while visiting his estate and the surrounding area. (Courtesy the Harriet Beecher Stowe Center, Hartford, Connecticut.)

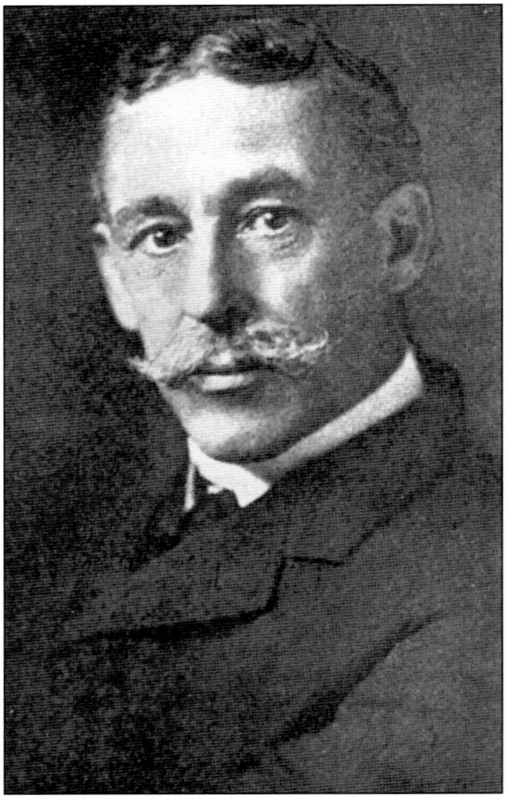

Journalist, editor, and author Kirk Munroe (1850–1930) traveled to Newport in 1883 for a brief stay at the home of Charles Beecher. While in Newport Munroe wrote the novel *Wakulla, A Story of Adventure in Florida*. Written for children, the novel details the adventures of the fictional Elmer family of Maine and is clearly influenced by the author's Newport surroundings. (Courtesy Mickler House Publishers.)

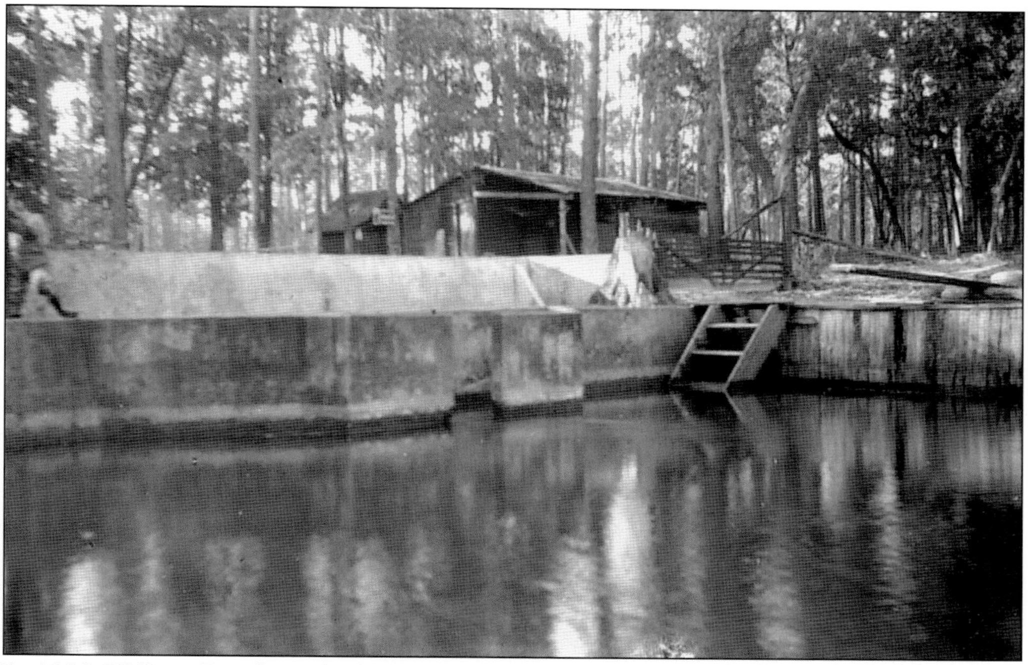

In 1846, William Daughtery built the Wakulla Hotel adjacent to a sulfur spring in Newport. Ezekiel Madden erected the Washington Hotel nearby and both establishments took advantage of the medicinal qualities of the mineral water. By the 1850s, Newport had gained the reputation of being a health resort. This 1921 photo shows the sulfur spring pool, remnants of which can still be seen today. (Courtesy Florida Photographic Collection.)

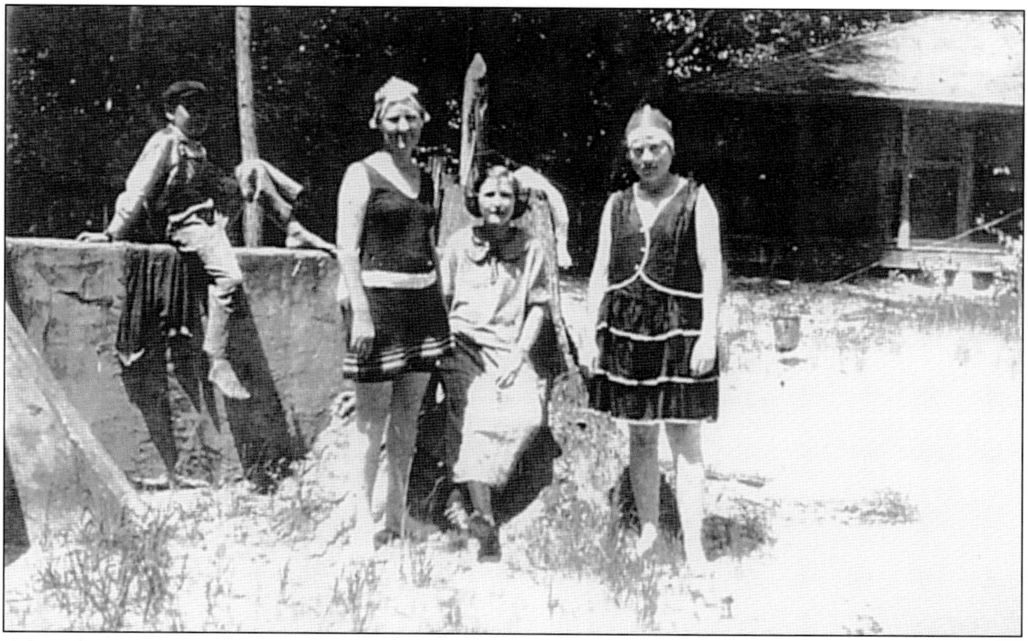

After the turn of the century several bath houses were built around the old sulfur spring pool, and it became a popular place for local residents to swim and picnic. Bathers from nearby Wakulla enjoy a pleasant afternoon in 1923. They are, from left to right, Frank Nesmith, Bruce Nesmith, unidentified, and Clara Page. (Courtesy author.)

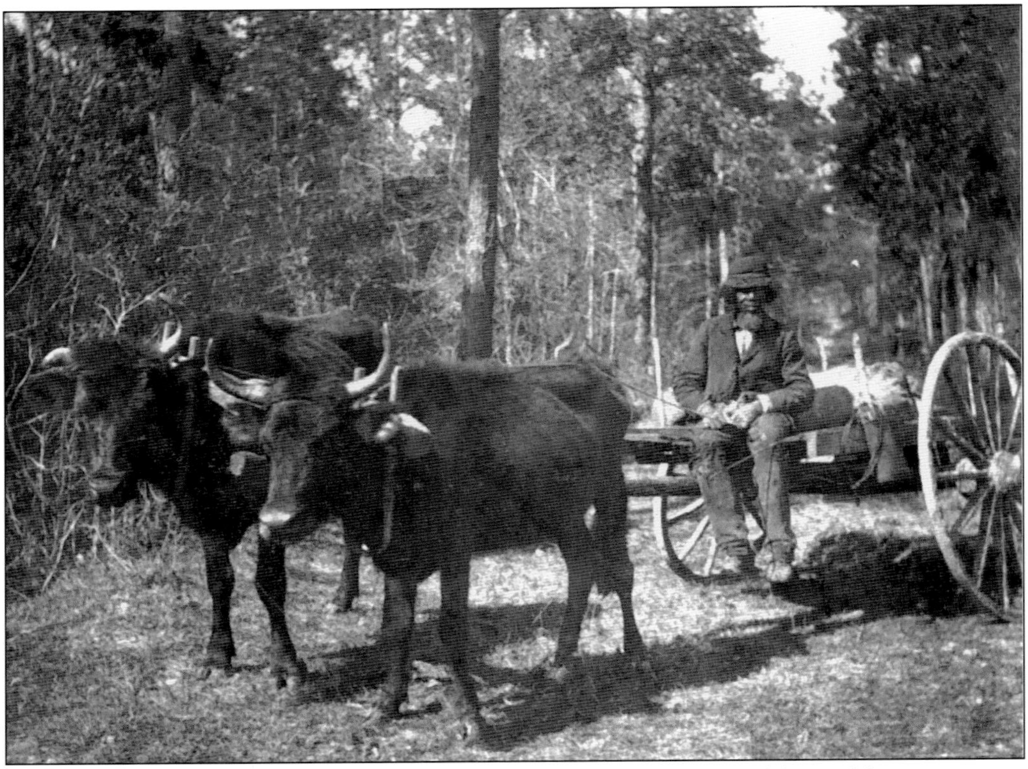

After the mail was delivered from Tallahassee to St. Marks by train Dave Morris would bring it back to Newport using his ox cart. Morris is seen here on his route in 1903. (Courtesy Florida Photographic Collection.)

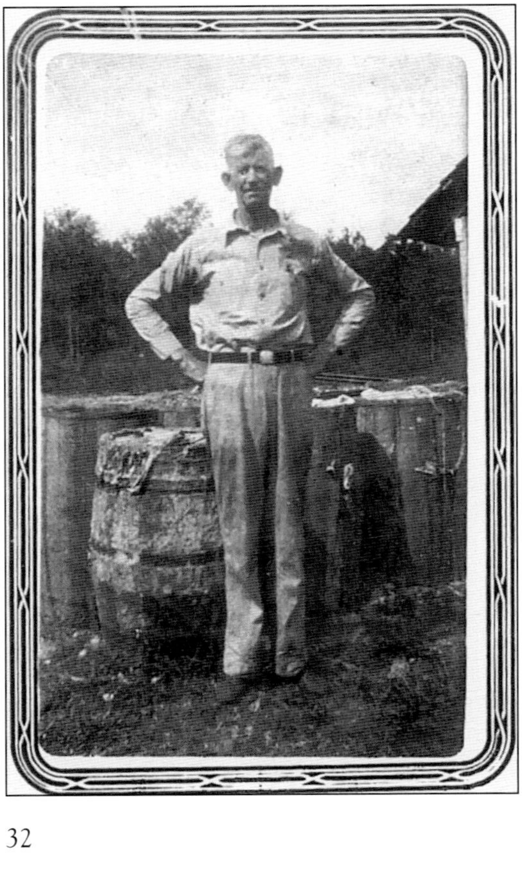

An employee of the U.S. Forestry Department from 1942 to 1951, Thomas Davidson Tadlock (1878–1951) manned the tall metal tower in Newport spotting for fire in the St. Marks Wildlife Refuge. Children who climbed the tower to visit Tadlock were rewarded with a quarter for their efforts. (Courtesy Monette Brooks.)

Three

CRAWFORDVILLE

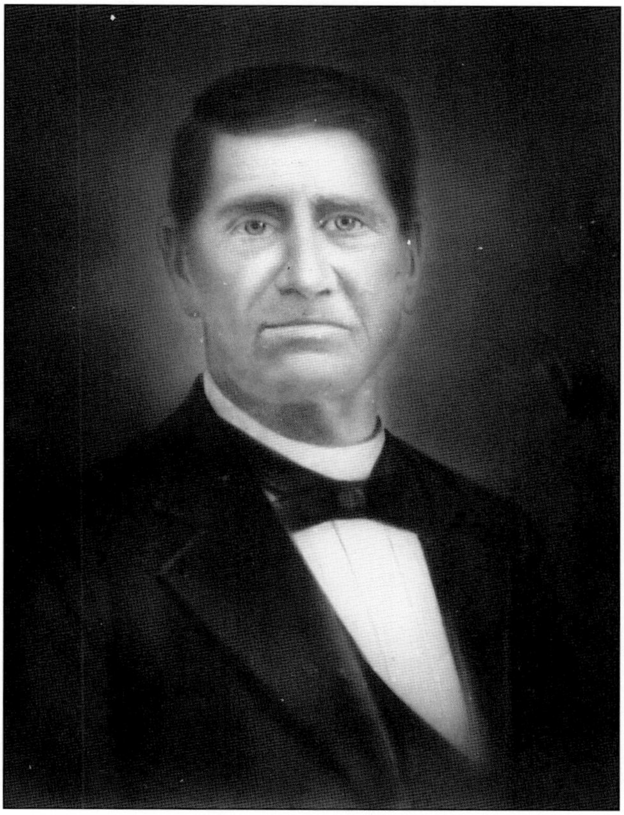

Moving to Wakulla in 1845 to practice medicine, Dr. John L. Crawford (1816–1902) became one of the county's most prominent citizens. In 1866 the county seat was moved from Newport and named in his honor. Elected to the Florida House of Representatives in 1847, he also served in the state senate from 1868 to1880. In 1881 he was appointed secretary of state, a post he held until his death. In a proclamation issued that same year, Gov. William Jennings hailed Crawford as "a public servant for nearly 40 years, distinguished for purity of character, honesty of purpose, and faithfulness of duty." (Courtesy Florida Photographic Collection.)

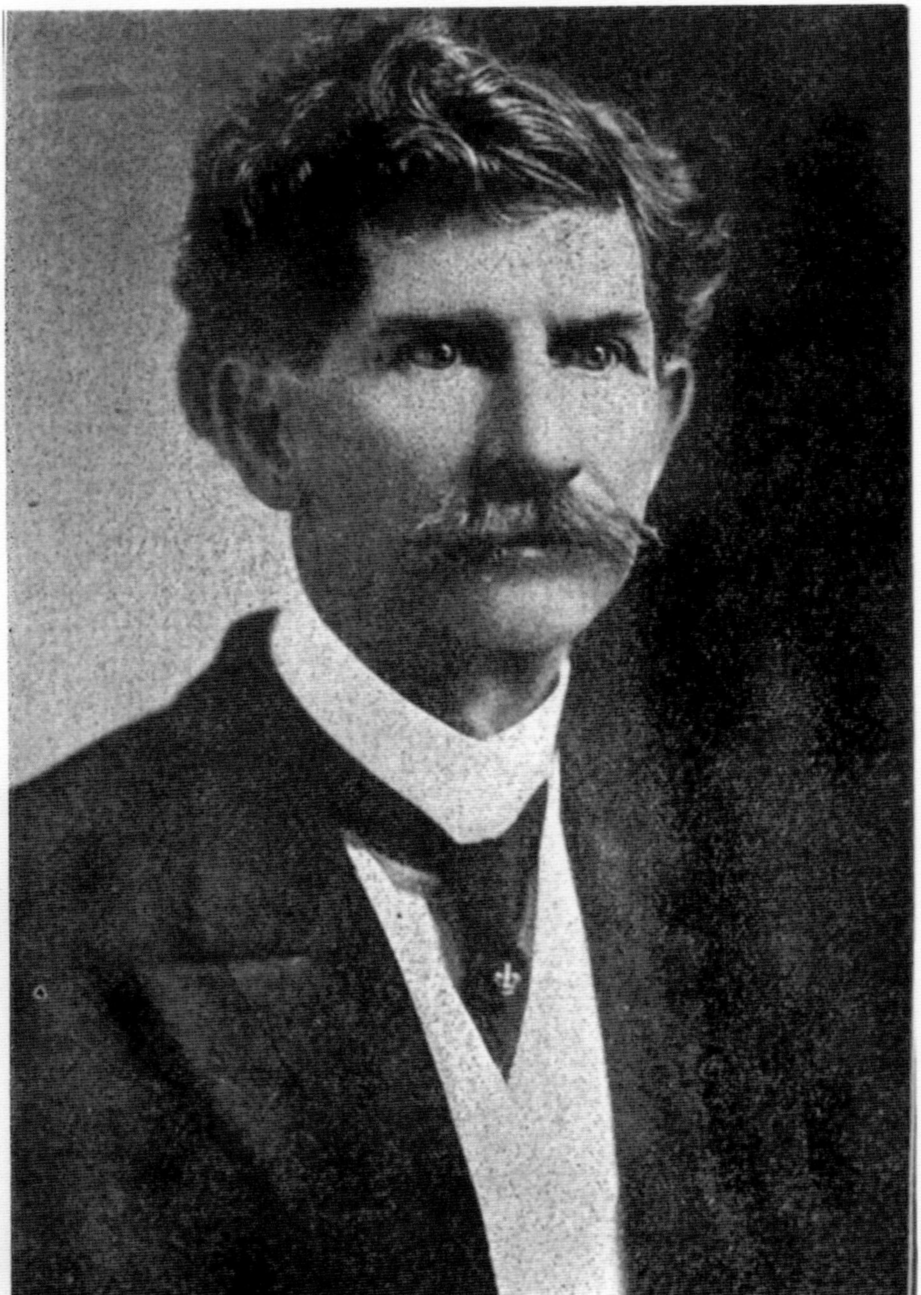

Henry Clay Crawford (1856–1929), the son of Dr. John L. Crawford, was elected as Wakulla's legislative representative in 1887 and was later appointed as a clerk in his father's office. Appointed secretary of state by Governor Jennings upon his father's death, the younger Crawford went on to serve in that capacity until his own death in 1929. The Crawfords of Wakulla served as Florida's secretary of state for a total of 48 years. (Courtesy Florida Photographic Collection.)

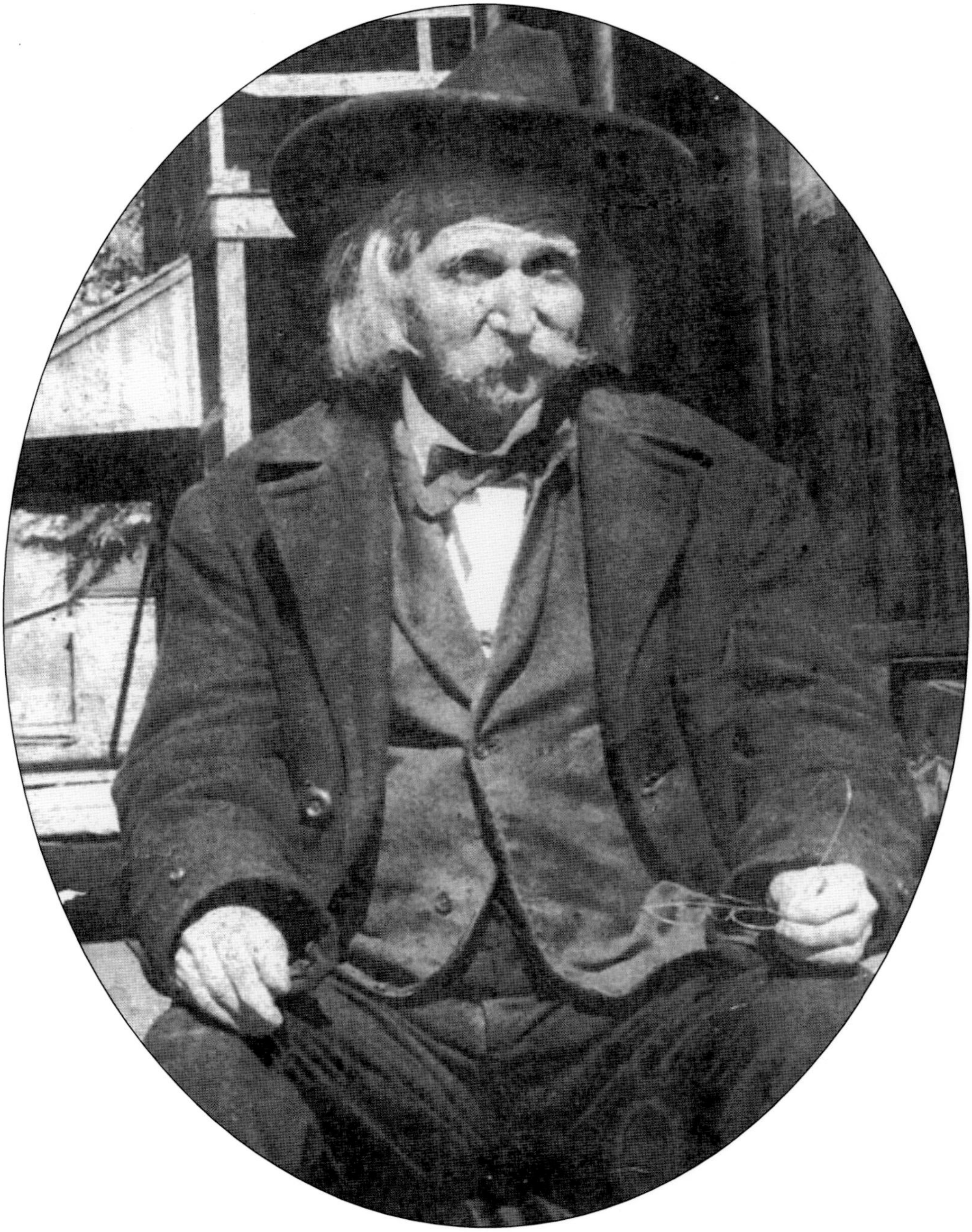

Described by historian Charlton Tebeau as "[o]ne of the most colorful and significant characters in the history of Florida," Wakulla-native Nat R. Walker (1852–1918) served a long career in both county and state politics. Receiving a law degree from Georgetown University, Walker served as county clerk from 1878 to 1887. He served three terms in the Florida legislature, was reading clerk of the House for over 25 years, was Wakulla's delegate to the democratic state convention from 1876 until his death, and as a delegate to the national democratic convention in 1896 was given the title "Boss Cracker of Florida." Upon his death, Gov. Sidney J. Catts issued a resolution mourning the state's loss of "so faithful, loyal, patriotic and serviceable a citizen." (Courtesy W. May Walker Jr.)

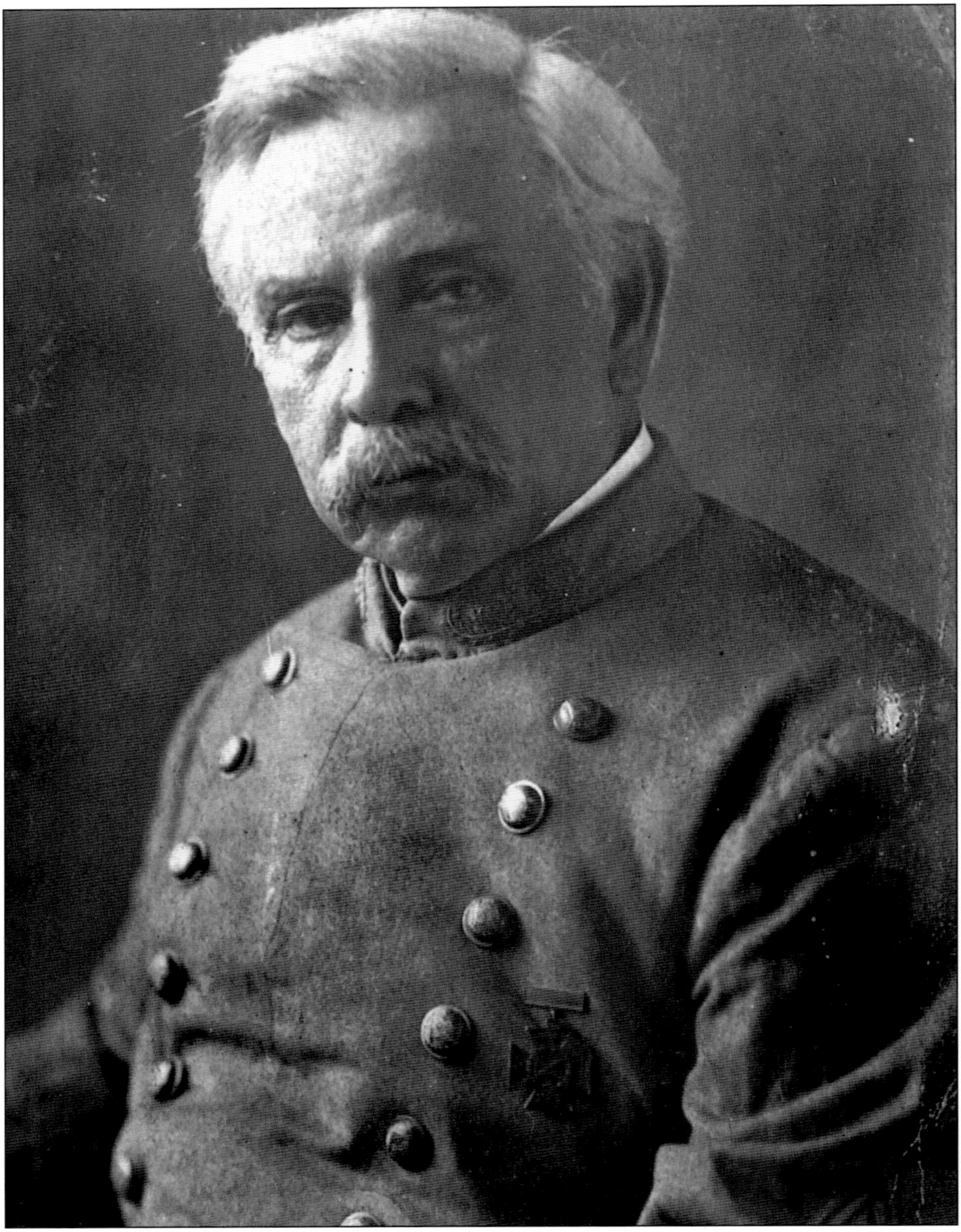

Born in Sumter County, Georgia, Roderick Donald McLeod (1848–1930) joined Company G of the 8th Georgia Reserves at the age of 16. Moving to Crawfordville in 1898 he served as county judge for 28 years, gaining the respect and admiration of his fellow citizens. Local legend holds that it was McLeod who issued the famous ruling that freed county fishermen arrested for catching mullet out of season. Due to his reasoning that because the mullet possesses a gizzard to digest its food it should be considered a fowl as opposed to a fish, the men were released. (Courtesy Florida Photographic Collection.)

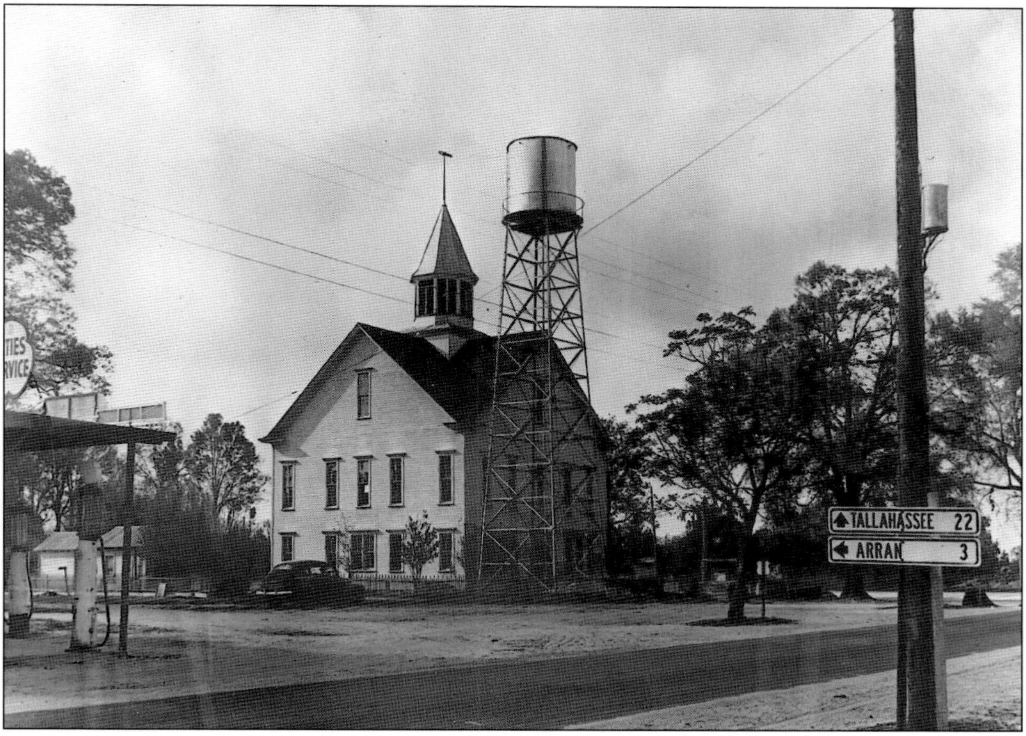

Completed in August of 1894, this three-story building served as the county's courthouse for 55 years. The building is included in the National Register of Historic Places and is one of three existing wooden courthouses in the state. (Courtesy Florida Photographic Collection.)

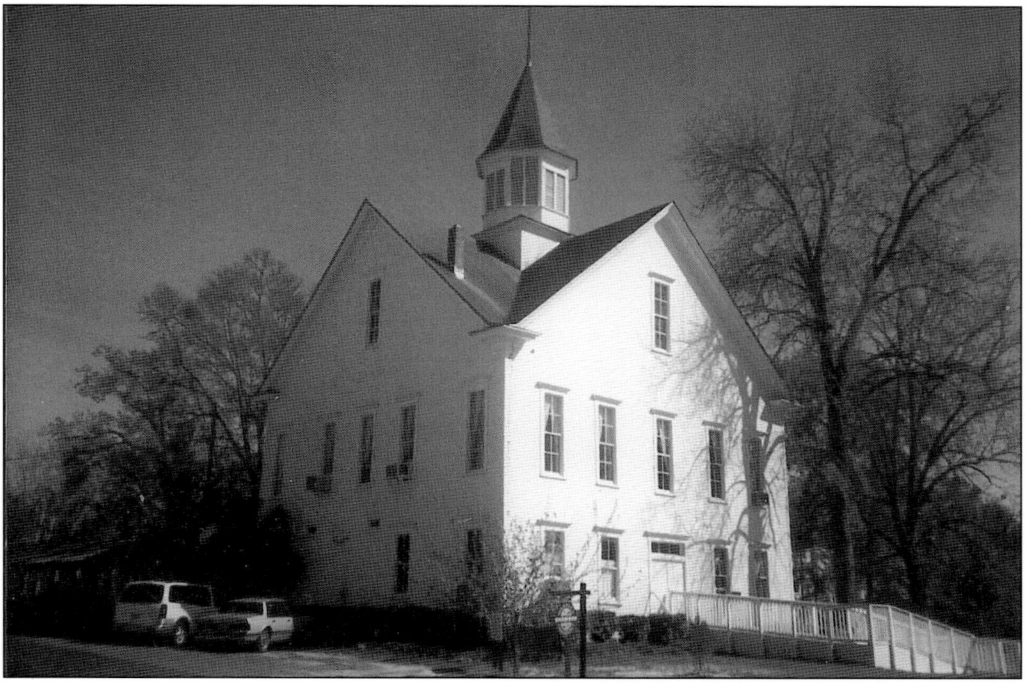
For many years the old courthouse served as home to the county's public library. It is currently the home of the Wakulla Chamber of Commerce. (Courtesy Peggy Page.)

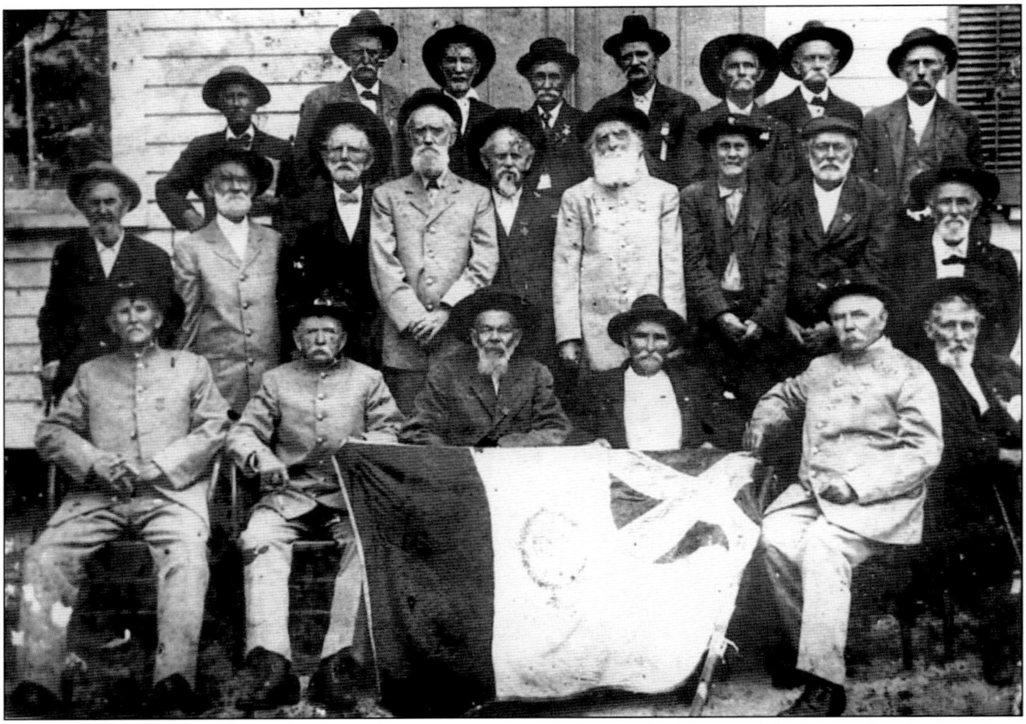

Members of the George W. Scott Camp Number 1557 United Confederate Veterans pose in front of the Crawfordville Courthouse on July 4, 1904. From left to right are (seated) Charles Patrick Alligood, Jack J. Pearce, James Ezell, Allison Brown, R. Don McLeod, and William Sasser; (middle row) R.B. Forbes, Thomas H. Moore, Capt. Arthur Lewis, James Sauls, Wesley Dugger, Henry Braswell, Nathaniel Singletary, Tom Vause, and Stephen Pigott; (back row) Lawrence Wilkerson, William H. Walker, George Core, Joseph Allen, John Stokley, Wiley Haskins, Stephen S. Causseaux, and Louis Gwaltney. (Courtesy Florida Photographic Collection.)

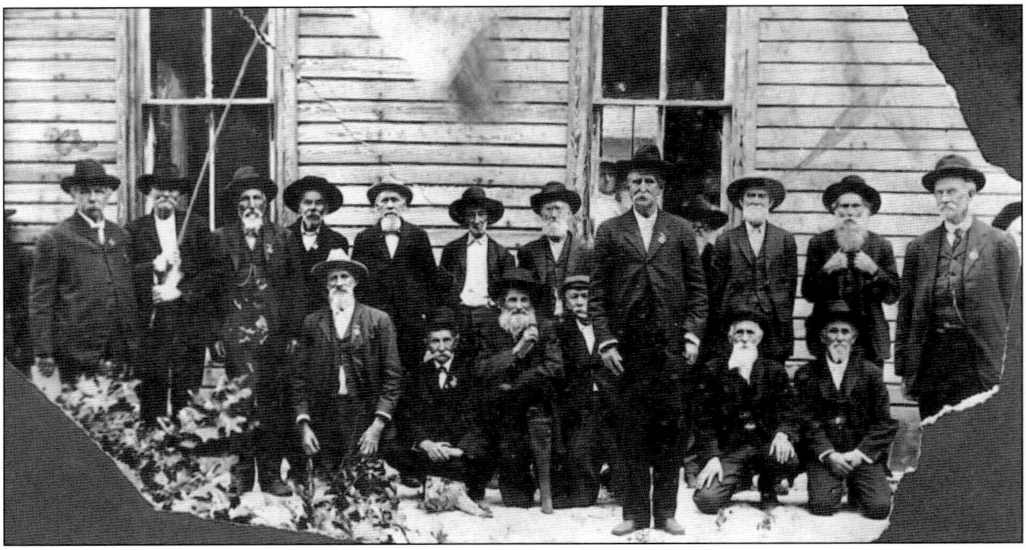

These are members of the same group in a photo taken a few years later. (Courtesy Florida Photographic Collection.)

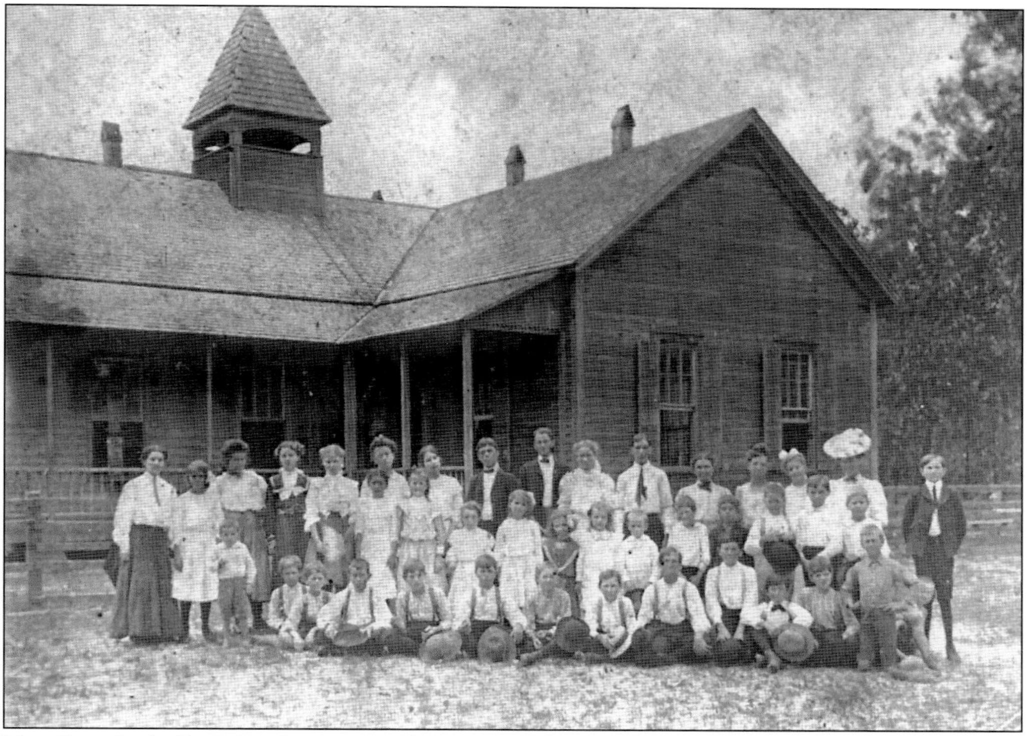

The Crawfordville School is seen in this c. 1908 photo. Teacher Ethel Rehwinkel is at far left with future county school superintendent C.K. Allen in the back row, eighth from right. When the new Crawfordville High School was built in 1933–1934, it was constructed around this wooden structure, which was built in 1897–1898. (Courtesy Florida Photographic Collection.)

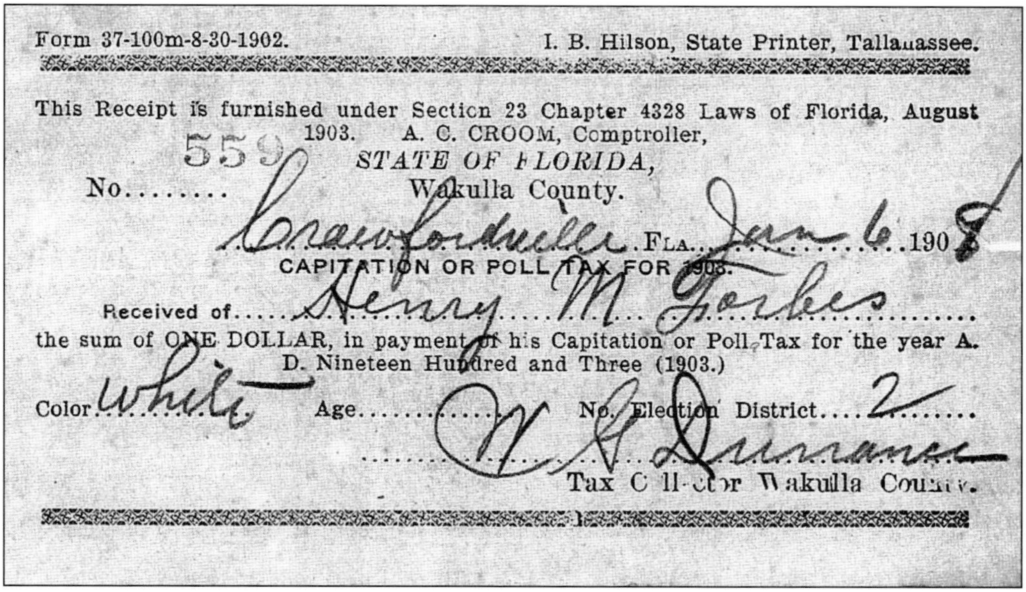

Form 37-100m-8-30-1902. I. B. Hilson, State Printer, Tallahassee.

This Receipt is furnished under Section 23 Chapter 4328 Laws of Florida, August 1903. A. C. CROOM, Comptroller,

STATE OF FLORIDA,
Wakulla County.

No. 559

Crawfordville FLA. Jan 6 1908

CAPITATION OR POLL TAX FOR 1903.

Received of Henry M Forbes

the sum of ONE DOLLAR, in payment of his Capitation or Poll Tax for the year A. D. Nineteen Hundred and Three (1903.)

Color White Age .... No. Election District 2

W G Durrance
Tax Collector Wakulla County.

This receipt acknowledges the payment of $1 by Henry M. Forbes for poll taxes for the year 1908, signed by Wakulla county tax collector W.G. Durrance. (Courtesy Lila Porter.)

FLORIDA TEACHER'S AGENCY
205 CAPITOL SQUARE BUILDING
TALLAHASSEE, FLA.

Affiliated with National Teacher's Agency, Philadelphia, Pa
Other Offices Listed: Pittsburgh, Pa.; Syracuse, N. Y.; Northampton, Mass.; Cincinnati, Ohio; New Haven, Conn.; Providence, R. I.; Bowling Green, Ky.; Washington, D. C.

The masses of the common people are like the mullet fish; The best fish and the best people on God's Green Earth and the most prayed on by sharks.

Nat. Walker.

The above is an excerpt from a speach made by Hon. Nat Walker at Concord Florida 1908.

This bit of wisdom from the "Boss Cracker of Florida," the honorable Nat Walker, was taken from a speech delivered in Concord, Florida in 1908. (Courtesy W. May Walker Jr.)

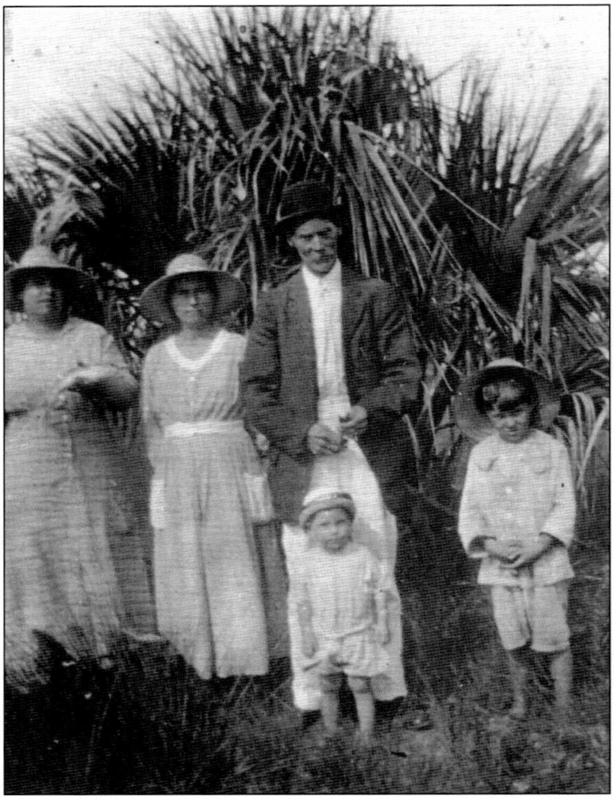

Dr. Joseph Harper (1866–1942) provided medical services to the county for 35 years. A native of Atlanta, Georgia, Harper attended the Georgia Medical School and Johns Hopkins University before moving to Crawfordville in 1907. Traveling the county by horse and buggy and Model-T Ford, Harper also served neighboring Jefferson and Franklin Counties in addition to operating a drug store in Crawfordville. Pictured *c.* 1920, from left to right, are Lizzie Harper, Ora Allen Harper, Dr. Joseph Harper, Johnny Harper, and Joseph Harper. (Courtesy Naomi Harper Buchan.)

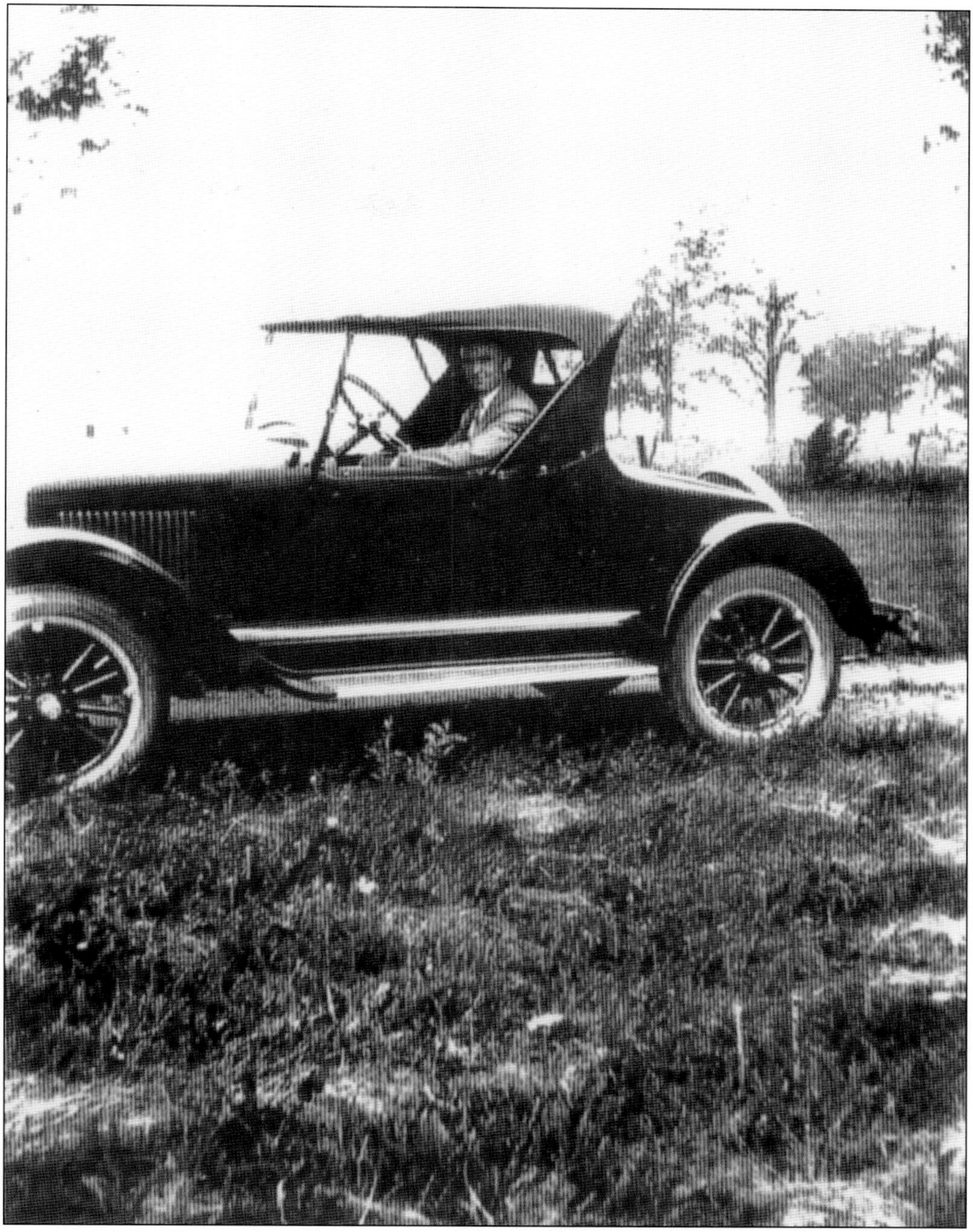

A native of Mt. Pleasant, Texas, A.L. Porter (1898–1992) was one of the county's most esteemed citizens. Accepting the position of principal of the Sopchoppy School in 1924, Porter began a legal career, which lasted over 60 years, in 1925. Serving as county attorney under Judge R. Don McLeod from 1926 to 1932, he was appointed as county judge in 1932 by Gov. Doyle Carlton, a position he held until 1960. In private practice until his death in 1992, Judge Porter was the county's authority on land deeds and titles, displaying a compassion for his fellow man, which characterized his years on the bench. (Courtesy Robert Porter.)

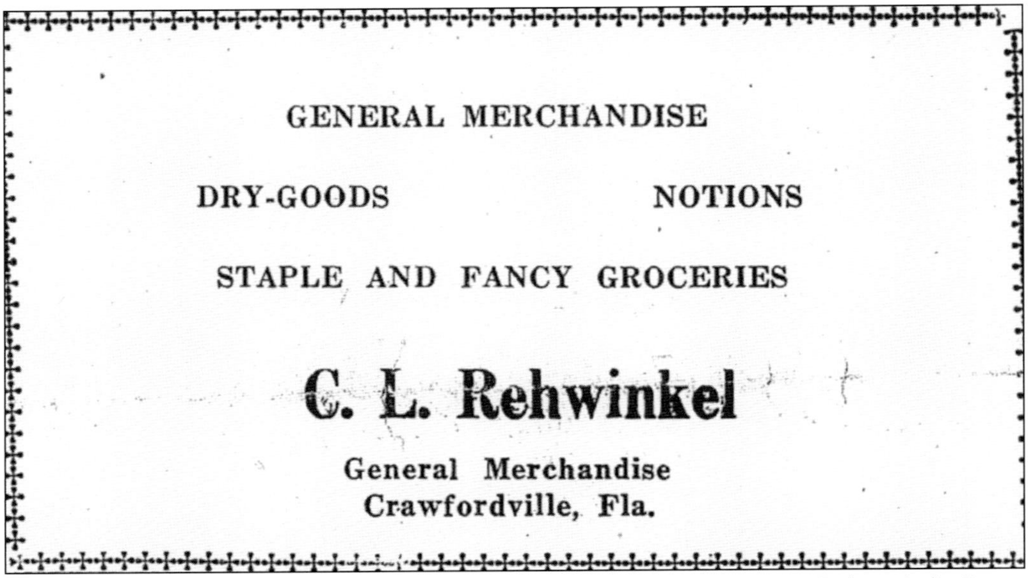
GENERAL MERCHANDISE

DRY-GOODS NOTIONS

STAPLE AND FANCY GROCERIES

C. L. Rehwinkel

General Merchandise
Crawfordville, Fla.

One of Crawfordville's most successful general mercantile businesses was Rehwinkel's Store, which was owned and operated by C.L. "Roy" Rehwinkel (1899–1974). Taking over the store from his brother Jennings in 1924, Rehwinkel provided local residents with such things as dry goods, work clothes, and farm implements until the store's closing in 1974. (Courtesy *Wakulla County News*.)

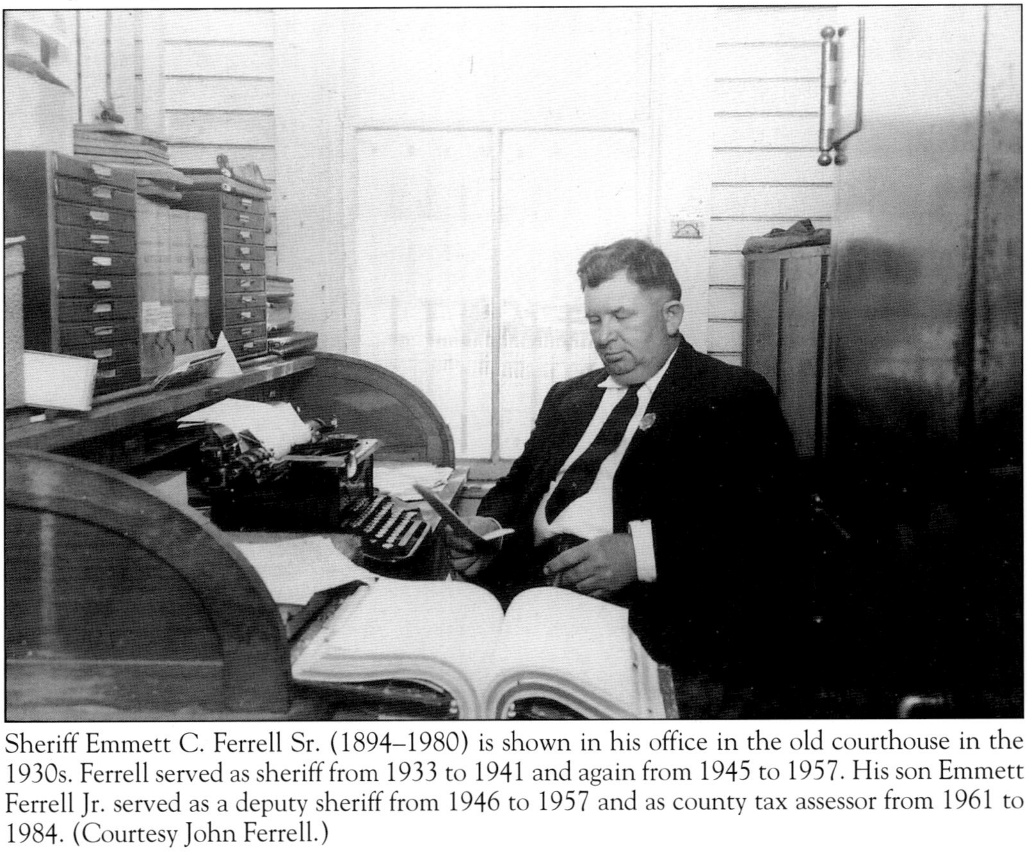

Sheriff Emmett C. Ferrell Sr. (1894–1980) is shown in his office in the old courthouse in the 1930s. Ferrell served as sheriff from 1933 to 1941 and again from 1945 to 1957. His son Emmett Ferrell Jr. served as a deputy sheriff from 1946 to 1957 and as county tax assessor from 1961 to 1984. (Courtesy John Ferrell.)

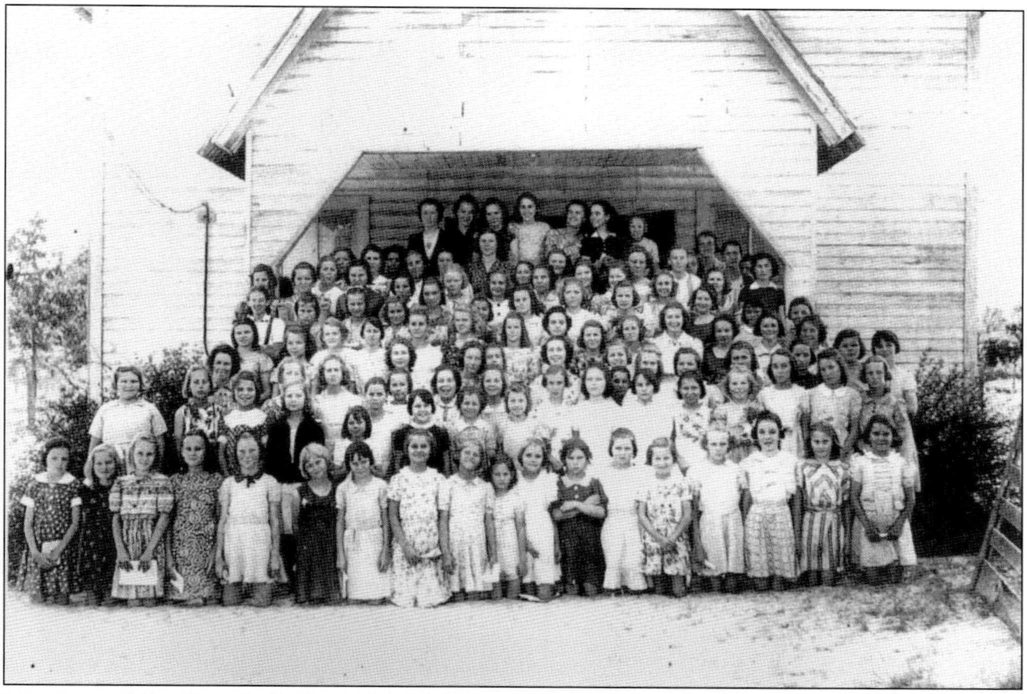

Members of the Crawfordville 4-H Girls Club pose in front of the old Crawfordville Methodist Church in 1938. (Courtesy Mable Roberts.)

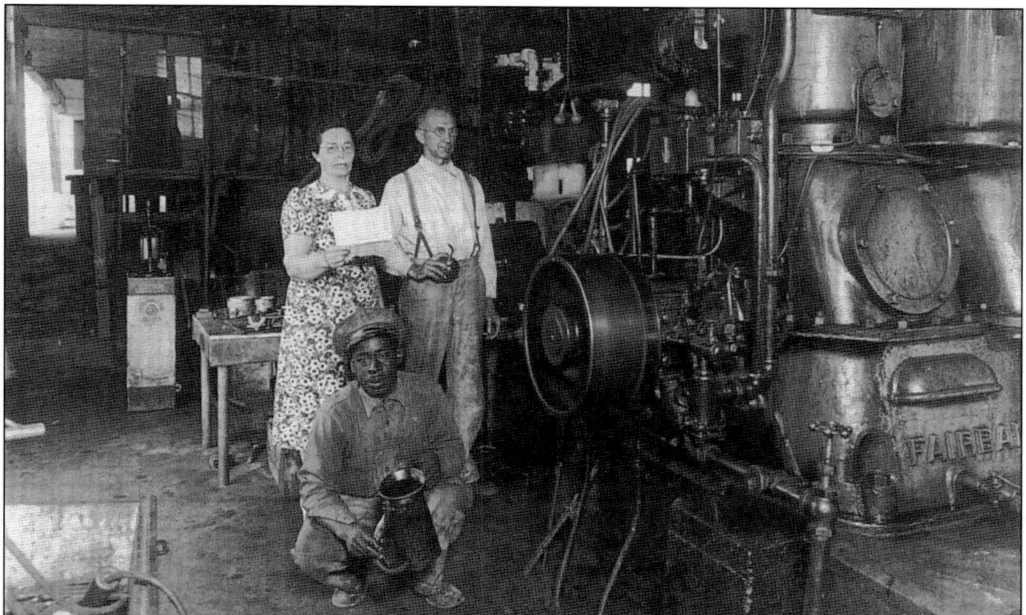

In 1933, Traube Woodbery (1883–1973) moved to Crawfordville and set up the county's first ice-making plant. Seen here with his wife, Susan Lambert Woodbery (1885–1963), and an unidentified employee inside the plant in 1935, Woodbery and his two sons, Warren and Gerald, operated the company until after World War II when it was sold to V.L. Cooper of Crawfordville. (Courtesy Mildred Musgrove.)

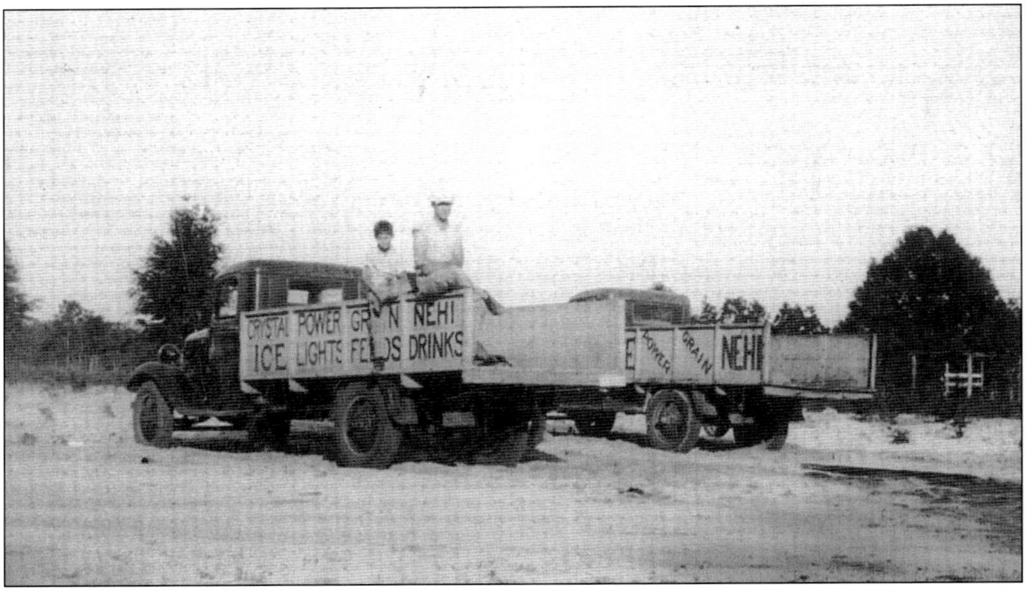

Seen here are the two delivery trucks used by the Woodbery Ice Company, *c.* 1935. The plant used water drawn from a well next to it to make ice in 300 pound blocks, which were then scored into 10, 15, 25, and 50 pound sections and delivered to area residents and businesses. Delivery men would chip off by hand the amount of ice needed. Woodbery's diesel-powered plant also generated electricity, which was sold to several Crawfordville businesses. (Courtesy Mildred Musgrove.)

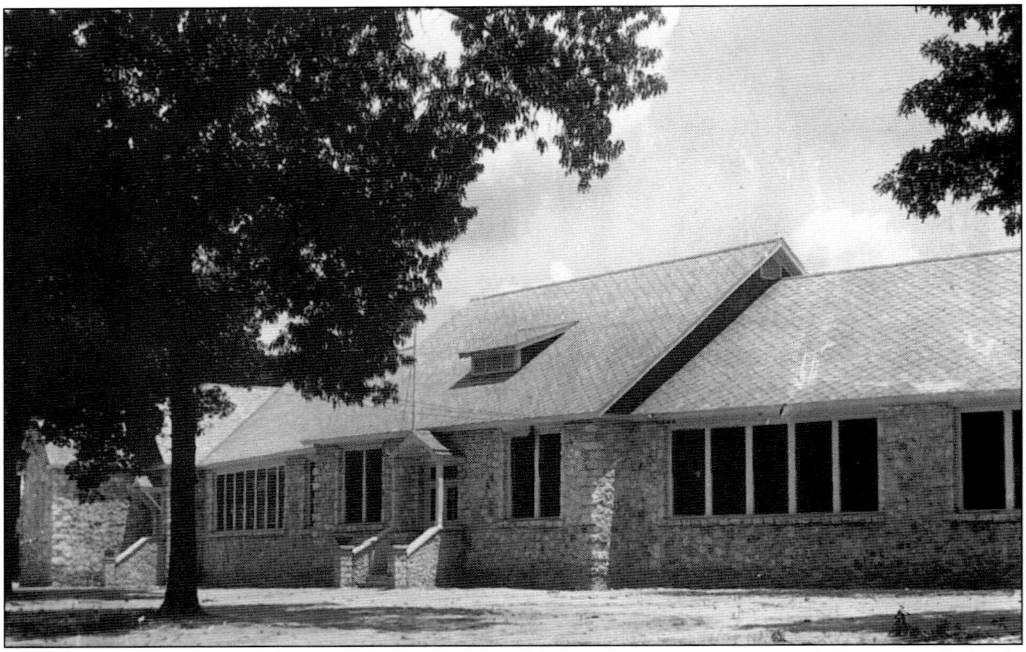

Built in 1933–1934 as a Work Projects Administration (WPA) project, the Crawfordville High School is seen here in 1935, its first year of operation. Serving grades 1 through 12 it was the county's second high school. In 1967, after the completion of the new Wakulla High School, it became an elementary school teaching grades 1 through 6. (Courtesy Florida Photographic Collection.)

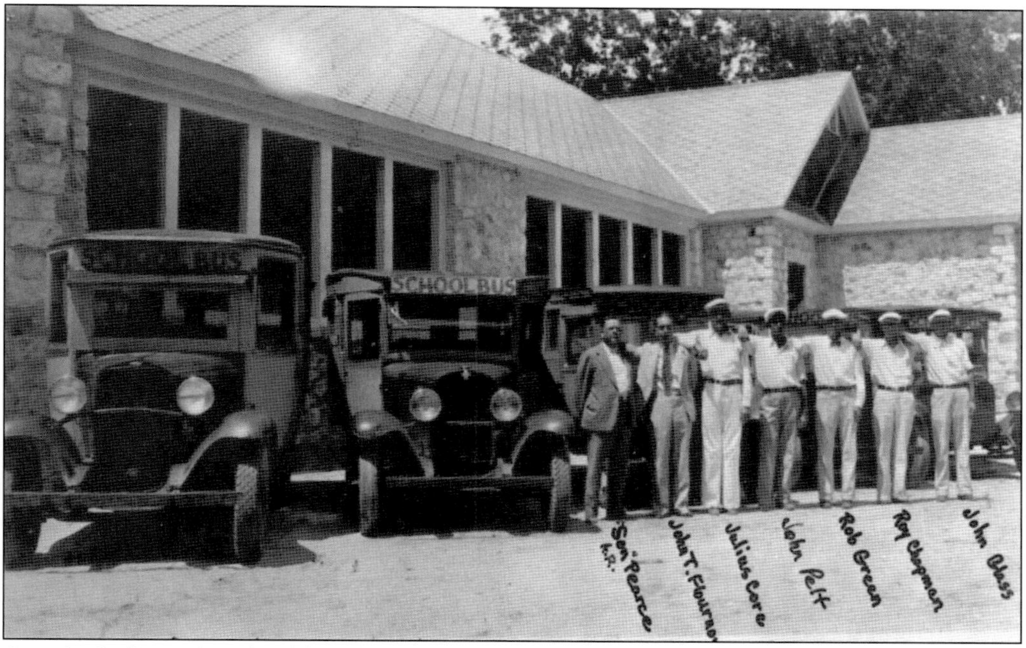

Crawfordville High School bus drivers pose in front of their vehicles in this 1935 photo. Each driver owned his own vehicle and contracted with the school board for his route. Pictured, from left to right, are School Superintendent A.R. Pearce; Principal John Flournoy; and drivers Julius Core, John Pelt, Rob Green, Roy Chapman, and John Glass. (Courtesy Florida Photographic Collection.)

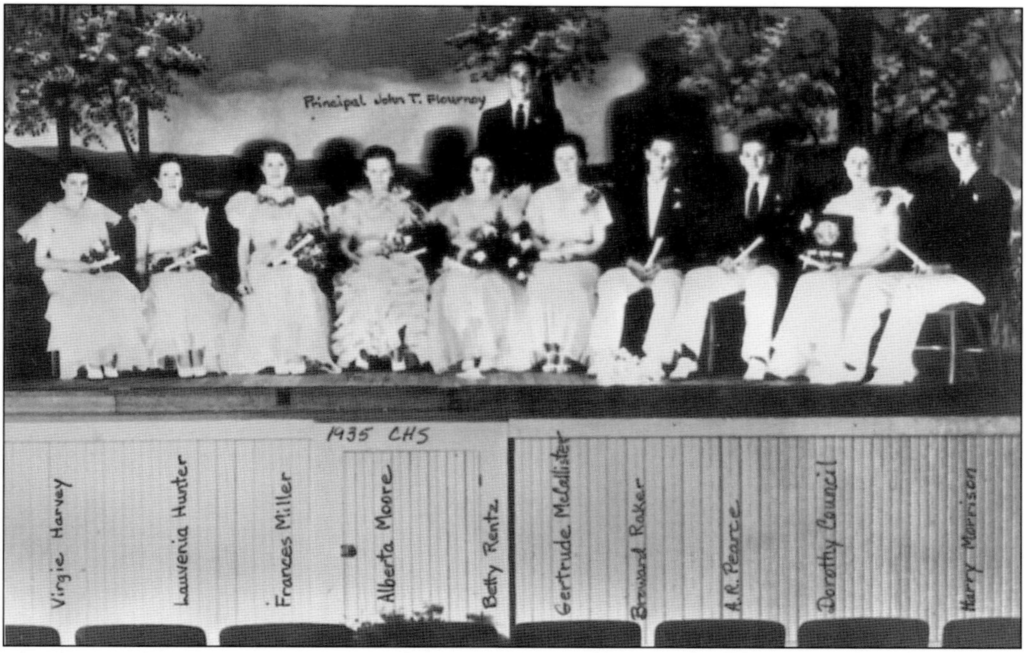

The first graduating class of the Crawfordville High School is seen here in 1935. Pictured, from left to right, are Virgie Harvey, Lauvenia Hunter, Frances Miller, Alberta Moore, Betty Rentz, Gertrude McCallister, Broward Raker, A.R. Pearce, Dorothy Council, and Harry Morrison. Principal John Flournoy is standing in the rear. (Courtesy Florida Photographic Collection.)

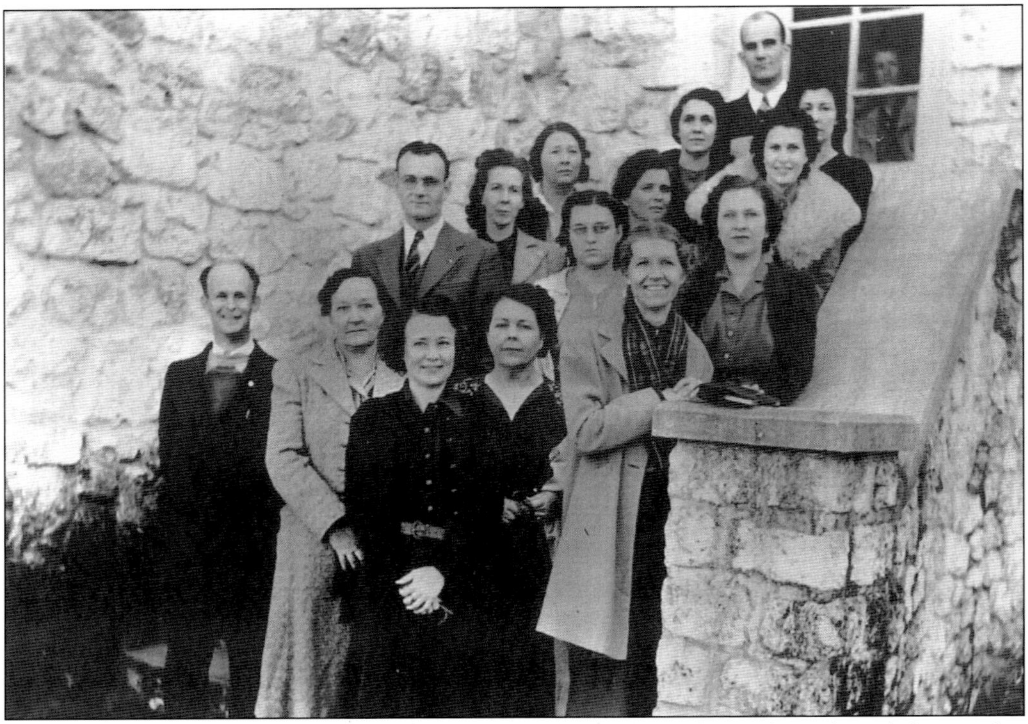

Members of the Crawfordville High School faculty in 1942, shown here from left to right, are (front row) Flournoy Moore, Mary Bell Ferrell, Laura Ward Neubauer, Viola Revell, and Estelle Taff; (second row) Principal Larry Williams, Dovie Cotton, and Etta Maud Kirkland; (third row) are Frances Raker, Audrey Walker, Mabel Roberts, and Beulah Tucker; (fourth row) Alene Gillespie and Ruth Ferrell; (top row) Coach Gabbard. (Courtesy Mabel Roberts.)

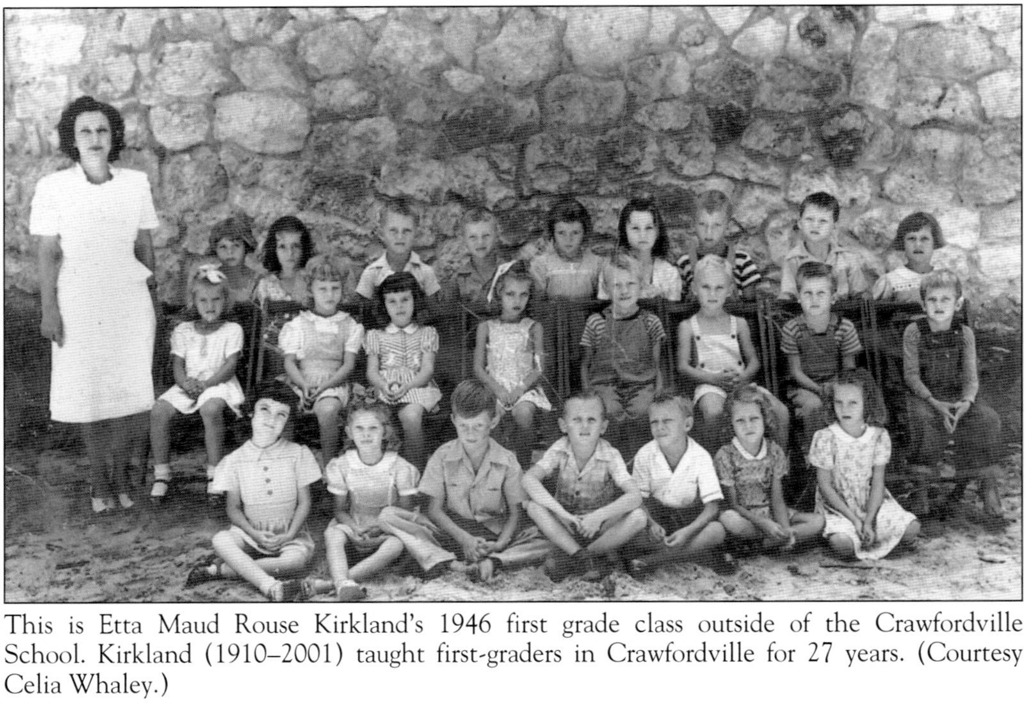

This is Etta Maud Rouse Kirkland's 1946 first grade class outside of the Crawfordville School. Kirkland (1910–2001) taught first-graders in Crawfordville for 27 years. (Courtesy Celia Whaley.)

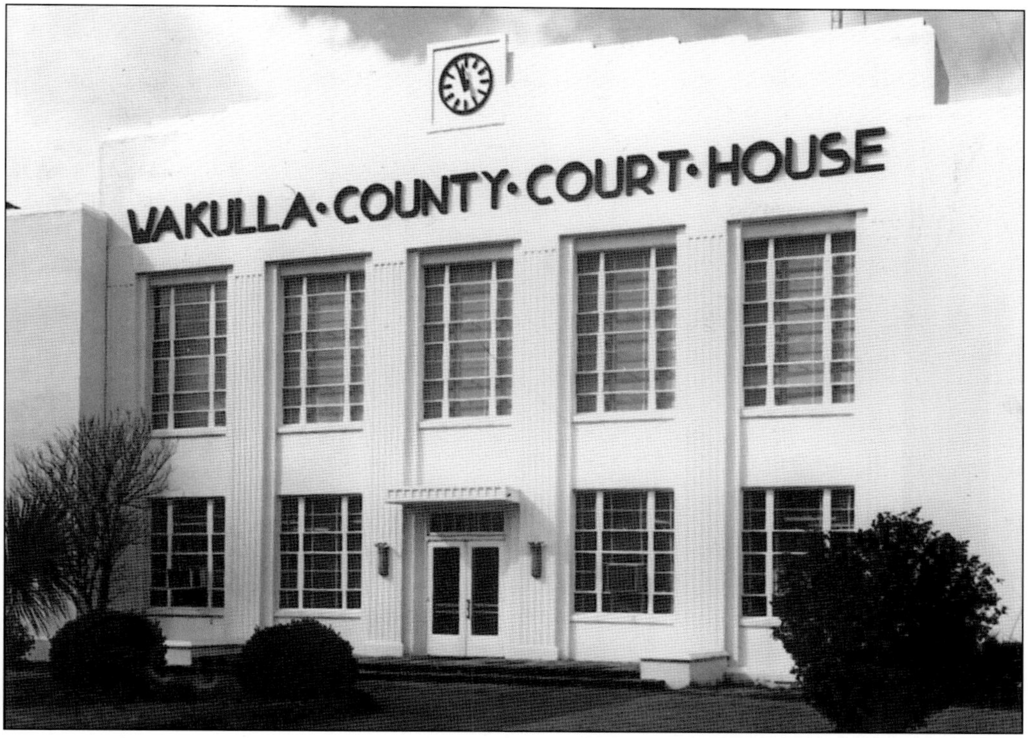

In September of 1949, in a ceremony presided over by circuit judge W. May Walker (1905–1974), the county's new courthouse was dedicated. The old wooden courthouse was moved approximately 500 feet to the south with a hand-powered wench and wooden rollers to make way for the new building. (Courtesy Florida Photographic Collection.)

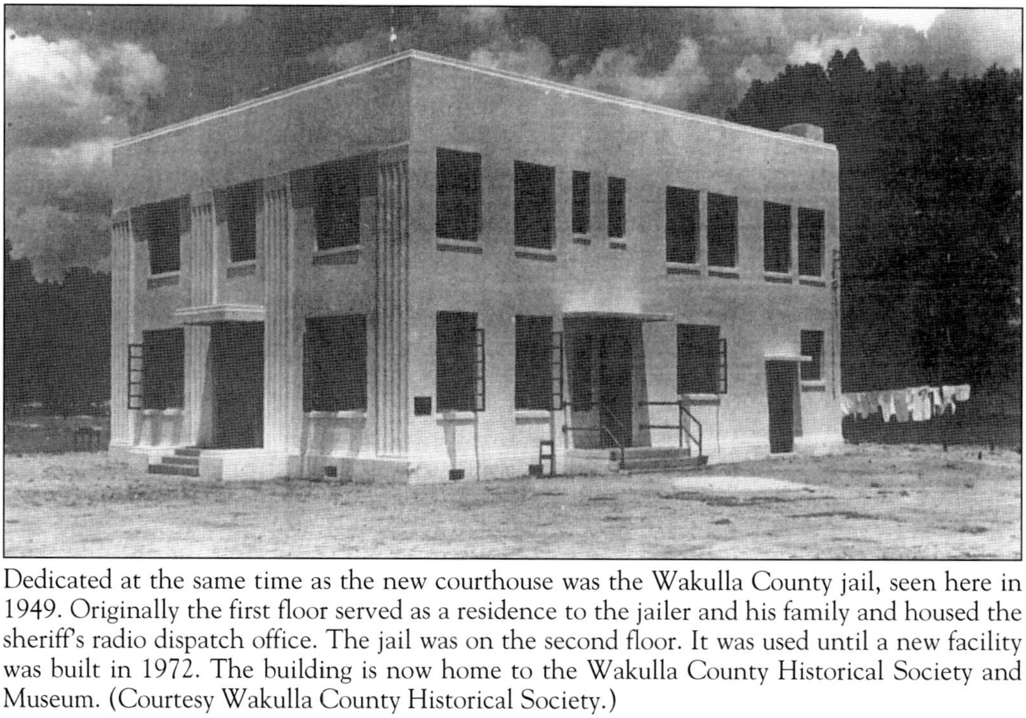

Dedicated at the same time as the new courthouse was the Wakulla County jail, seen here in 1949. Originally the first floor served as a residence to the jailer and his family and housed the sheriff's radio dispatch office. The jail was on the second floor. It was used until a new facility was built in 1972. The building is now home to the Wakulla County Historical Society and Museum. (Courtesy Wakulla County Historical Society.)

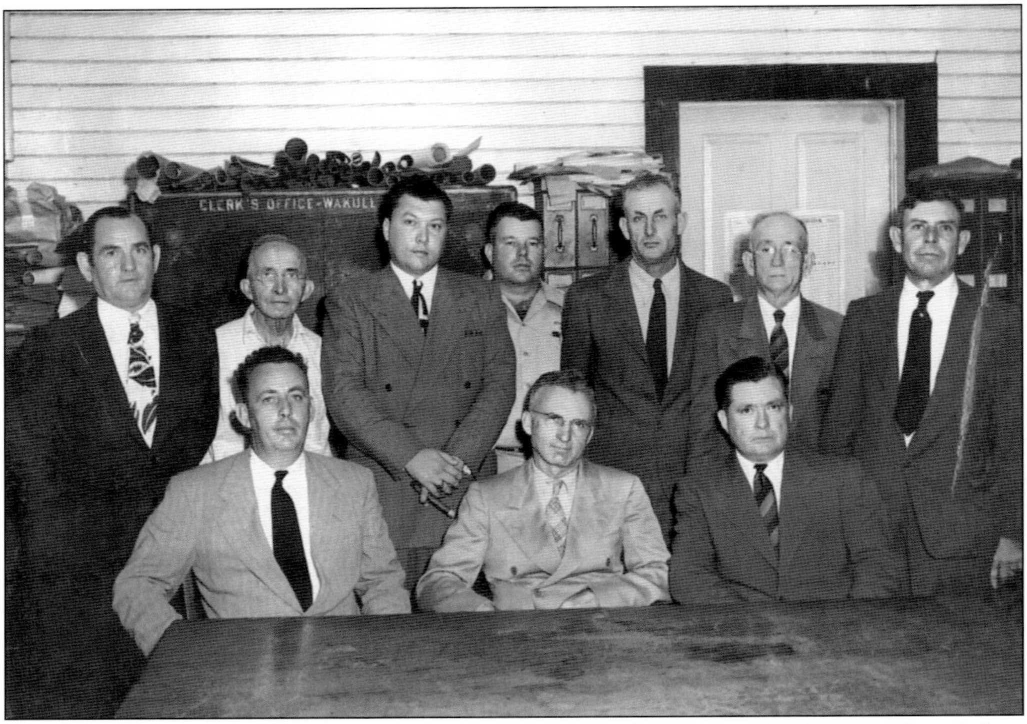

Officers of the Wakulla Chamber of Commerce are seen here in 1947. They are, from left to right, (seated) William Schley, secretary; A.L. Porter, president; and George Nesmith, vice president; (standing) Bennie Rogers, W.E. Rehwinkel, U.G. Fayard, V.L. Cooper, E.W. Roberts, Steve Moore and Jake Pigott, directors. (Courtesy author.)

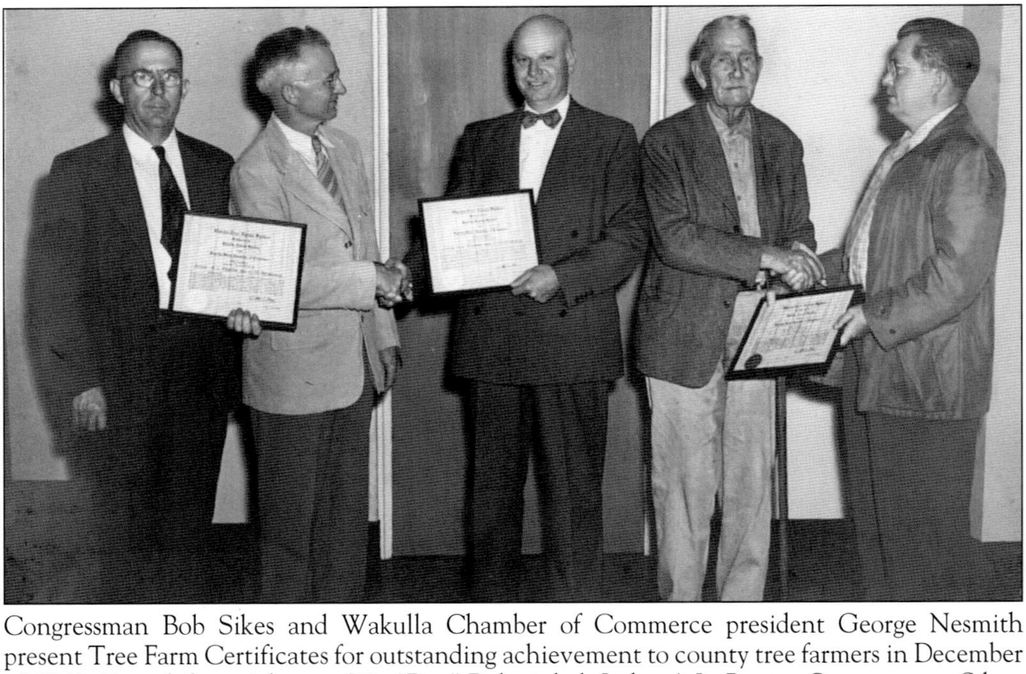

Congressman Bob Sikes and Wakulla Chamber of Commerce president George Nesmith present Tree Farm Certificates for outstanding achievement to county tree farmers in December of 1949. From left to right are C.L. "Roy" Rehwinkel, Judge A.L. Porter, Congressman Sikes, J.L. Trice Sr., and President Nesmith. (Courtesy author.)

Many county residents served with great distinction and bravery in World War II. Among them was James A. Cox (1922–1999) of Crawfordville. Captured in France in July of 1944, after having participated in the Normandy invasion, Cox was incarcerated in eight different prisons in France and Germany before being liberated by Russian forces in April of 1945. Shown here is Cox's German prisoner of war identification sheet listing the camps where he was held. (Courtesy Genie Cox.)

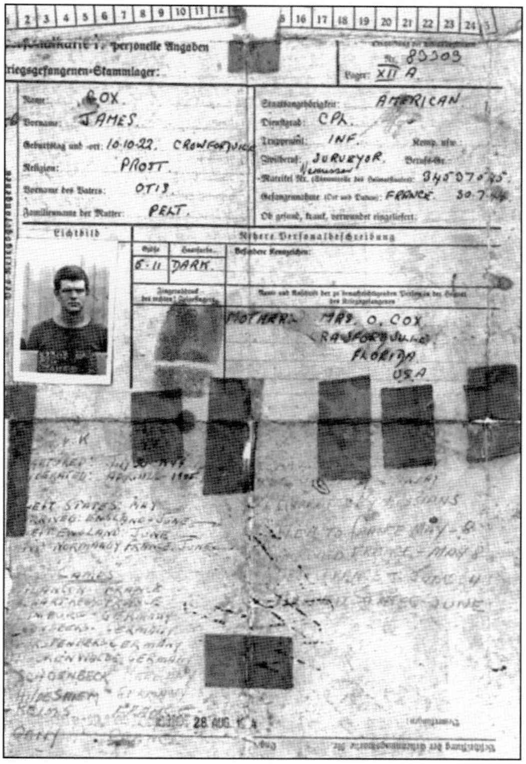

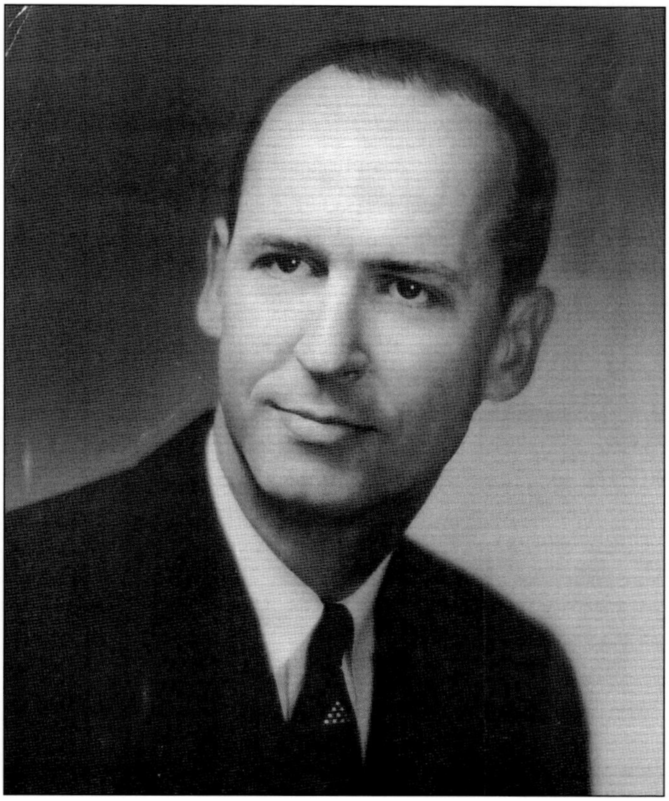

From 1936 to 1940 Crawfordville native Harry C. Morrison (1917–1980) worked for the state Bureau of Identification specializing in the new crime solving technique of fingerprinting. In 1940 he was appointed as a special agent for the FBI engaged in internal security investigations. Appointed first assistant state attorney of the second judicial circuit, Morrison was responsible for all criminal prosecutions in Wakulla and Franklin Counties for 23 years. In 1972 he was elected state attorney, a post he held until his death. (Courtesy Chip Morrison.)

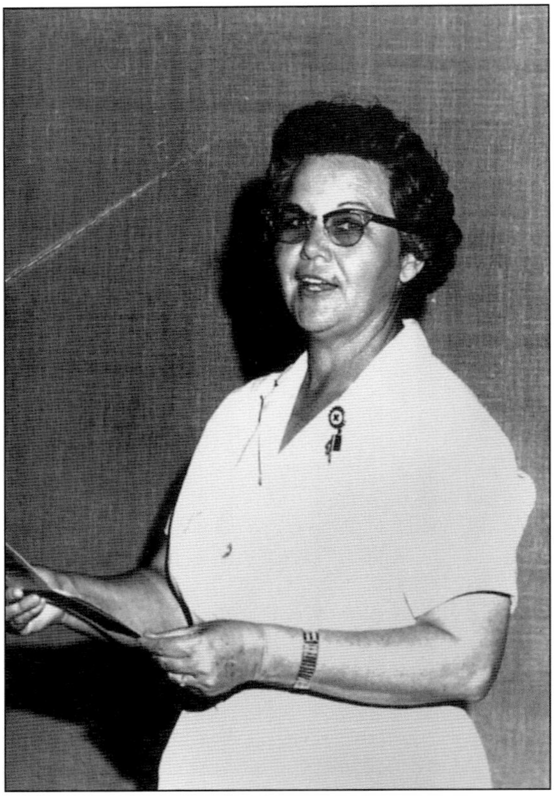

During a 44-year career in the public health field Anita Townsend was responsible for helping to establish a comprehensive public health program in Wakulla County. Among her many accomplishments were securing full-time medical professionals and staff for the county, implementing school health programs, and improving public awareness of health and health services. In 1988 the Wakulla County Health Department was named in her honor. (Courtesy Anita Townsend.)

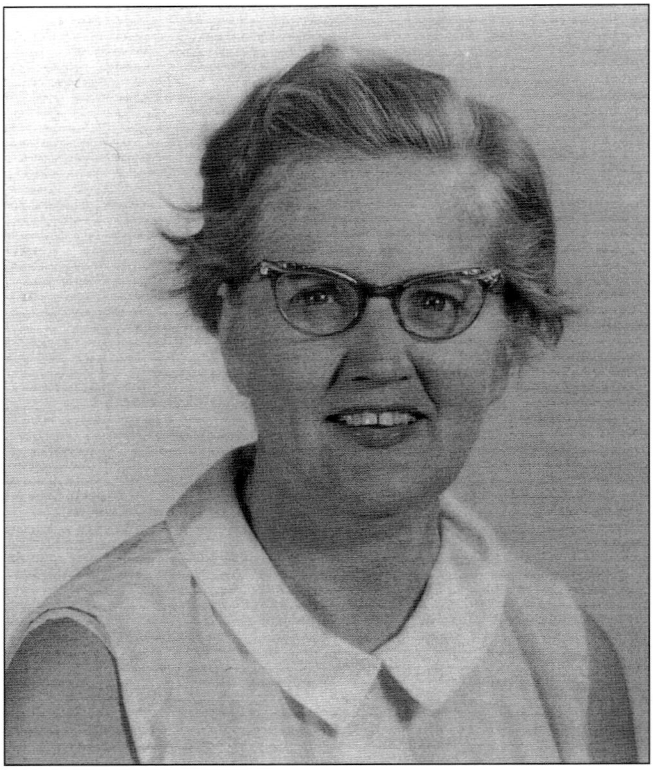

Moving to Crawfordville in 1953, Pennsylvania native Elizabeth Fisher Smith (1920–1977) wrote, edited, and published the *Magnolia Monthly*. Publishing the first issue in October of 1963, Smith documented the county's history and that of its people through extensive research and interviews with many older residents. Smith's work makes up one of the largest collections of county history available today. The last issue appeared shortly before her death in 1977. (Courtesy Jenny Druda.)

Four

SOPCHOPPY

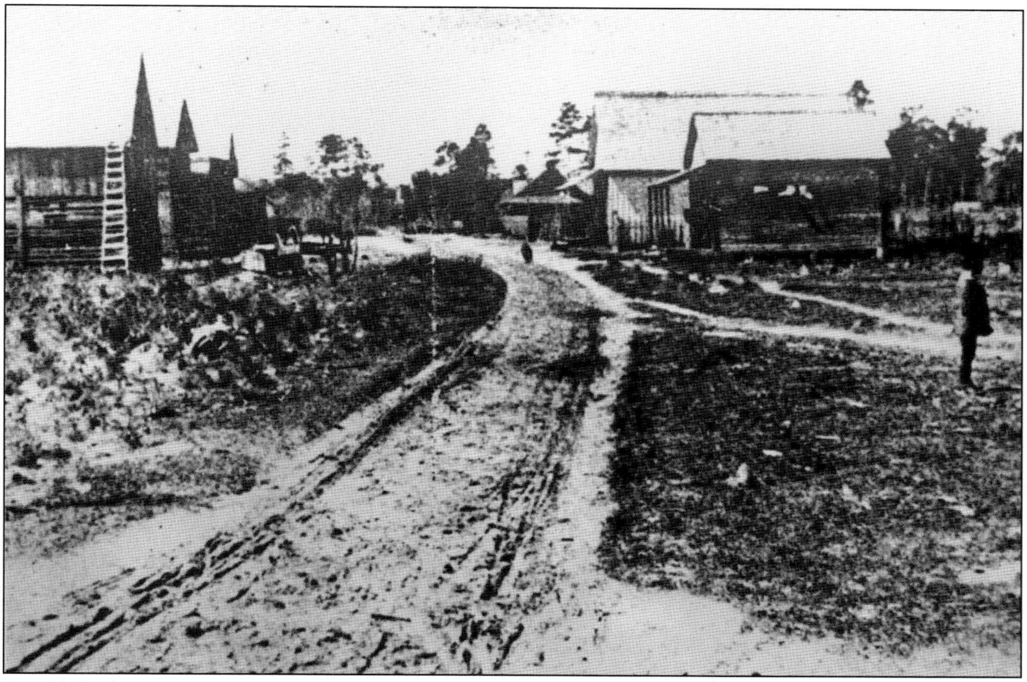

Possibly deriving its name from the Creek Indian words "sokhe" meaning "twisted" and "chapke" meaning "long," the town of Sopchoppy, located along the river of the same name, is seen here in the late 1890s. In 1893 the Georgia, Florida, and Alabama (GF&A) Railroad was built through the area, prompting the Scottish Land and Improvement Company to survey the town in 1895. This work was completed by county native John Calhoun Hodge (1855–1950), referred to as the founder of Sopchoppy. By 1910 Sopchoppy was the largest and only incorporated town in the county serving as the hub to surrounding communities such as Greenough, Ashmore, Smith Creek, Sanborn, and Buckhorn. (Courtesy Florida Photographic Collection.)

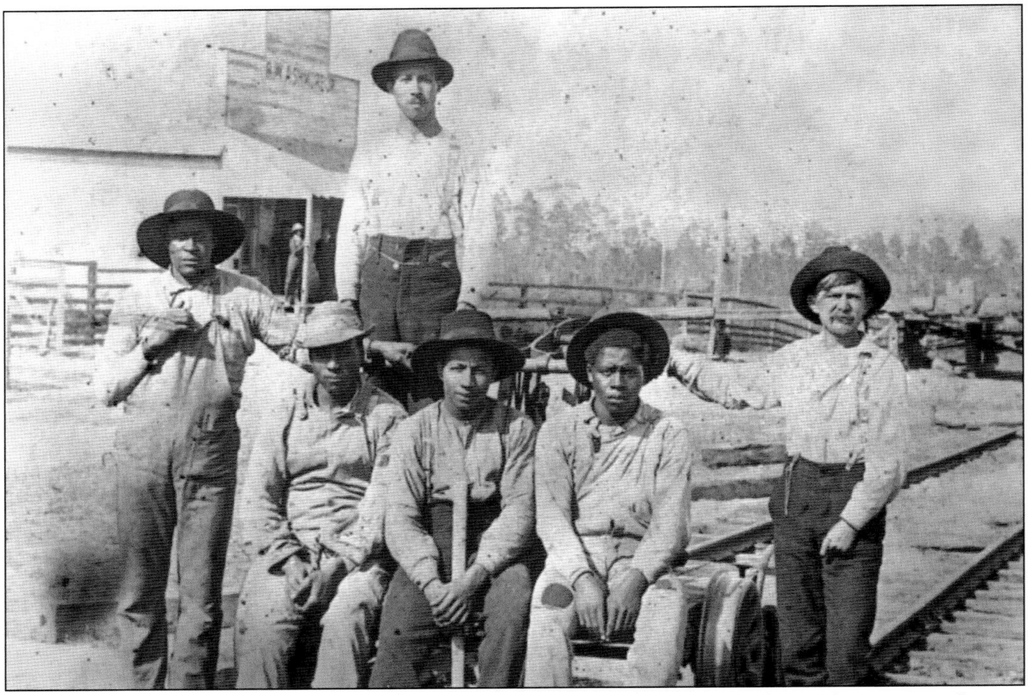

Pictured here is a railroad section crew on the Georgia, Florida, and Alabama line in Sopchoppy in the 1920s. In the background is the R.W. Ashmore store. Opened by Robert Walter Ashmore (1833–1902) before the turn of the century, it was later run by Ashmore's son Joseph (1867–1958) until it was closed in 1949. (Courtesy Florida Photographic Collection.)

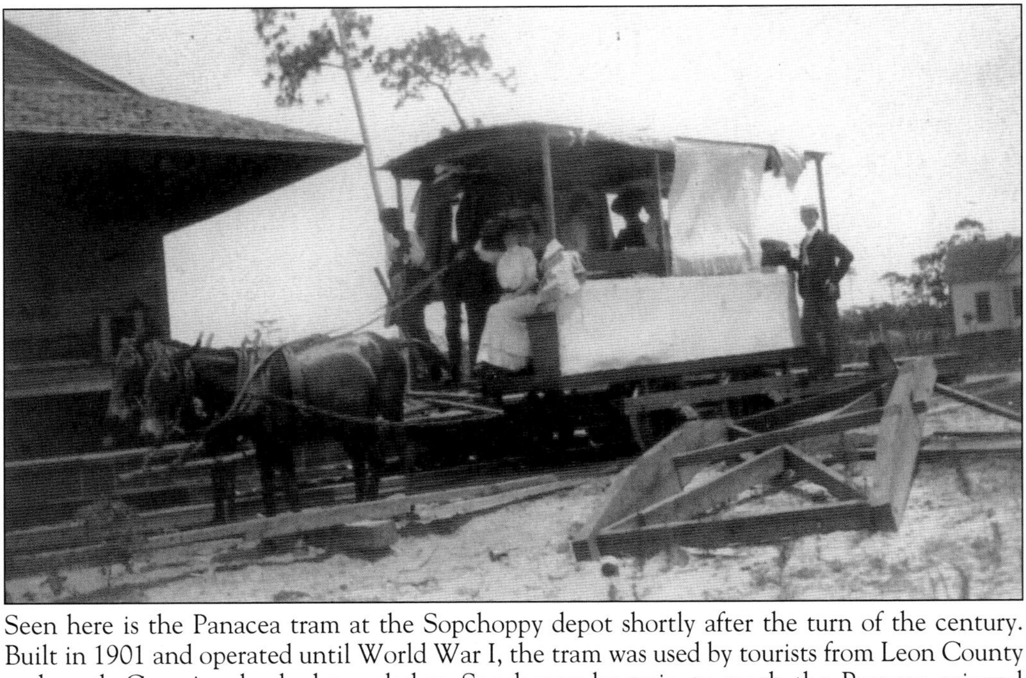

Seen here is the Panacea tram at the Sopchoppy depot shortly after the turn of the century. Built in 1901 and operated until World War I, the tram was used by tourists from Leon County and south Georgia who had traveled to Sopchoppy by train to reach the Panacea mineral springs and hotels. The mule-drawn tram was pulled along wooden tracks laid down in the sand. (Courtesy Florida Photographic Collection.)

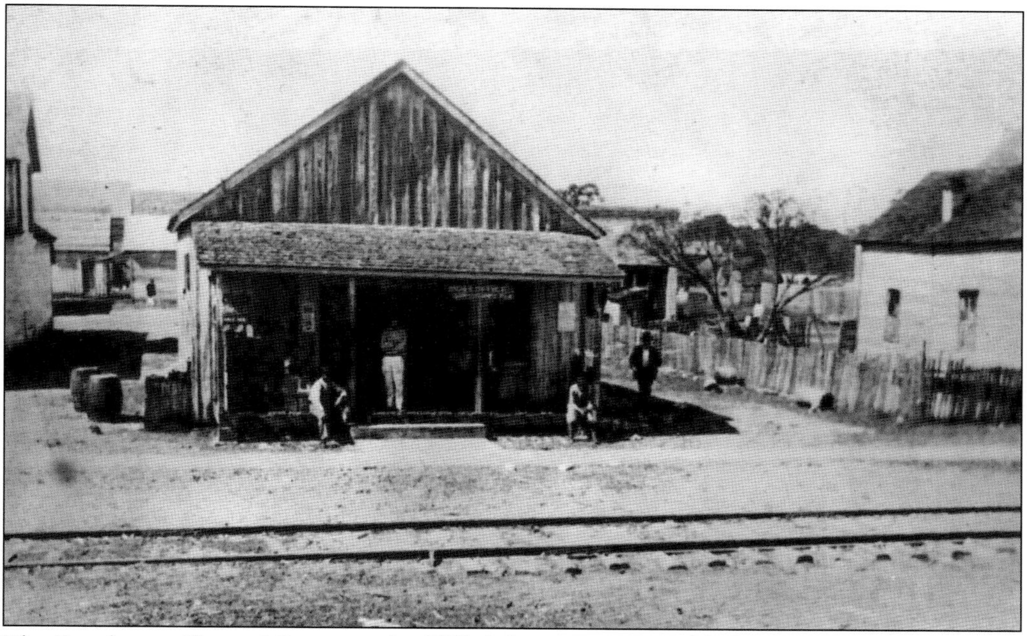

The Sopchoppy General Store on the GF&A line was operated before World War I by Maud Gwynn Pelestine. In 1917 it was taken over by Sally Lewis and included a soda fountain, barber shop, and post office. Lewis's son Nat operated the barber shop for many years after his mother moved to Jacksonville in 1928. (Courtesy Florida Photographic Collection.)

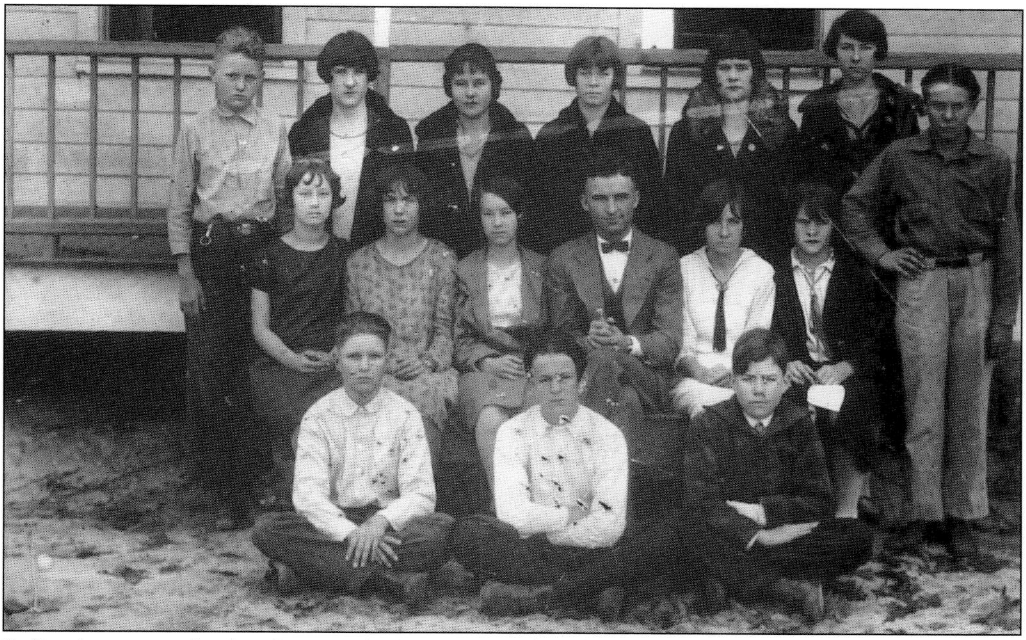

Before beginning his legal career A.L. Porter taught school in Sopchoppy and also served as the school's principal. Shown here in 1924, from left to right, are (front row) C.S. Alligood, Bill Moore, and V.L. Cooper; (middle row) Grace Spears, Mary Raker, Varol Beatrice Spears, A.L. Porter, Jessie Vause (?), Effie Edwards (?), and Joseph Harper (standing); (back row) Archie Alligood, Bessie Martin, Ruby Raker, Gertrude McCallister, Elzie Martin, and unidentified. (Courtesy Florida Photographic Collection.)

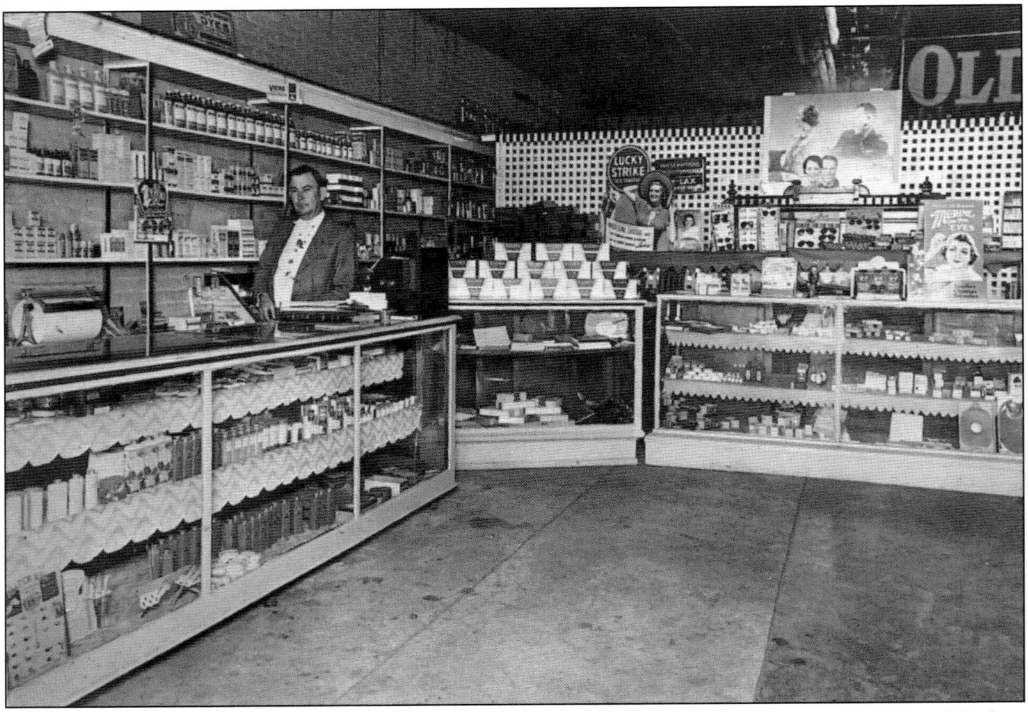

Opened in 1925, the Sopchoppy Drug Company was run for several years by Beno Hodge, seen here inside the store in the late 1930s. After Hodge's death his sister Coryne operated the business before closing it in the early 1970s. (Courtesy Florida Photographic Collection.)

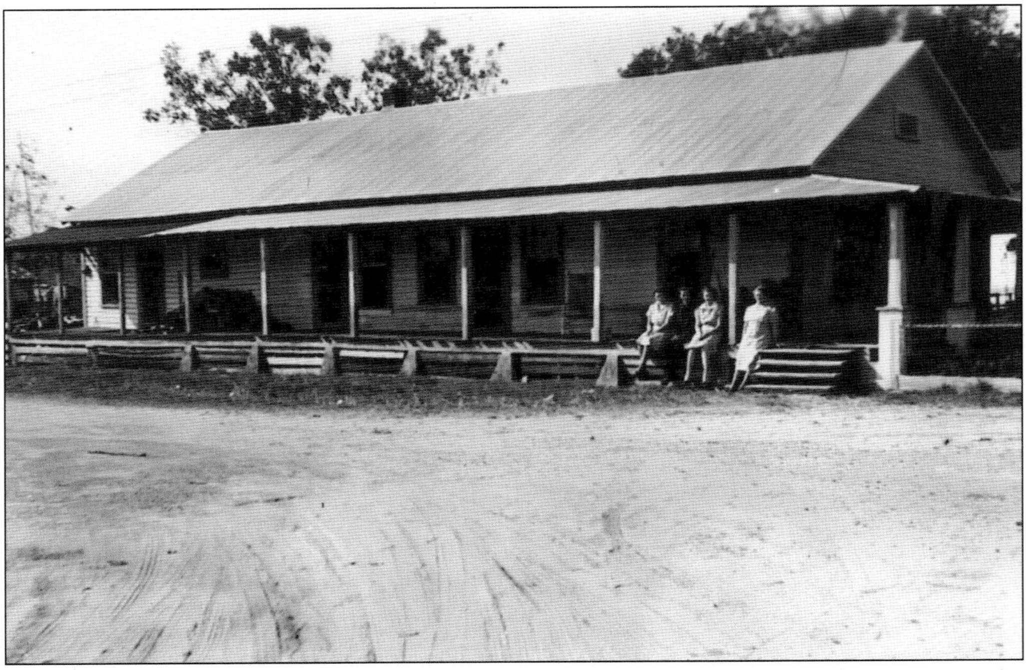

This boarding house, pictured here in the 1940s, was operated in Sopchoppy for many years by Martha Syfrett Revell (1859–1949). A portion of the old building is still standing. (Courtesy Florida Photographic Collection.)

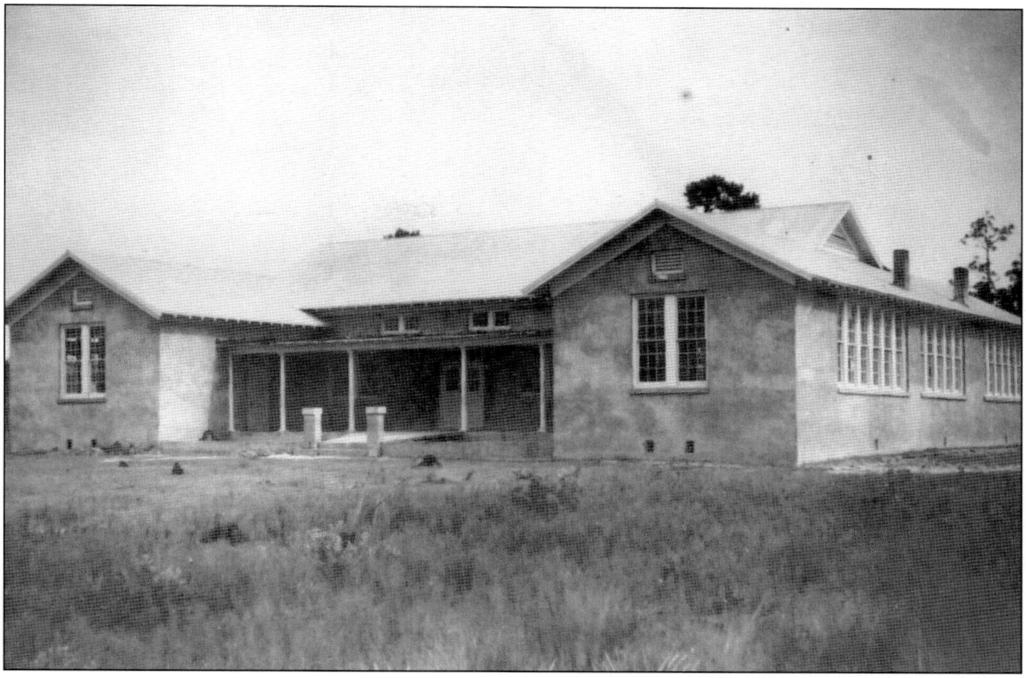

Originally built in 1924, the Sopchoppy High School was the first high school in the county to offer grades 1 through 12. Additions were made as WPA projects in 1933 and 1938. It became an elementary school in 1967 and was closed in 1996. The school is seen here in 1938 before its lime rock façade was added in the 1930s. (Courtesy Celia Whaley.)

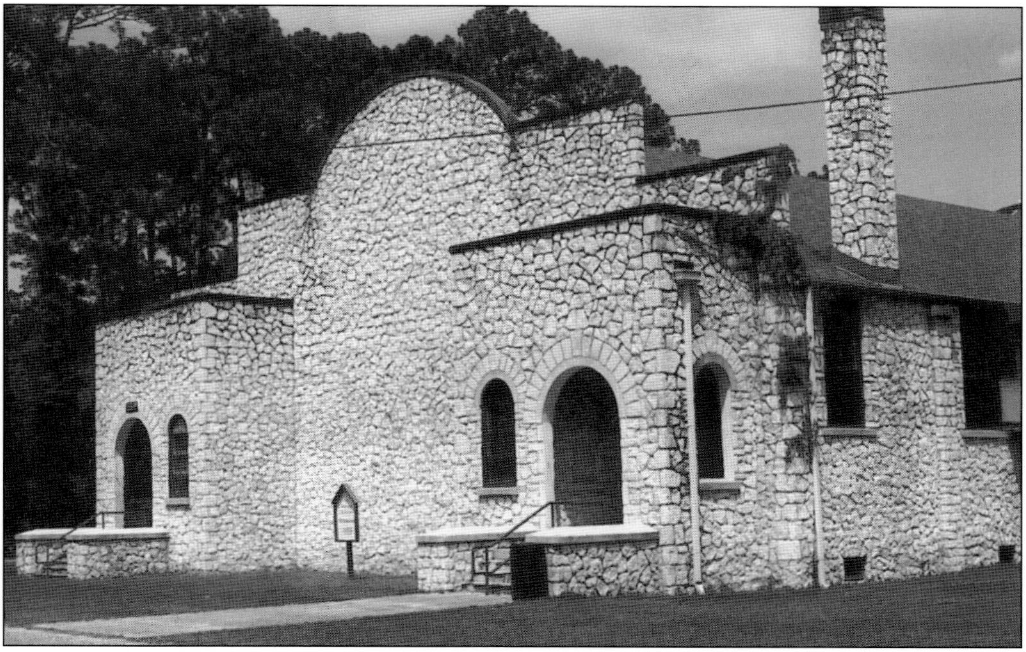

Built in 1938–1939 the Sopchoppy High School gymnasium sits adjacent to the main building. It features an exterior of lime rock quarried in nearby Medart. Local labor was used to construct both the gym and the school building. The gym was recently renovated and is now used for social functions. (Courtesy Terri Johnson.)

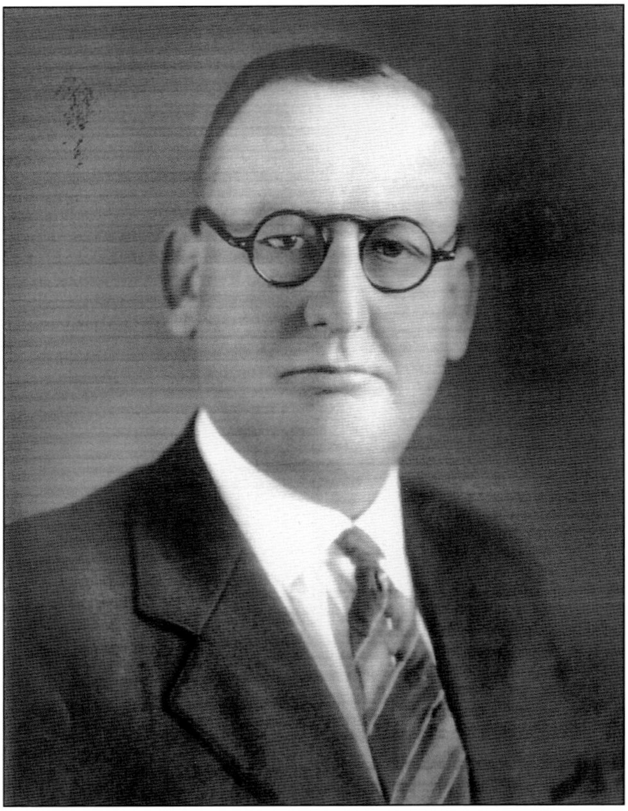

In 1912, Angus Morrison (1886–1937) of Sopchoppy was elected sheriff of Wakulla County, a position he held for 20 years. Named democratic committeeman from Wakulla in 1932, Morrison was elected as the county's legislative representative in 1937. He was a charter member of the Florida Sheriffs Association and was one of the sponsors in the creation of the Gulf Coast Scenic Highway, now U.S. Highway 98. (Courtesy Chip Morrison.)

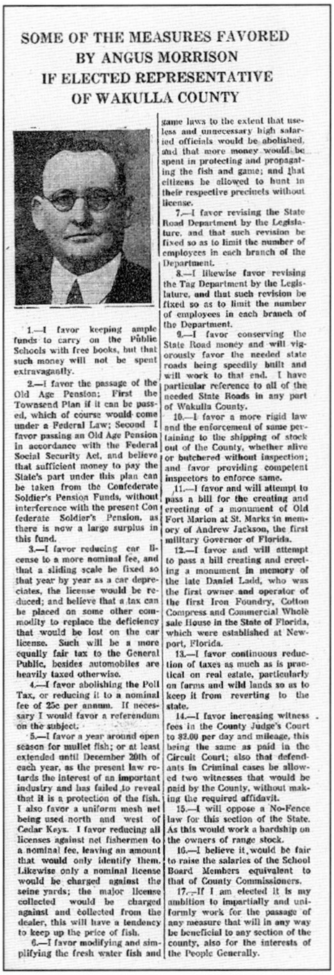

SOME OF THE MEASURES FAVORED BY ANGUS MORRISON IF ELECTED REPRESENTATIVE OF WAKULLA COUNTY

1.—I favor keeping ample funds to carry on the Public Schools with free books, but that such money will not be spent extravagantly.

2.—I favor the passage of the Old Age Pension: First the Townsend Plan if it can be passed, which of course would come under a Federal Law; Second I favor passing an Old Age Pension in accordance with the Federal Social Security Act, and believe that sufficient money to pay the State's part under this plan can be taken from the Confederate Soldier's Pension Funds, without interference with the present Confederate Soldier's Pension, as there is now a large surplus in this fund.

3.—I favor reducing car license to a more nominal fee, and that a sliding scale be fixed so that year by year as a car depreciates, the license would be reduced; and believe that a tax can be placed on some other commodity to replace the deficiency that would be lost on the car license. Such will be a more equally fair tax to the General Public, besides automobiles are heavily taxed otherwise.

4.—I favor abolishing the Poll Tax, or reducing it to a nominal fee of 25c per annum. If necessary I would favor a referendum on the subject.

5.—I favor a year around open season for mullet fish; or at least extended until December 20th of each year, as the present law retards the interest of an important industry and has failed to reveal that it is a protection of the fish. I also favor a uniform mesh net being used north and west of Cedar Keys. I favor reducing all licenses against net fishermen to a nominal fee, leaving an amount that would only identify them. Likewise only a nominal license would be charged against the seine yards; the major license collected would be charged against and collected from the dealer, this will have a tendency to keep up the price of fish.

6.—I favor modifying and simplifying the fresh water fish and game laws to the extent that useless and unnecessary high salaried officials would be abolished, and that more money would be spent in protecting and propagating the fish and game; and that citizens be allowed to hunt in their respective precincts without license.

7.—I favor revising the State Road Department by the Legislature, and that such revision be fixed so as to limit the number of employees in each branch of the Department.

8.—I likewise favor revising the Tag Department by the Legislature, and that such revision be fixed so as to limit the number of employees in each branch of the Department.

9.—I favor conserving the State Road money and will vigorously favor the needed state roads being speedily built and will work to that end. I have particular reference to all of the needed State Roads in any part of Wakulla County.

10.—I favor a more rigid law and the enforcement of same pertaining to the shipping of stock out of the County, whether alive or butchered without inspection; and favor providing competent inspectors to enforce same.

11.—I favor and will attempt to pass a bill for the creating and erecting of a monument of Old Fort Marion at St. Marks in memory of Andrew Jackson, the first military Governor of Florida.

12.—I favor and will attempt to pass a bill creating and erecting a monument in memory of the late Daniel Ladd, who was the first owner and operator of the first Iron Foundry, Cotton Compress and Commercial Whole sale House in the State of Florida, which were established at Newport, Florida.

13.—I favor continuous reduction of taxes as much as is practical on real estate, particularly on farms and wild lands so as to keep it from reverting to the state.

14.—I favor increasing witness fees in the County Judge's Court to $2.00 per day and mileage, this being the same as paid in the Circuit Court; also that defendants in Criminal cases be allowed two witnesses that would be paid by the County, without making the required affidavit.

15.—I will oppose a No-Fence law for this section of the State. As this would work a hardship on the owners of range stock.

16.—I believe it would be fair to raise the salaries of the School Board Members equivalent to that of County Commissioners.

17.—If I am elected it is my ambition to impartially and uniformly work for the passage of any measure that will in any way be beneficial to any section of the county, also for the interests of the People Generally.

Seen here is the campaign platform used by Angus Morrison in his successful bid as Wakulla's representative in 1937. Among those things favored were an old age pension, the abolition of the poll tax, and the erection of a monument to Daniel Ladd in Newport. (Courtesy Chip Morrison.)

Appointed by Gov. Fuller Warren to the Florida Supreme Court in 1949, Sopchoppy native B.K. Roberts (1907–1999) served on the court for 27 years with three terms as chief justice before retiring in 1976. Roberts also helped establish the Florida State University College of Law. Upon retiring from the court, he practiced law until 1994. (Courtesy Florida Photographic Collection.)

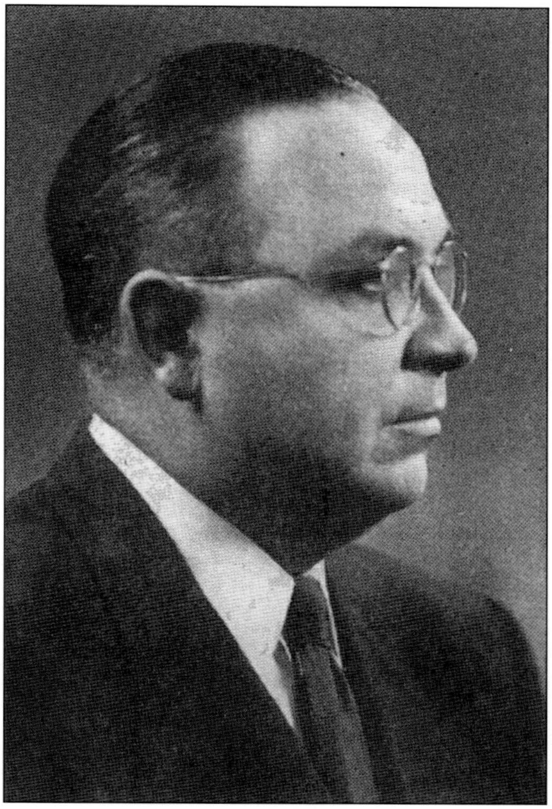

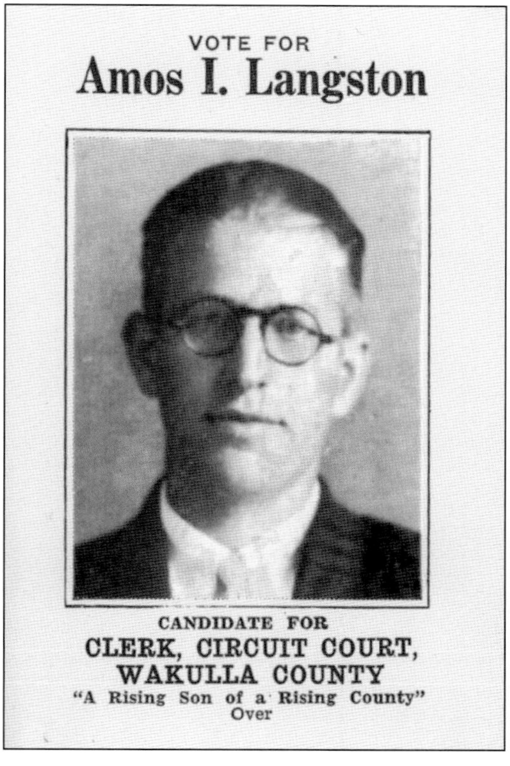

In 1932 Amos I. Langston (1911–1991) of Sopchoppy ran an unsuccessful campaign for clerk of the circuit court. Eight years later his brother Gilbert Langston (1914–1971) was elected to the office, which he held for 16 years. (Courtesy Eloise Strickland.)

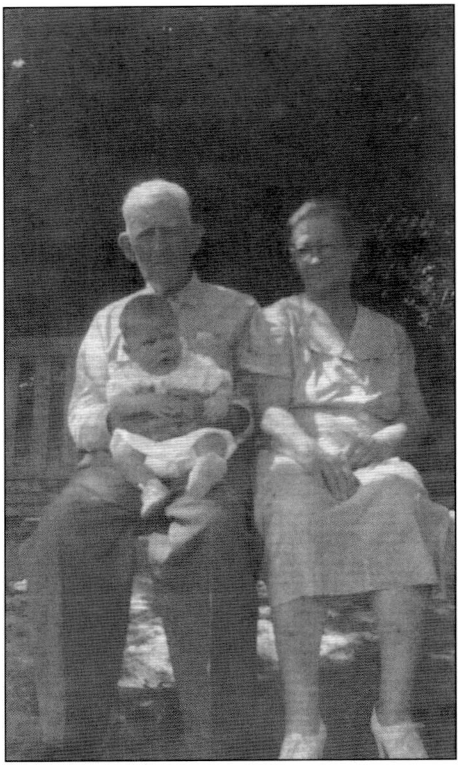

Melvin O. Strickland (1875–1966), pictured here with his wife, Sarah Langston Strickland (1878–1957), and grandson, was one of Sopchoppy's first commercial bee keepers. In addition to processing honey, Strickland also operated a grist mill that ground corn for area residents each Saturday. (Courtesy George Strickland Sr.)

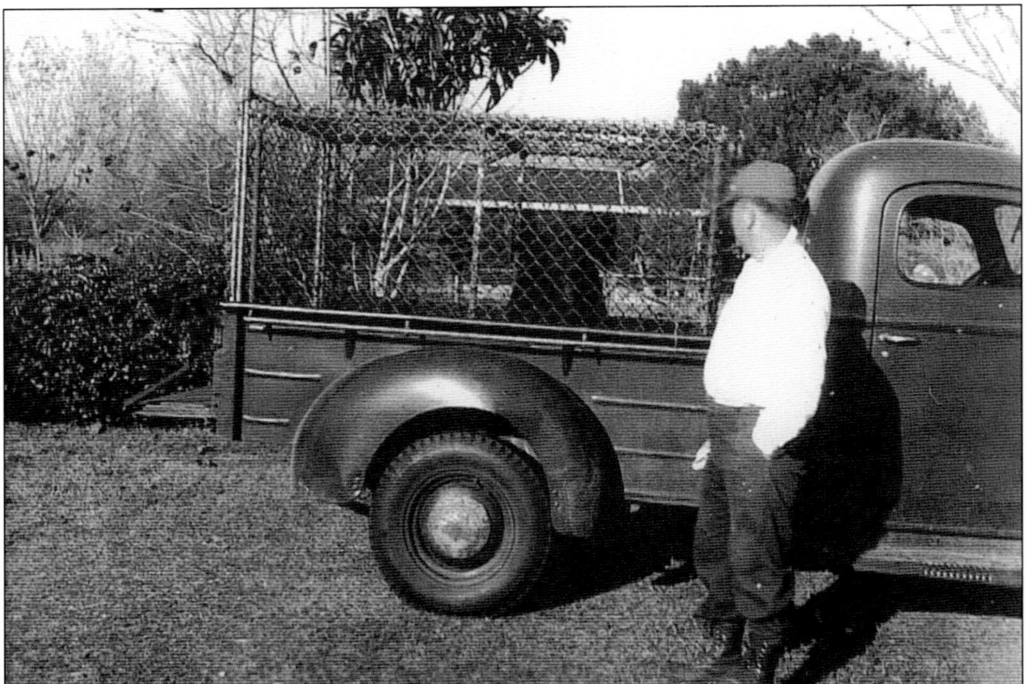

Taking over his father, M.O. Strickland's, honey business, George Strickland Sr. operated S&K Honey Company for many years with partner Bernie Kemp. Strickland is seen here in the late 1940s with a black bear that he caught near his bee boxes. (Courtesy George Strickland Sr.)

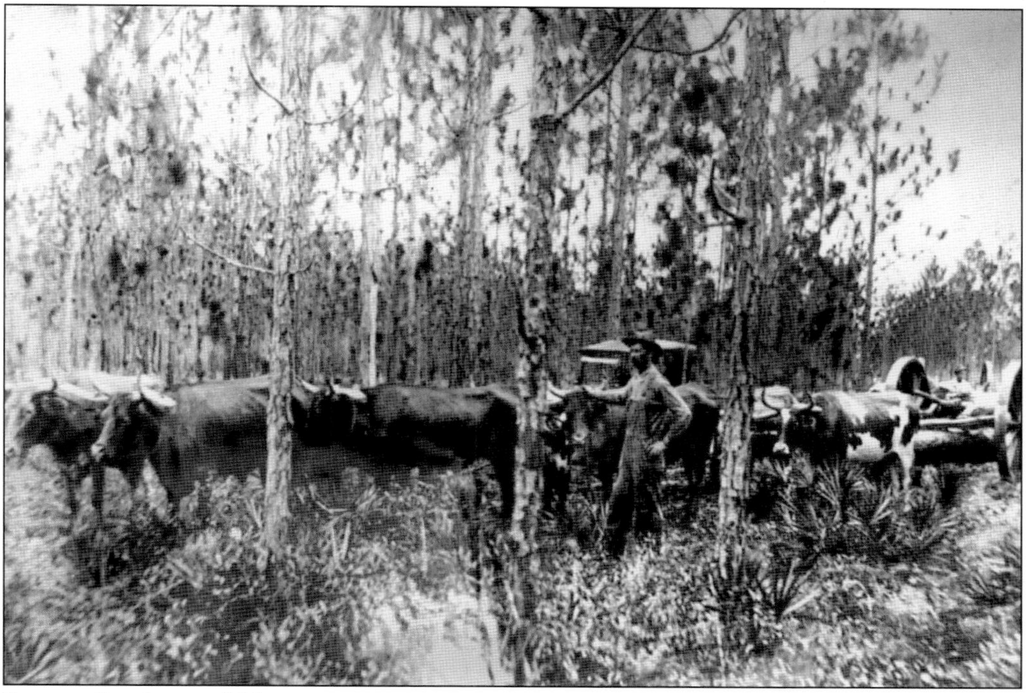

Born in Sopchoppy, Valarious Lafayette Roberts (1875–1948) is seen here with the ox team he used to "snake" logs out of the woods and swamps before hauling them to area sawmills. Roberts also operated a passenger boat on the Ochlockonee River in the 1910s and 1920s and served as a county commissioner in the 1930s. The names of his oxen were Red, Pet, Rat, Lewis, Brood, Bright, and Jack. (Courtesy Florida Photographic Collection.)

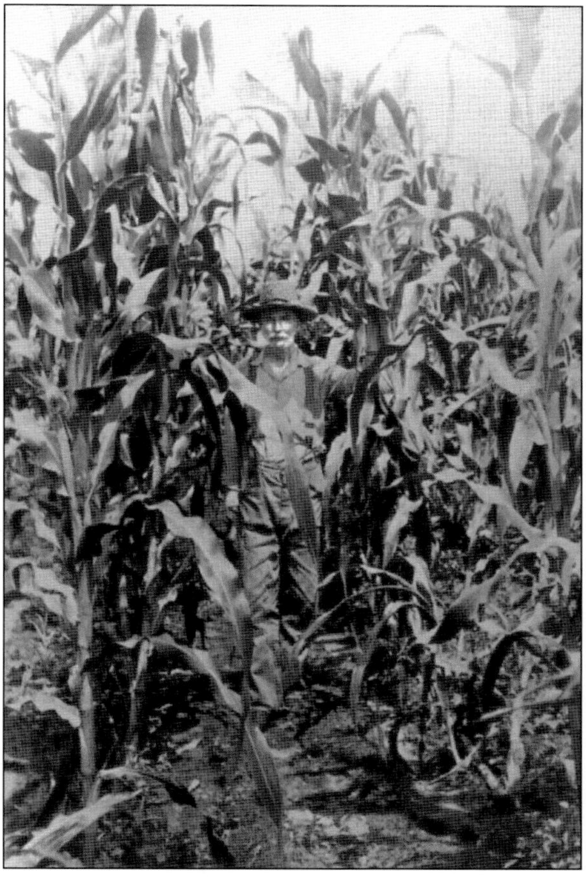

Seen here is John Edward Houston (1863–1930) on the family farm just outside of Sopchoppy in the 1920s. He is standing in a cornfield planted by his son Royce Houston (1906–1998). The prize-winning crop earned the younger Houston a trip to both the state and world's fair. (Courtesy Shirley Ann Sanders.)

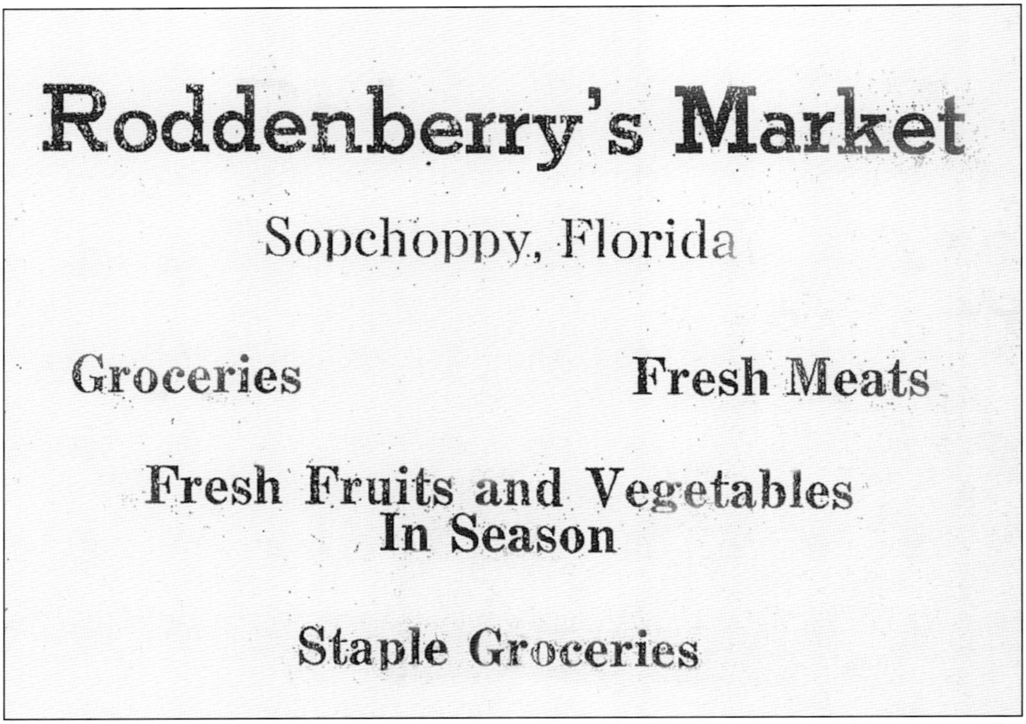

Opened in the 1920s by R.L. Roddenberry (1876–1963), the business was taken over in the early 1940s by Roddenberry's son Ernest Roddenberry (1905–1971), who was joined by partner Amos Langston (1911–1991). It then became the R&L Trading Company. Langston became the sole owner in the 1960s, renaming it the Sopchoppy Grocery. Over 70 years later the business is still in operation. (Courtesy *Wakulla County News*.)

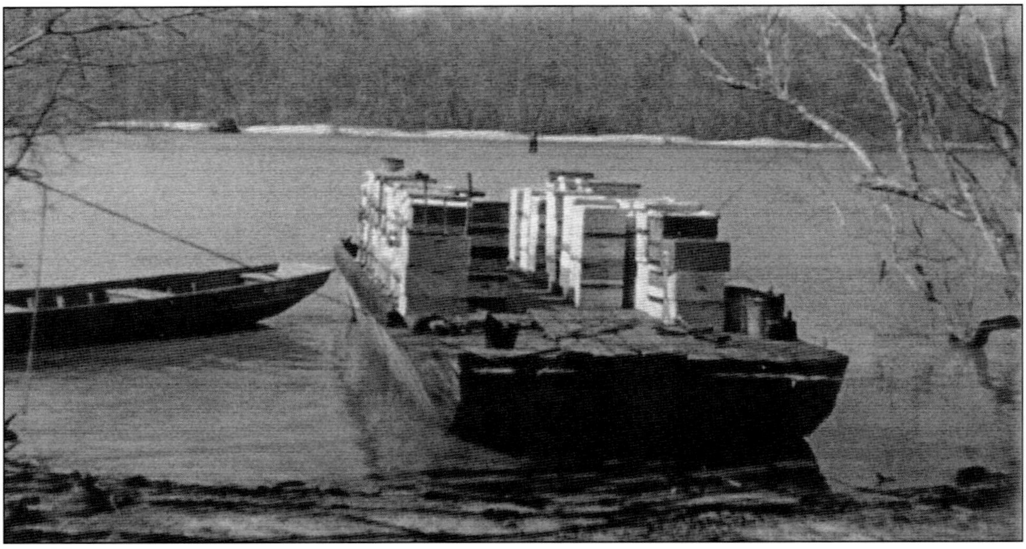

For 35 years Tony Strickland and his father, D.L. Strickland, operated Cindy's Tupelo Honey in Sopchoppy, and they took advantage of the tupelo trees that grow along the Sopchoppy, Ochlockonee, and Apalachicola Rivers. Seen here are bee boxes on a barge along the Apalachicola River used by Strickland to collect honey from the tupelo trees. (Courtesy Tony Strickland.)

Five

PANACEA

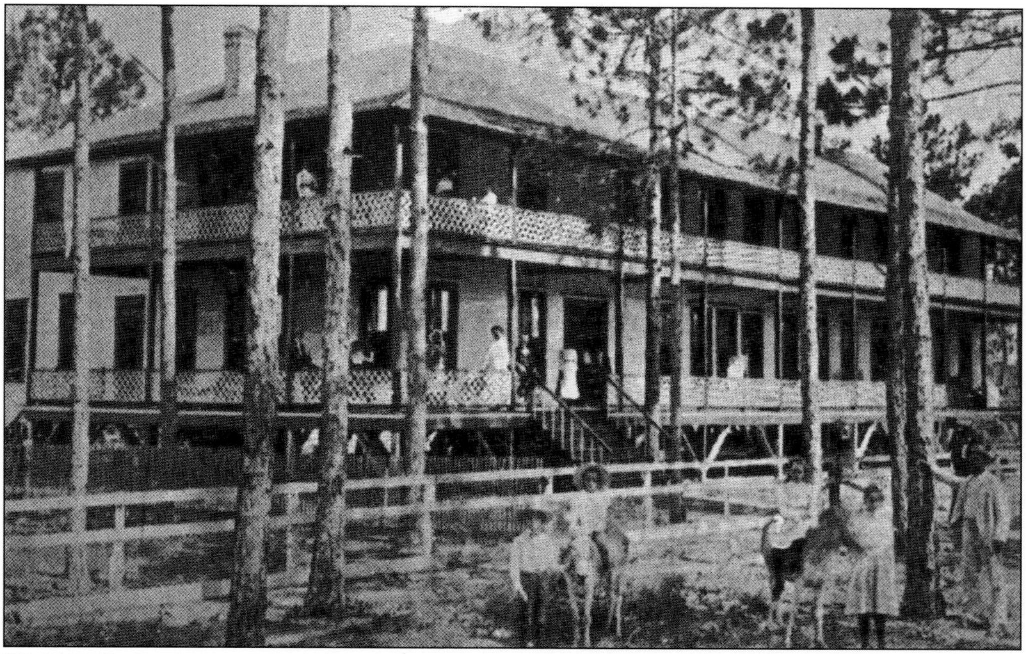

W.C. Tully Sr. (1841–1929) founded Panacea in 1895 and named it for the healing properties of its many mineral springs. In addition to building a post office and several cottages, Tully built the Panacea Mineral Springs Hotel, seen here at the turn of the century. Accommodating 125 guests, the hotel offered many amenities to its summer visitors during Panacea's heyday in the 1910s and 1920s. It was destroyed by fire in the 1920s. (Courtesy Florida Photographic Collection.)

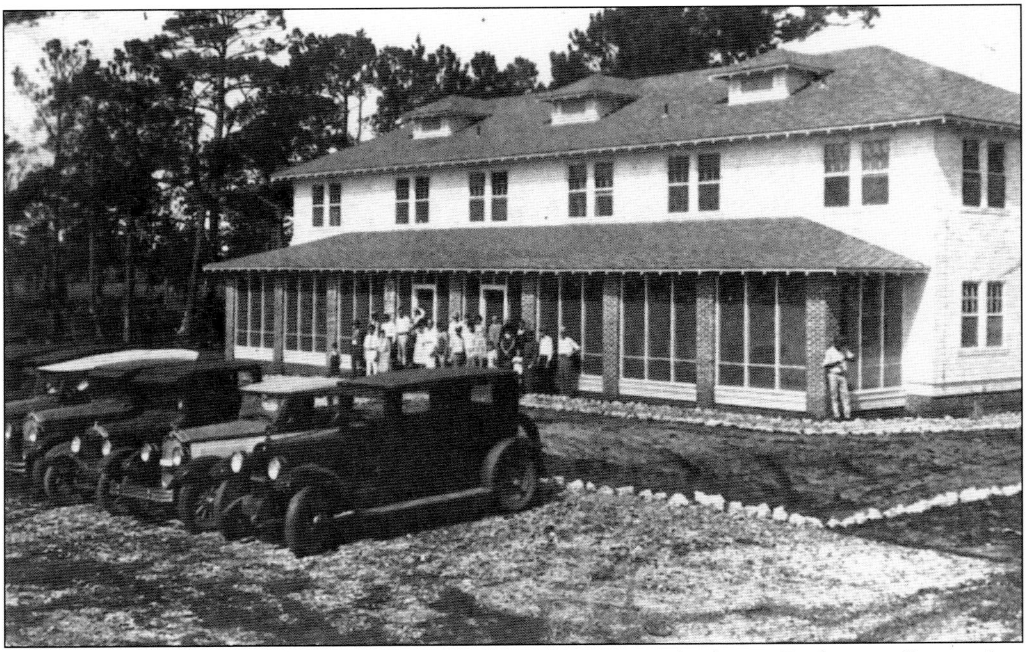

Another of Panacea's large hotels, the Bay View Inn was built on Dickerson Bay and is seen here in 1929. Originally a dormitory for men, the hotel was remodeled in 1901 and opened to the general public. Together with the Panacea Hotel, the Bay View offered visitors a relaxing and pleasant time. The hotel was torn down in the 1950s. (Courtesy Florida Photographic Collection.)

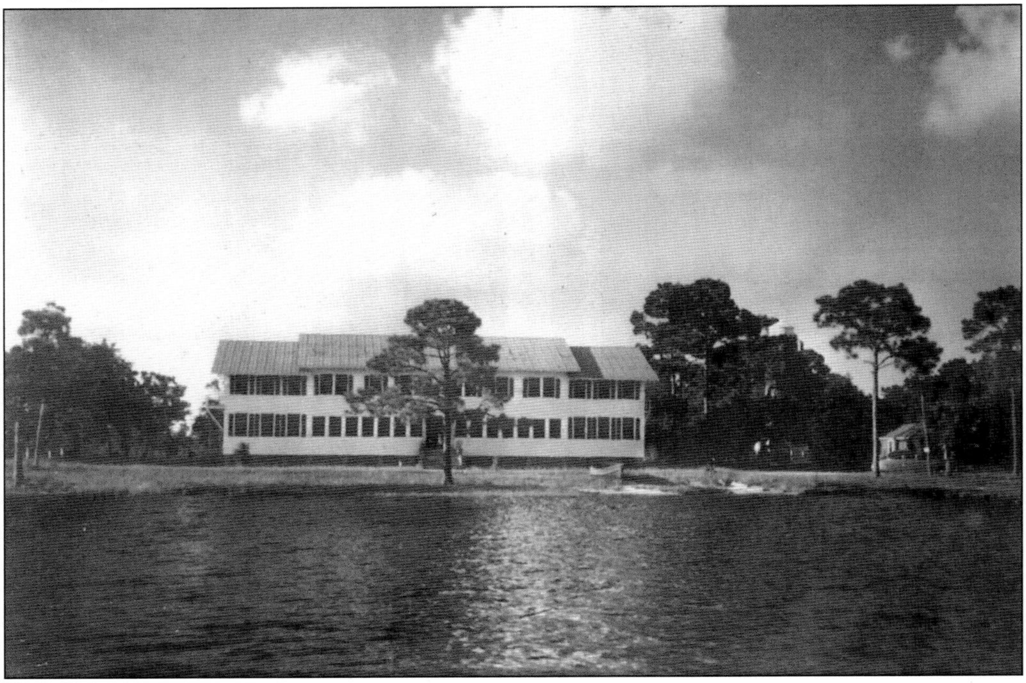

The Tallahassee Yacht Club is located at the head of Ochlockonee Bay c. 1950. Originally constructed as a hunting and sportsman's lodge, the building was later home of the Coast Guard Auxilliary Division 8. (Courtesy author.)

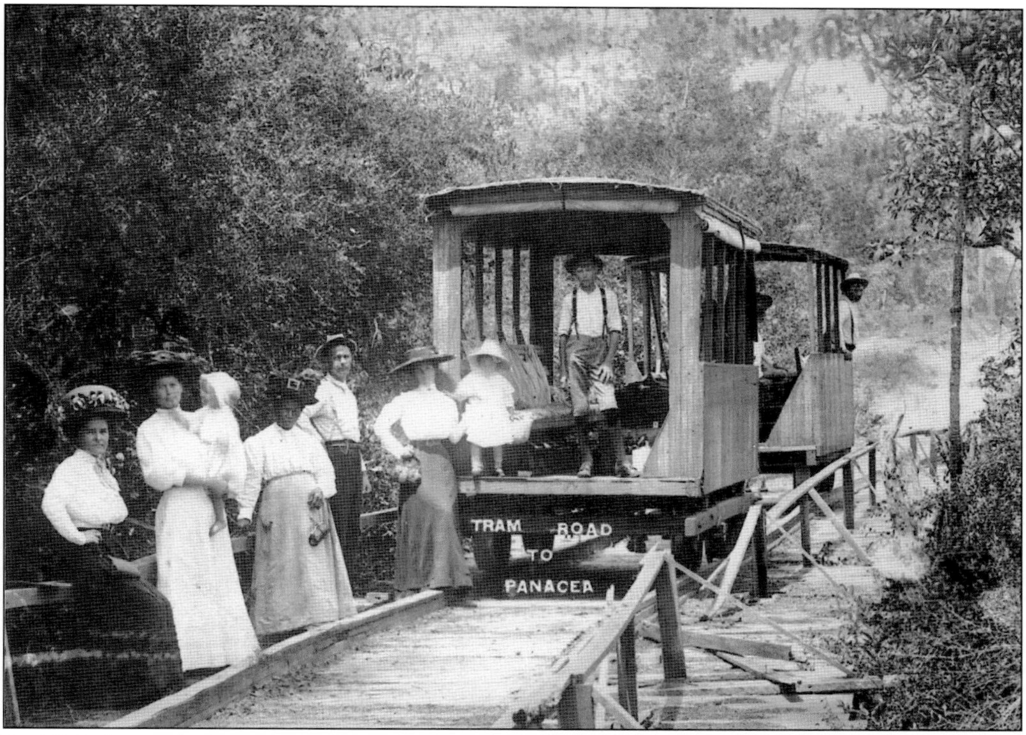

In 1901 this mule-drawn tram line was completed between Sopchoppy and Panacea, replacing the old stage coach that had previously carried both mail and visitors to the resort. Pulled along wooden rails the little tram often jumped its tracks. It was used up until World War I. (Courtesy Florida Photographic Collection.)

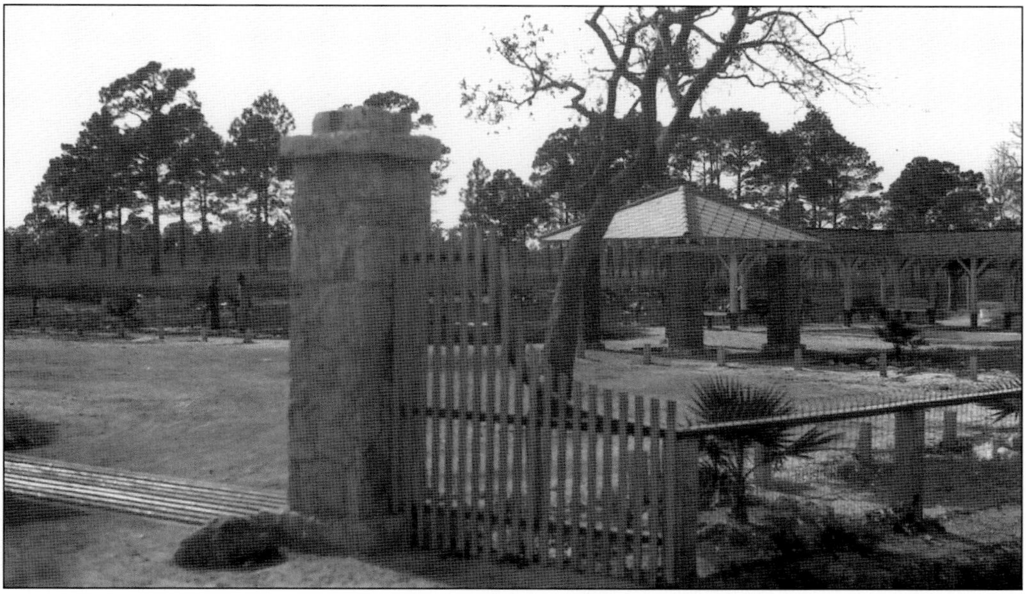

Here is the pavilion at Panacea Springs as it appeared in the late 1920s. Located between the Panacea Mineral Springs and Bay View hotels, the pavilion featured evening concerts, recitations, dancing, and cake walks at the turn of the century. (Courtesy Florida Photographic Collection.)

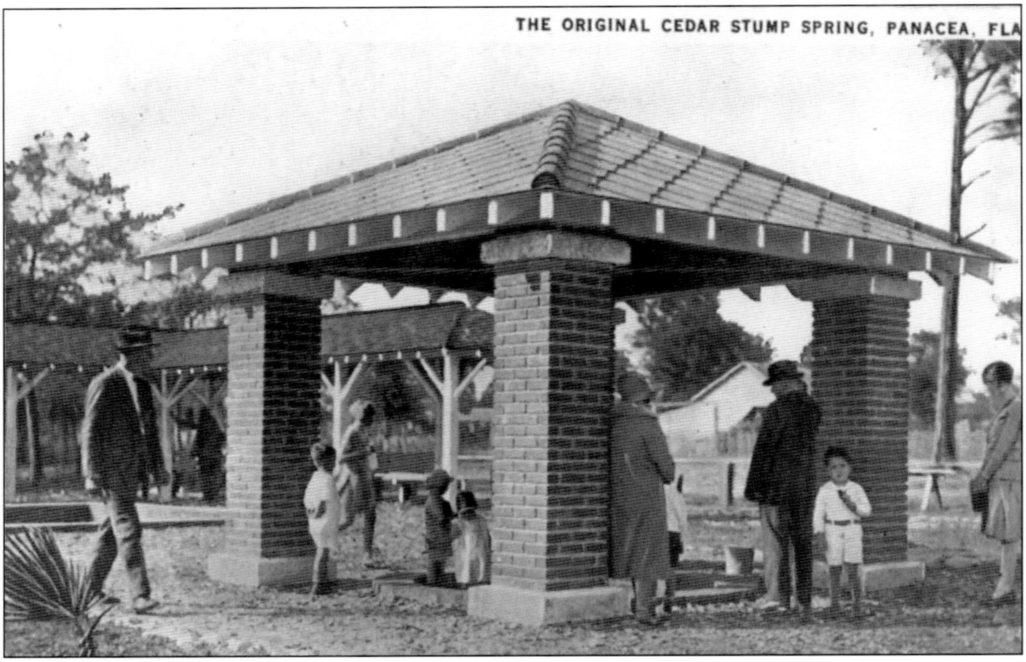

As many as 20 springs once flowed within the pavilion, each containing different mineral properties. Attracting visitors to the area for their restorative powers, the springs were named for the illnesses they were thought to cure. Seen here in the 1920s is the shed covering the original cedar stump spring. (Courtesy Florida Photographic Collection.)

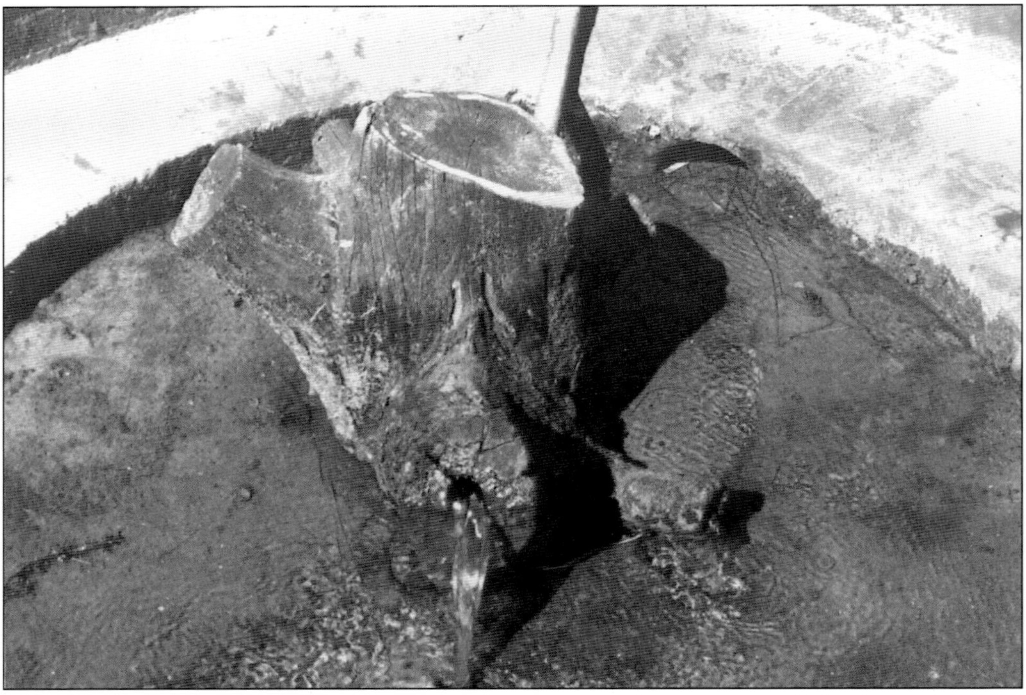

In order to facilitate the flow of the mineral springs, a cedar stump would be driven into the ground to allow the water to pour from holes bored in its branches. This stump was installed in 1926 by John Henry Roddenberry (1891–1932). (Courtesy Florida Photographic Collection.)

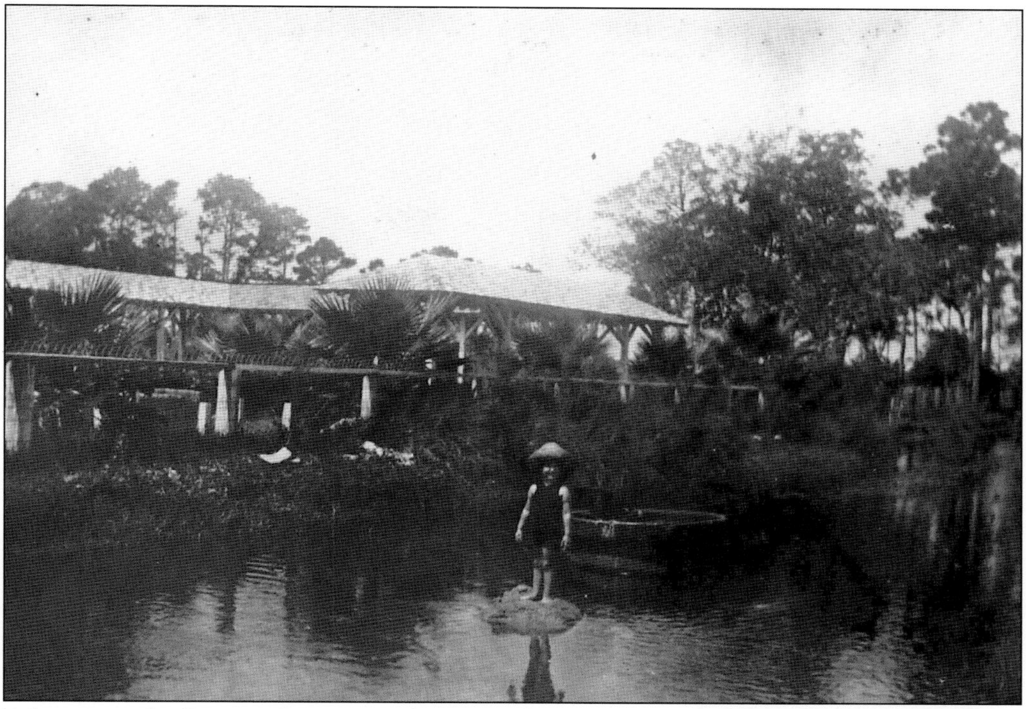

Adjacent to the Panacea Springs pavilion was a large mineral pool used for swimming. In 1901 a steam-powered pump, which replaced an old windmill pump, was installed to keep the pool filled. Water from this pool was also piped to the nearby hotels. This picture dates from the early 1920s. (Courtesy Florida Photographic Collection.)

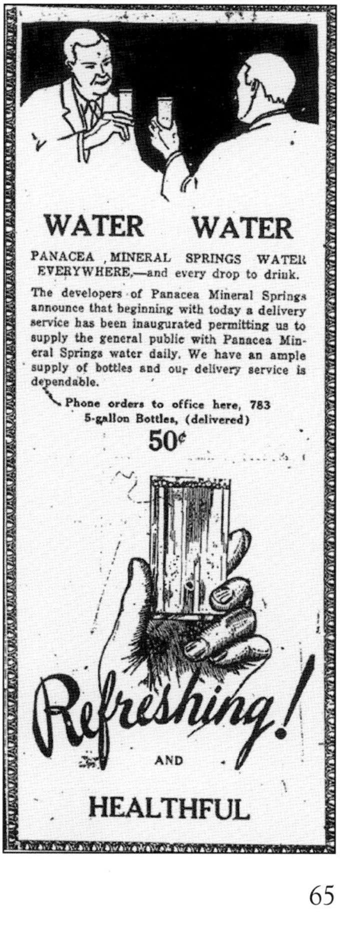

A June 23, 1929 advertisement announces the sale of water drawn from the Panacea Mineral Springs. An analysis done several years earlier by Professor V. Coblentz of New York showed the waters to contain elements such as sodium, magnesium, calcium chloride, and calcium carbonate and declared it to be "especially beneficial in kidney, stomach and bowel disorders." (Courtesy *Tallahassee Daily Democrat*.)

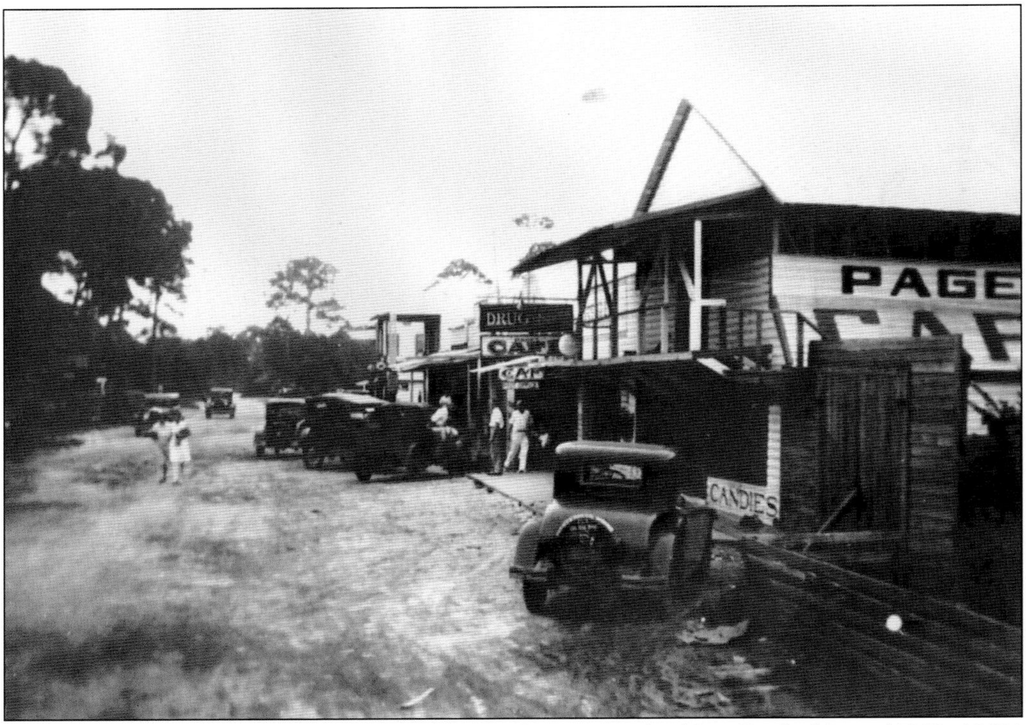

A view of downtown Panacea as it appeared in the 1930s. Thaddeus Raiford Page (1883–1959) moved to Panacea in the late 1920s and purchased a café, which can be seen here. He soon added a drug store, soda fountain, and hotel to his holdings. In later years a dance floor was installed complete with a small band. (Courtesy Florida Photographic Collection.)

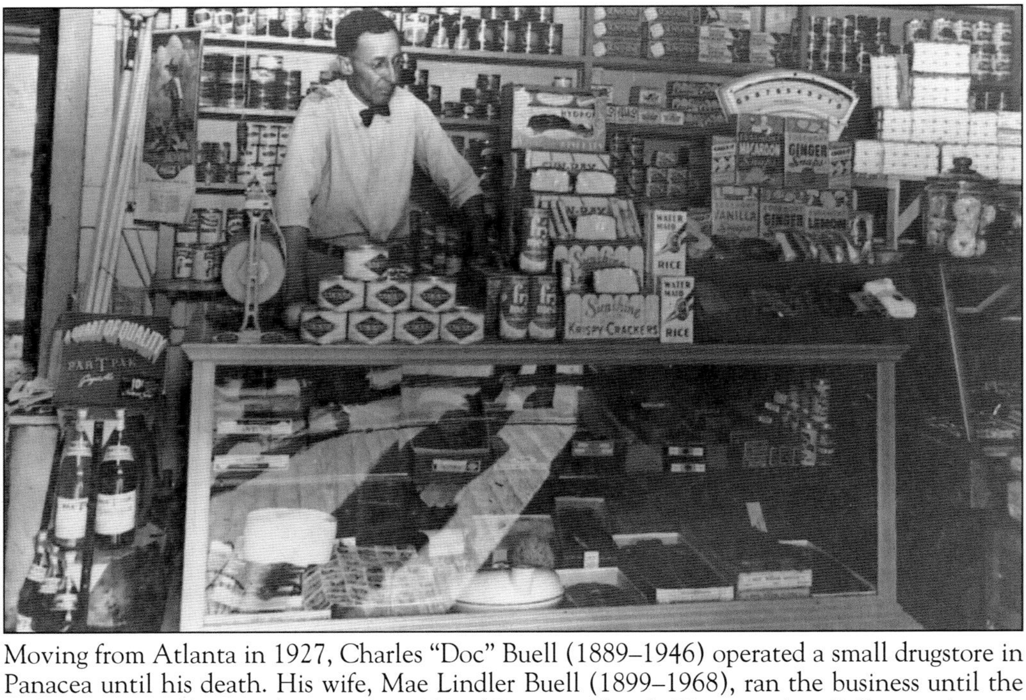

Moving from Atlanta in 1927, Charles "Doc" Buell (1889–1946) operated a small drugstore in Panacea until his death. His wife, Mae Lindler Buell (1899–1968), ran the business until the early 1950s. Buell is seen here in the 1930s. (Courtesy Florida Photographic Collection.)

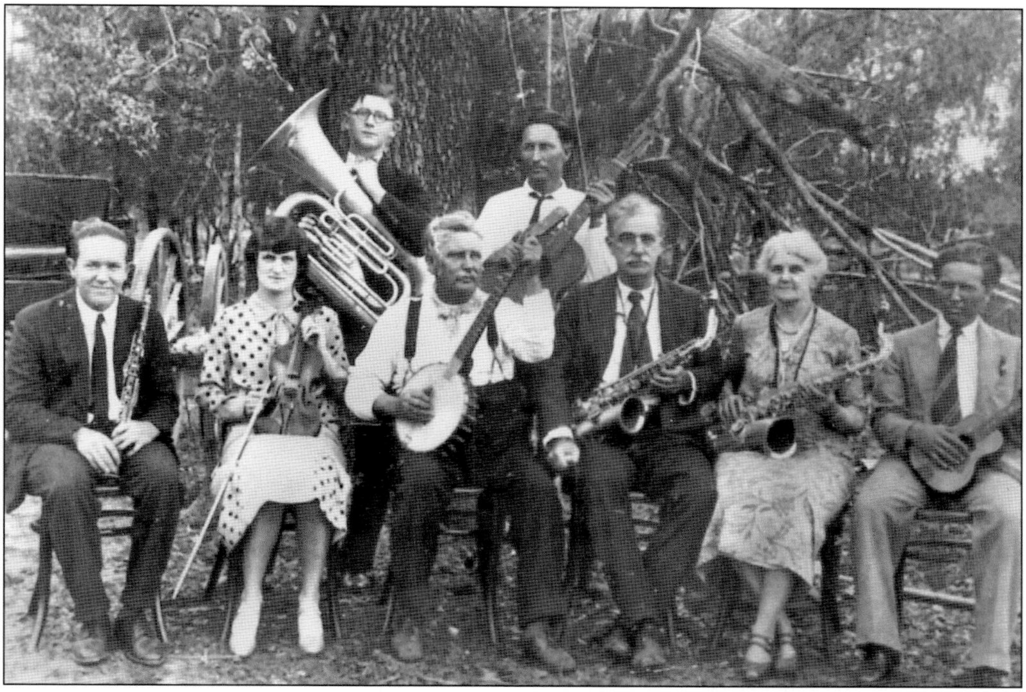

John Robertson Kelly (1867–1937) of Panacea was a traveling livestock trader who traveled throughout north Florida to make his living. Kelly is seen here with family and friends in 1928 at a campsite on the Suwannee River. From left to right are (seated) John Kelly, Aetha Scarbor, John Robertson Kelly, Paul Henry Scarbor, Mrs. ? Scarbor, and Taylor Kelly; (standing) Paul Scarbor Jr. and Patrick Kelly. (Courtesy Florida Photographic Collection.)

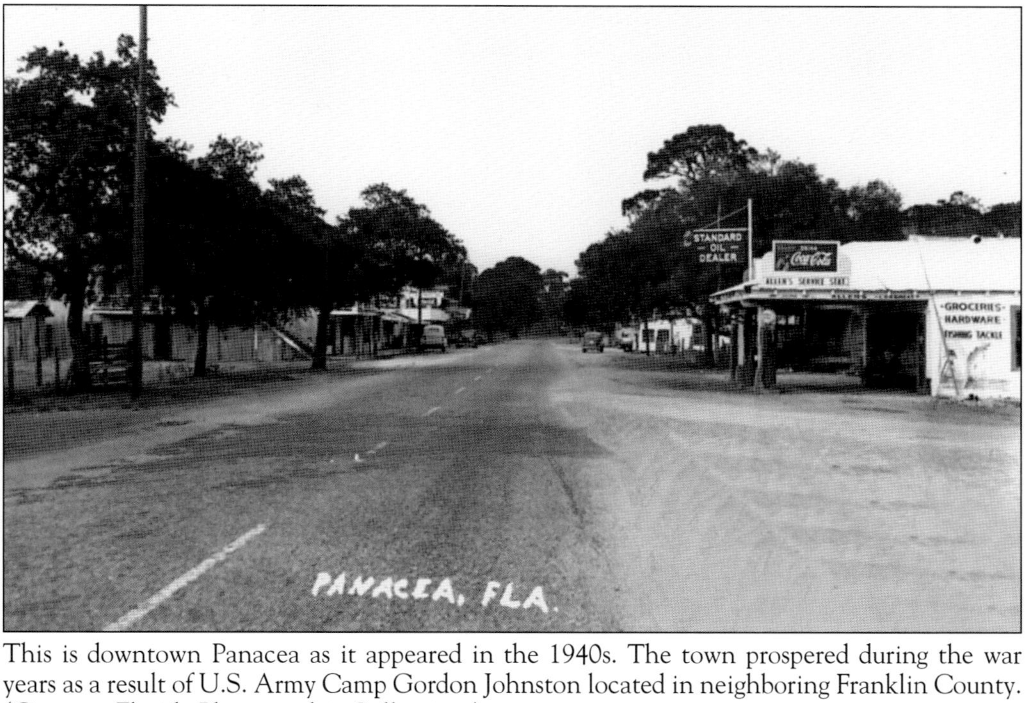

This is downtown Panacea as it appeared in the 1940s. The town prospered during the war years as a result of U.S. Army Camp Gordon Johnston located in neighboring Franklin County. (Courtesy Florida Photographic Collection.)

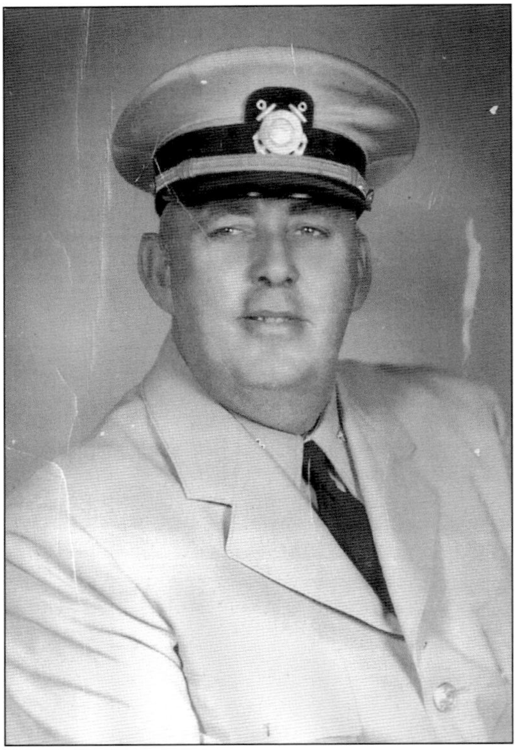

A native of New York City, William Schley (1906–1982) majored in journalism at the University of Minnesota and pursued an early career as a reporter. Moving to Panacea with his wife, Irene, in 1946, Captain Schley founded and was the first commander of the Wakulla County unit of the U.S. Coast Guard Auxiliary. Schley also served as Wakulla's civil defense director and was one of the county's leading environmentalists. (Courtesy Linda Thompson.)

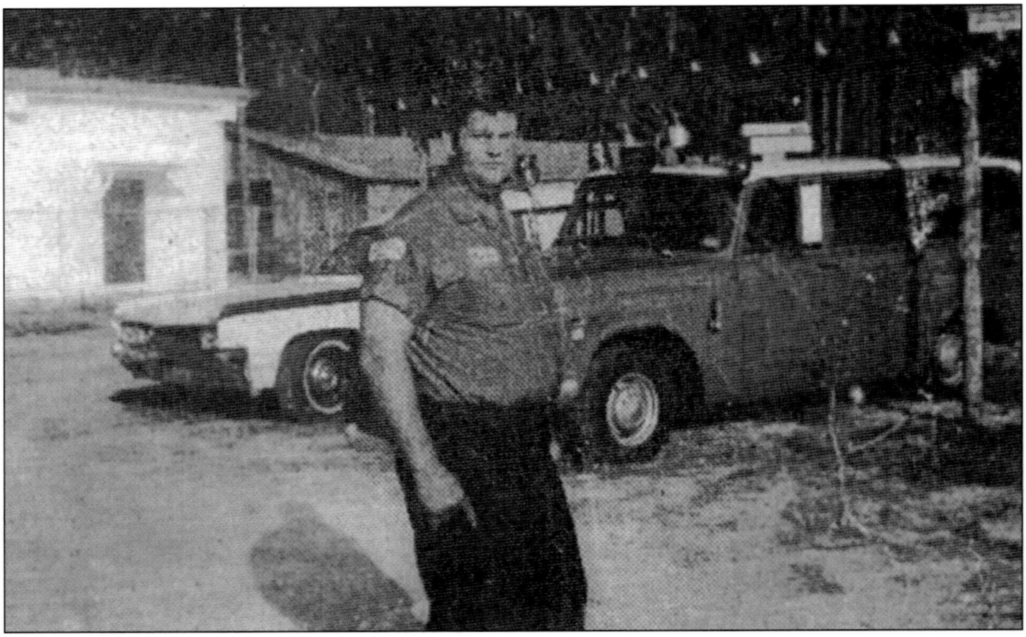

In 1970, Glynwood Crum of Panacea created the Wakulla County Ambulance Service, the county's first emergency response unit. Using a donated ambulance and financing the service himself, Crum and his four brothers—Donnie, Warren, Kenneth, and Ronald Fred—along with several volunteers, provided first aid to accident victims for two years until the operation was taken over by the county in 1972. Crum is seen here in front of his rescue vehicles in the early 1970s. (Courtesy Audrey Crum.)

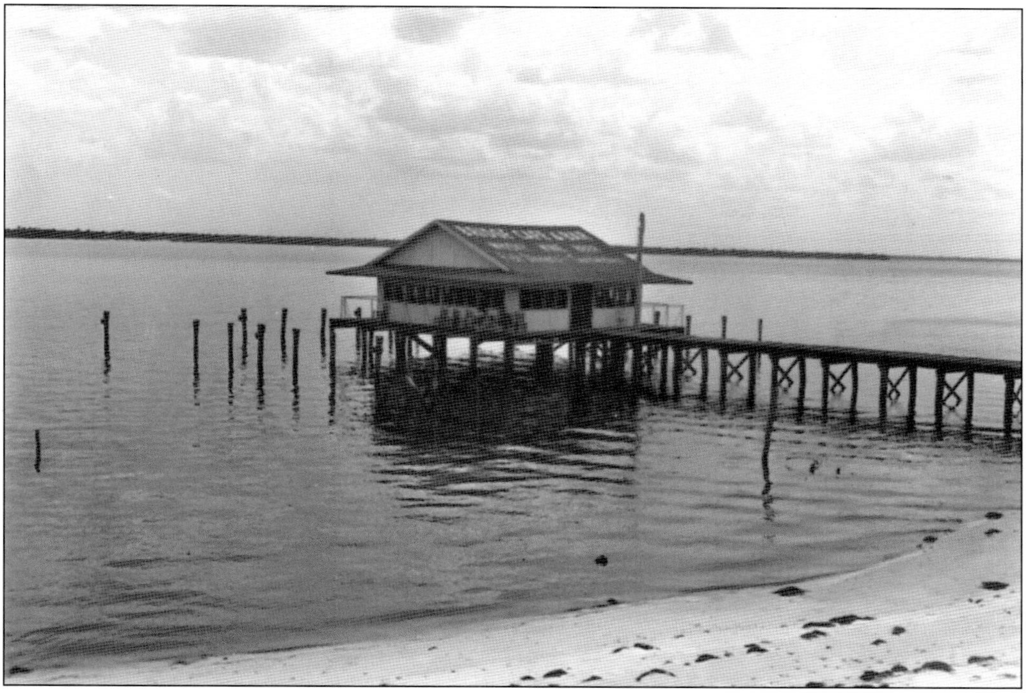

The Bridge Café and Bar is seen here in 1948. As Wakulla was a "dry" county in the 1940s and 1950s, the bar's off-shore location enabled it to serve liquor legally. It was torn down in the 1950s. (Courtesy Florida Photographic Collection.)

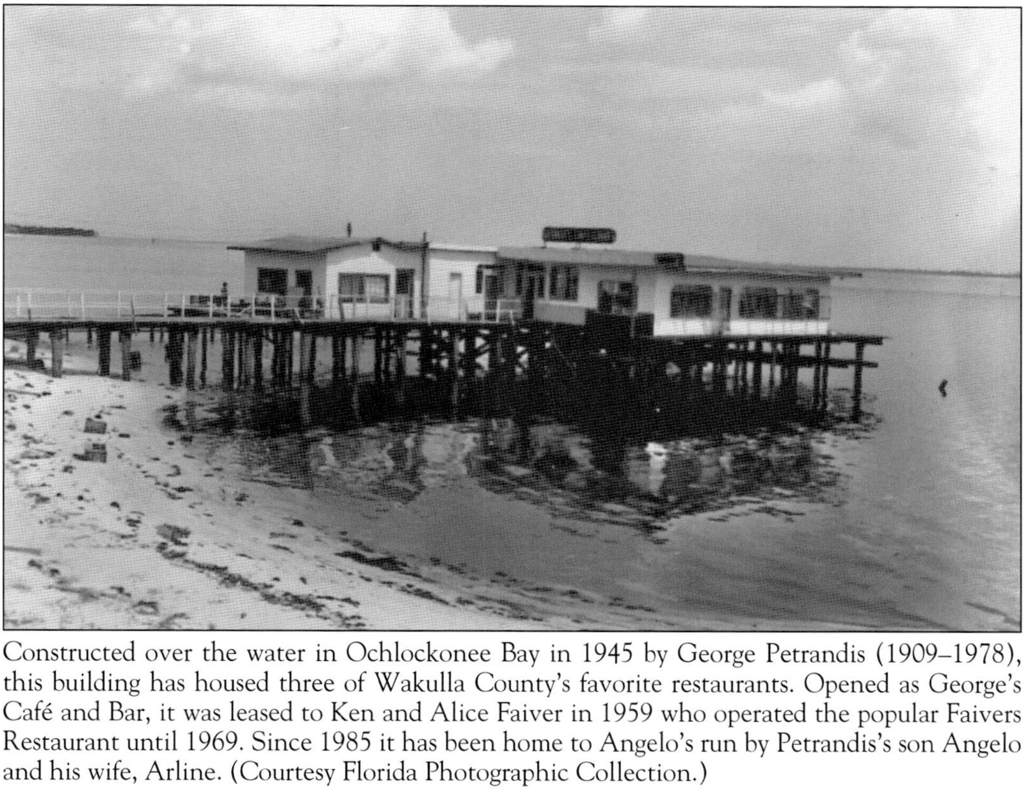

Constructed over the water in Ochlockonee Bay in 1945 by George Petrandis (1909–1978), this building has housed three of Wakulla County's favorite restaurants. Opened as George's Café and Bar, it was leased to Ken and Alice Faiver in 1959 who operated the popular Faivers Restaurant until 1969. Since 1985 it has been home to Angelo's run by Petrandis's son Angelo and his wife, Arline. (Courtesy Florida Photographic Collection.)

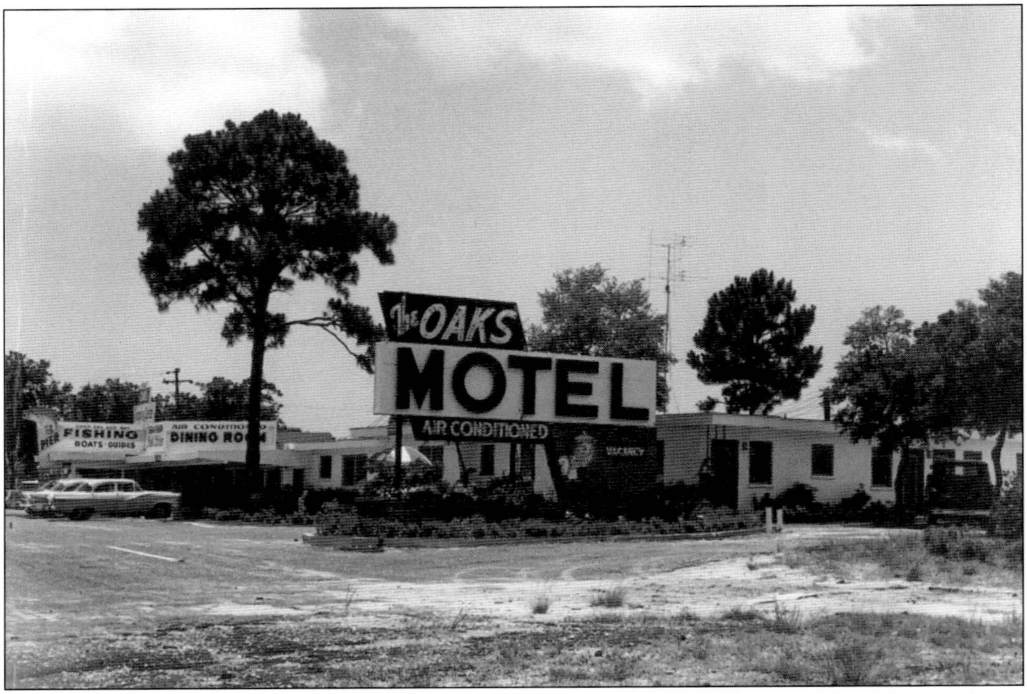

A familiar site in Panacea is the Oaks Motel and Restaurant opened in 1953 by Alton and Ora Strickland Oaks. Seen here in the late 1950s, the business was run by the family until 2000. (Courtesy Barbara Ann Linton.)

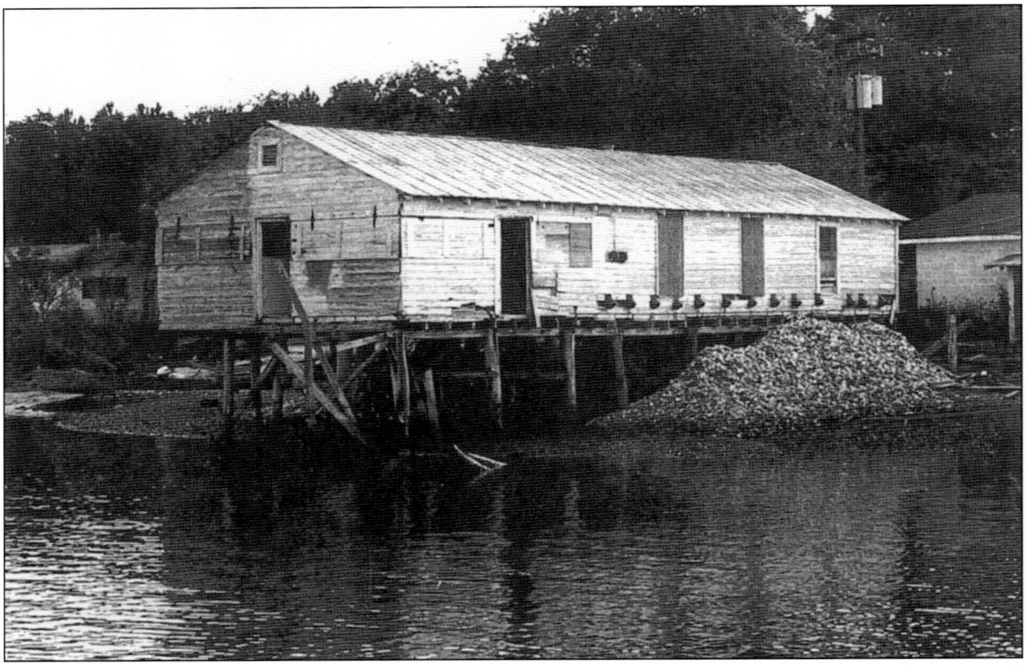

Panacea produces some of the best seafood on the gulf coast. Pictured here is the Metcalf and Son seafood business built in 1952 by Herman Metcalf. Metcalf and his son operated the business for 12 years, specializing in blue crabs and oysters. Note the large pile of empty oyster shells at right. (Courtesy Linda Thompson.)

Seven

SHADEVILLE

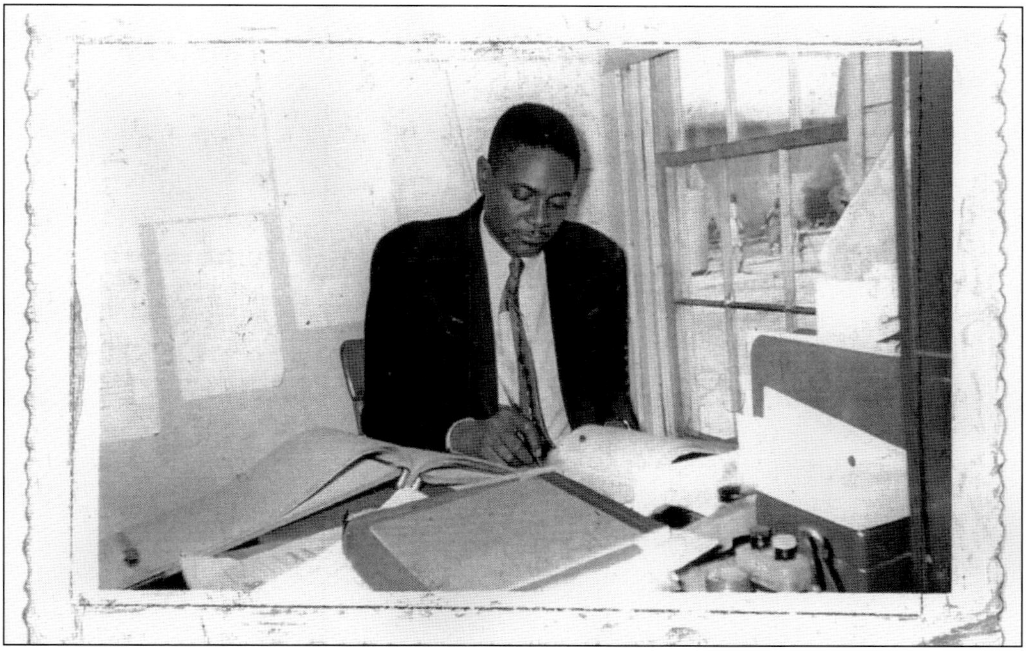

Receiving both his bachelor's and master's degrees from Florida A&M University, Rufus Williams (1911–1988) served as principal of the Shadeville High School from 1956 until 1970. In addition to his career as an educator in which he founded the Citizens League of Wakulla County and helped organize the Wakulla County Academic Boosters Club, Williams was also involved in many civic, social, and religious activities. (Courtesy Ruth Williams.)

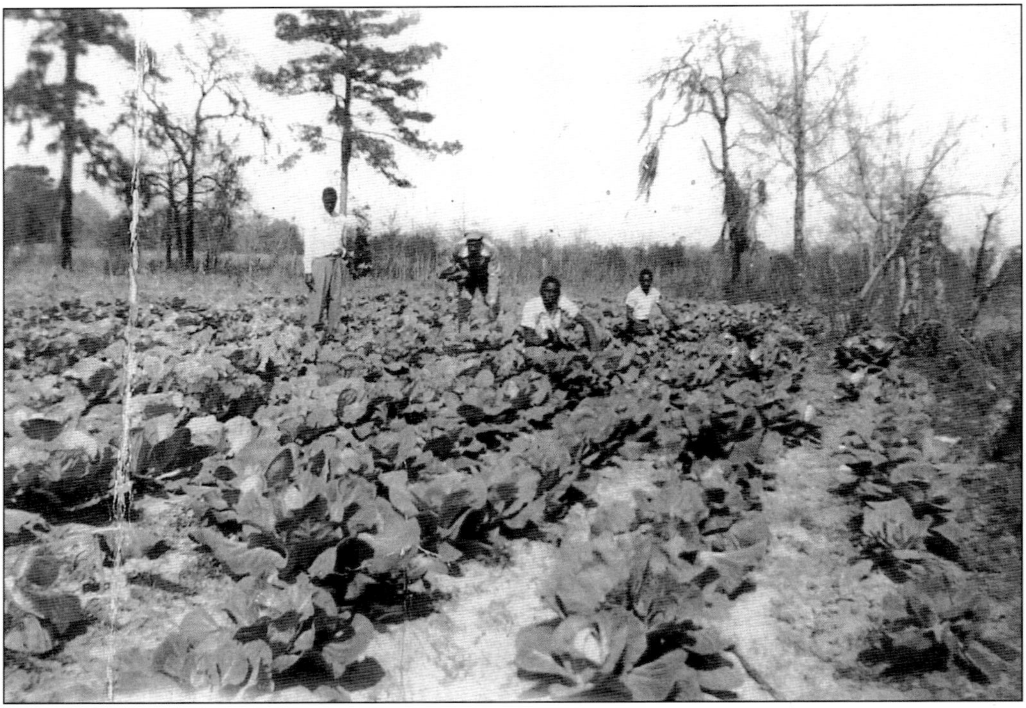

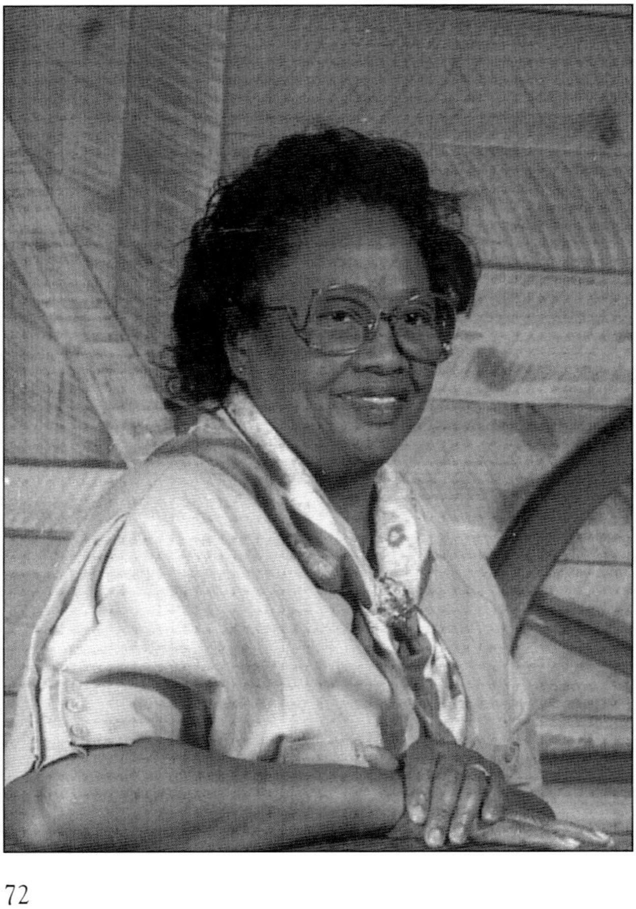

Beginning his educational career in Shadeville in 1947 as an instructor in agriculture, Rufus Williams, seen above at far left, served as head of New Farmers of America, the African-American community's equivalent of 4-H, where he was named outstanding teacher of the year. (Courtesy Ruth Williams.)

A 1944 graduate of Shadeville High School, Ruth Gavin Williams taught elementary school in Wakulla County for 41 years. Receiving her bachelor's and master's degrees in elementary education from Florida A&M University, Williams taught at Shadeville High School for many years before being transferred to the Crawfordville Elementary School where she taught for 21 years. (Courtesy Ruth Williams.)

Agnes McPherson Triplett (1891–1971) is one of three sisters-in-law who taught generations of students in the county's African-American communities. Teaching in many one-room schoolhouses in areas such as Medart, Hyde Park, Tintop, and Punch Bowl, Triplett, who received a degree from Florida A&M University, finished her 36-year career at Shadeville High School in 1958. (Courtesy Jerelene Howard.)

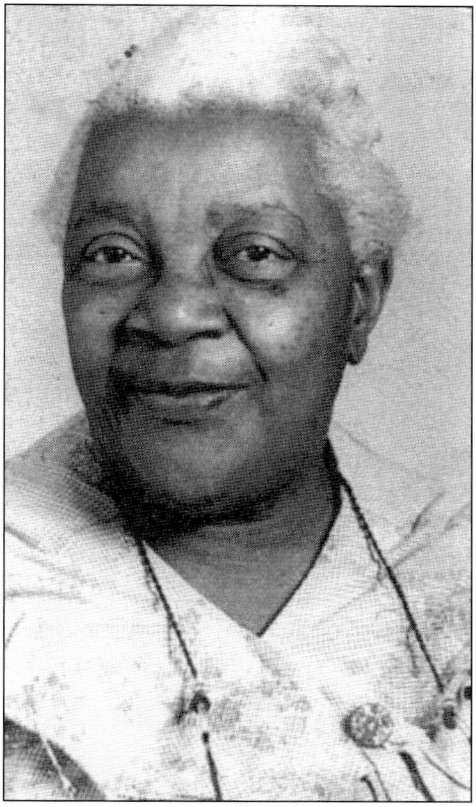

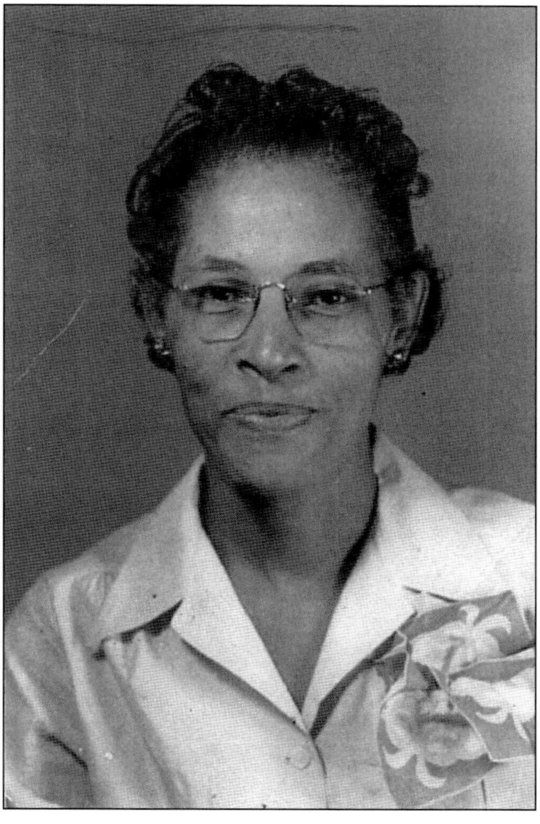

Queen Triplett (1906–1975) began teaching in 1923 in a career that lasted 47 years. Receiving a degree in elementary education from Florida A&M University in 1947, Triplett taught for many years in the Hyde Park and Shadeville schools. (Courtesy Mae Williams.)

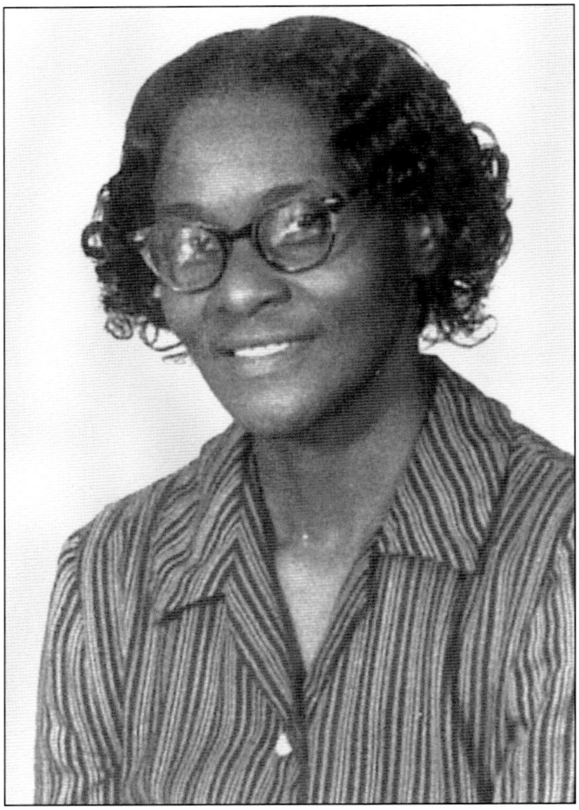

Mary Donaldson Triplett (1908–1995) began her teaching career in 1929. Receiving a master's degree in mathematics from Florida A&M University in 1951, Triplett retired from Shadeville High School in 1965 as a much beloved figure. (Courtesy Mae Williams.)

Members of the Shadeville High School home economics class are pictured here *c.* 1942. Miss Green, the instructor, appears in the front row, center. (Courtesy Frenchie Lewis.)

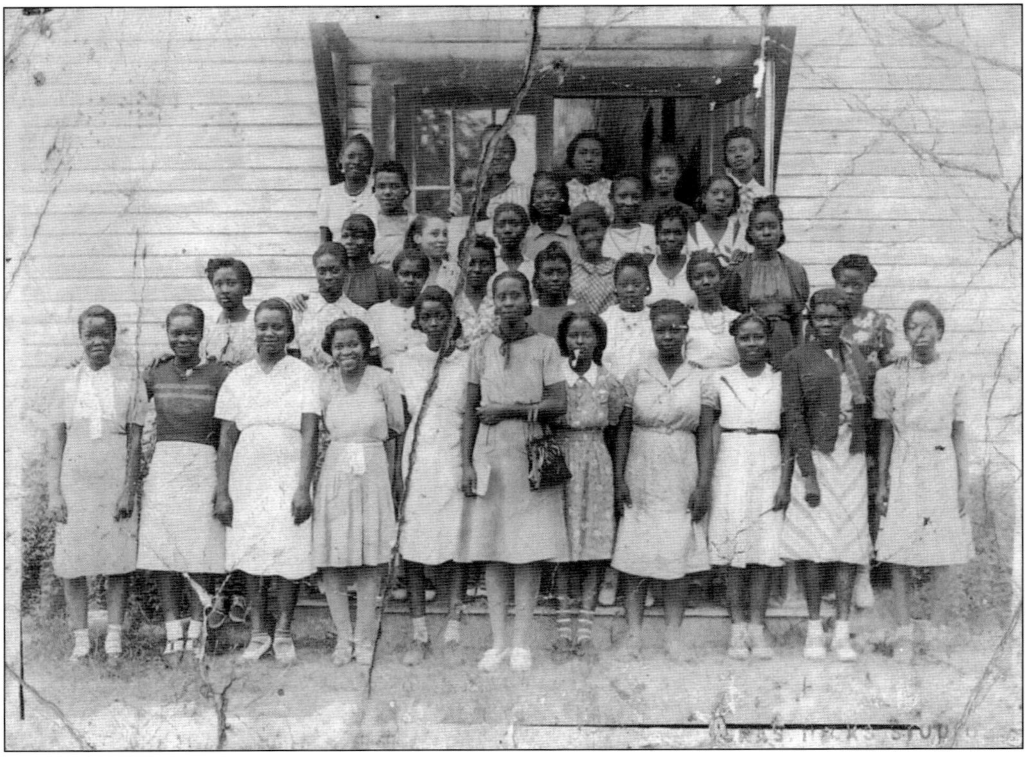

George Green, left, and Rev. Frank Mathews, right, were two of the first bus drivers for Shadeville High School in 1935. Each man provided his own bus and was paid by the county for his services. Interestingly, Green could not drive so his son Emmett, who was a student at the time, did the driving for him. (Courtesy Mae Williams.)

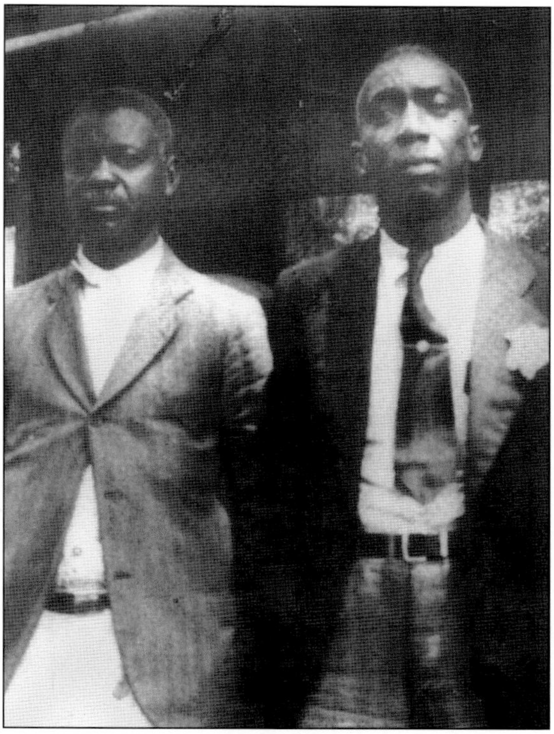

Established in 1909 as a grade school, Shadeville High School was created in 1930. Graduating its first class of three seniors in 1934, the school served as the county's only black high school until 1968. Members of the graduating class of 1945, from left to right, are (front row) Nursey Donaldson, Pauline McPherson, and Catherine Poole; (back row) Bertell Greene, Rachel Melton, Charles Ana Allen, and Josephus Shingles. (Courtesy Jessie Shingles.)

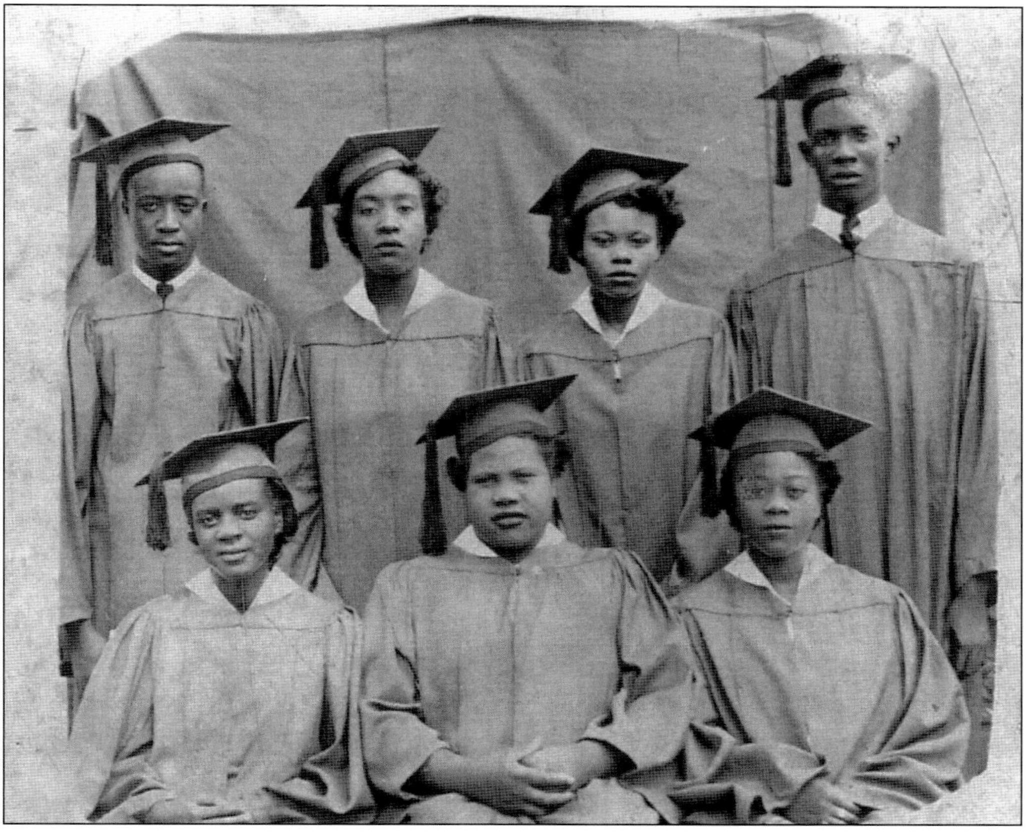

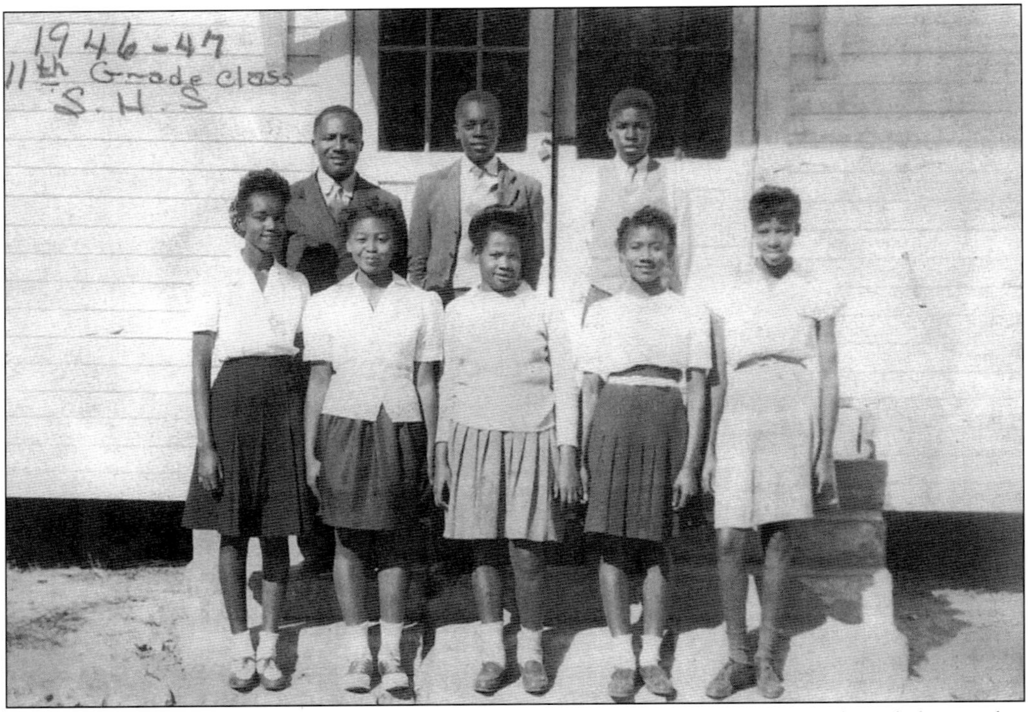

Members of the 1946–1947 11th-grade class at Shadeville High School are, from left to right, (front row) Rosette Gavin, Vera Mae Hargrett, Ernestine McPherson, Pauline Donaldson, and Winifred Donaldson; (back row) Principal S.J. Cooper, Eddie Thomas, and Herbert Hargrett. (Courtesy Jerelene Howard.)

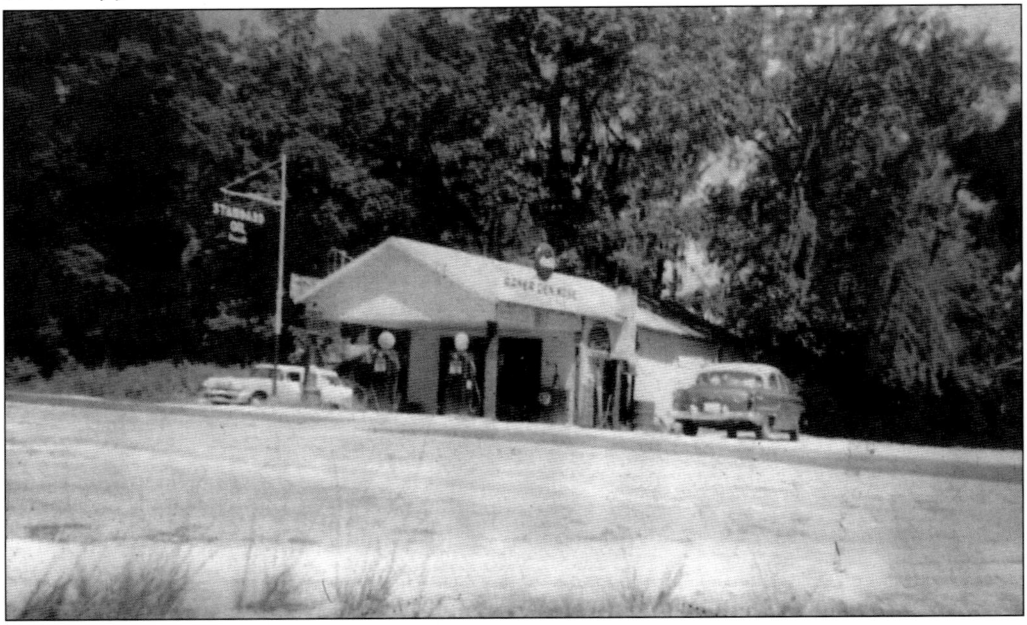

Built by John Adams in Shadeville around 1900, the store in this early 1950s photo was purchased by T.A. Raker (1912–1990) and his wife, Inez Raker (1910–1998), in 1938. The Rakers also opened a sawmill and lumberyard in the early 1950s, building another store nearby. The second store was run by Inez Raker until her death in 1998. (Courtesy Mike Begley.)

Eight

WAKULLA

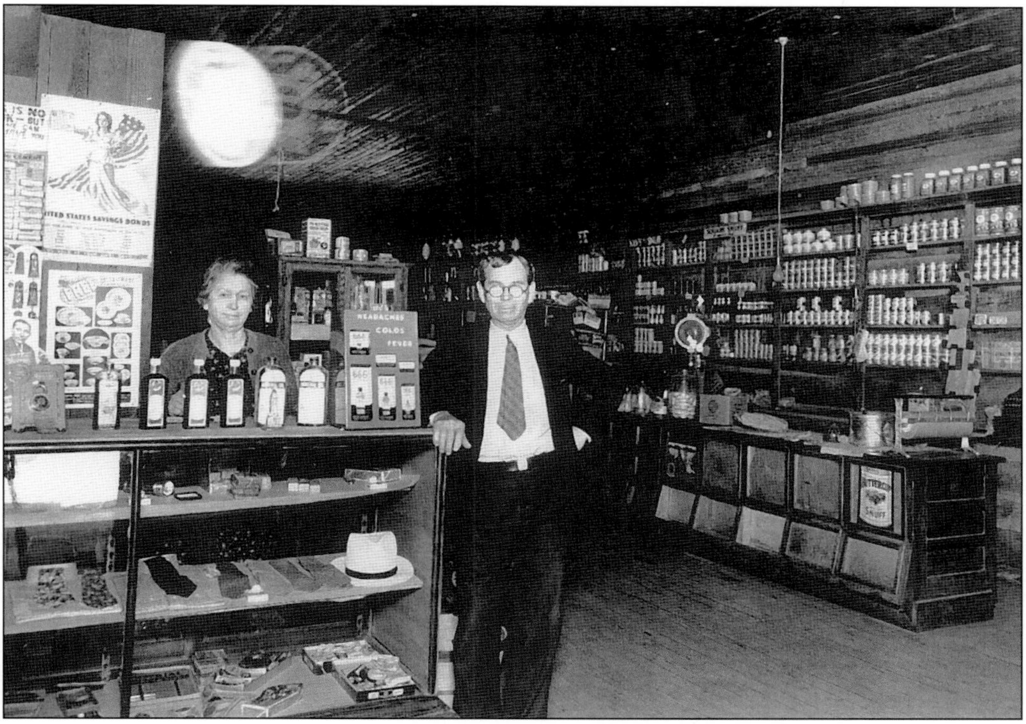

Moving to the community in 1897 when it was called Oil Still, Walter Page Sr. (1877–1956), shown here in the 1930s with his wife, Jessie Kinsey Page (1880-1964), was one of Wakulla's leading citizens. Elected as a delegate to the state democratic convention in 1900, Page also served as the county's legislative representative in 1908–1909, as Wakulla's postmaster from 1902 to 1925, and as a member of the county's democratic executive committee for 50 years. He administered the federal Civil Works Administration (CWA) program in the 1930s, and during World War II, he served as chairman of the county's finance committee. (Courtesy author.)

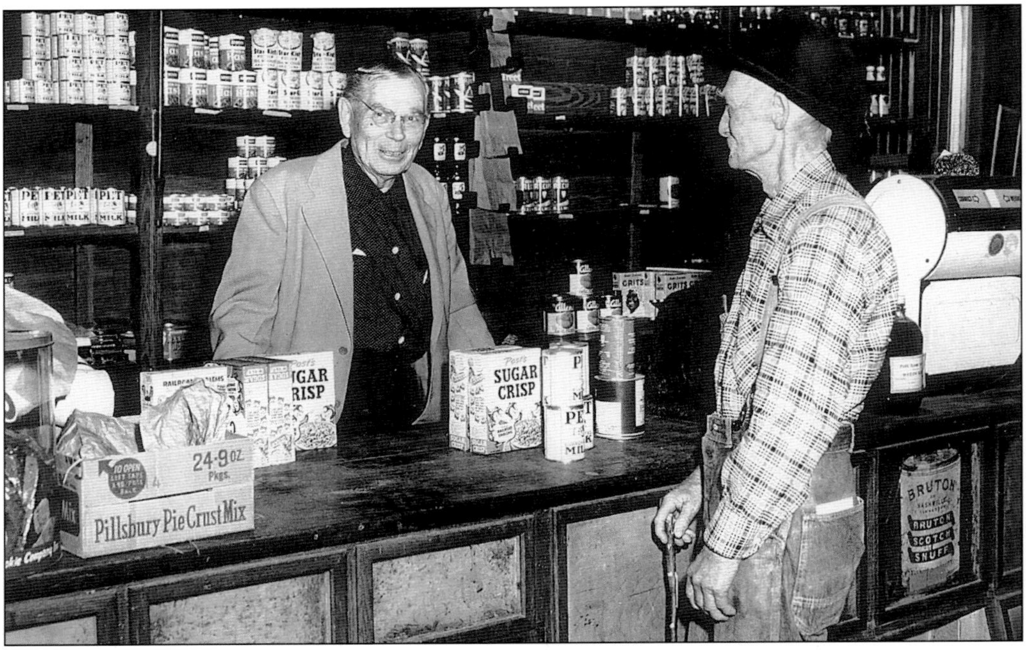

At the time of its closing in 1955, Walter Page's store in Wakulla was the oldest in the state, having opened in 1897. Shown here on his last day in business, Page serves his final customer Aquilla Nail (1873–1967), who, incidentally, had been his first customer 58 years earlier. (Courtesy Ann Little.)

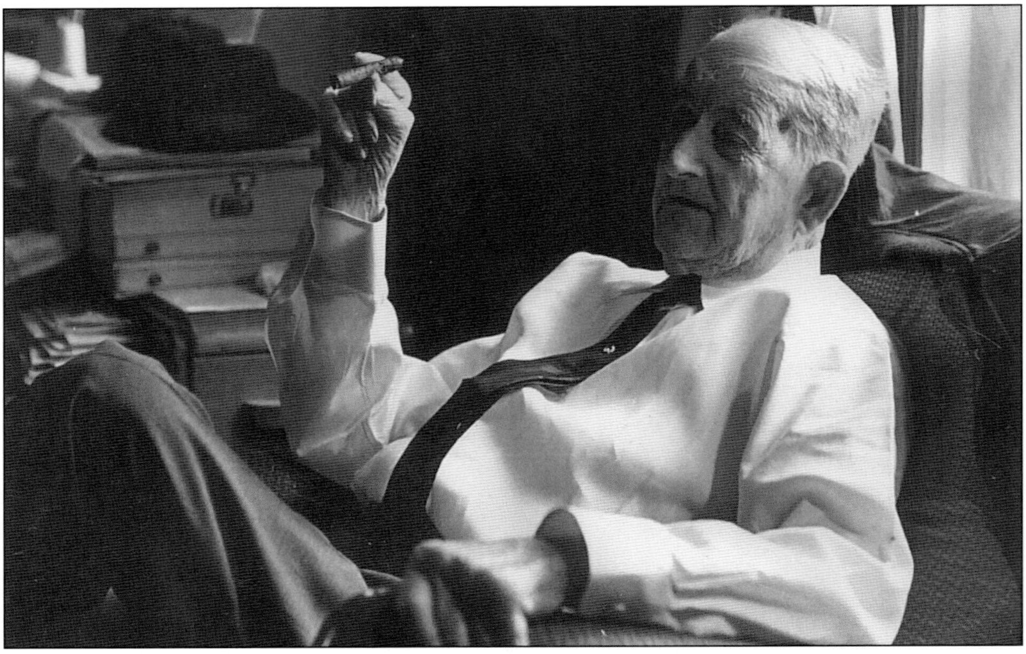

Moving to Wakulla in the 1890s, Newton Culbreath (1882–1970) established the Wakulla Turpentine Company in 1910 with George Russ. Purchasing his first tract of timber in 1904 and applying his motto of "All Things Cometh to He Who Waiteth, if He Worketh like Hell while He Waiteth," Newt Culbreath became the largest private land-owner in the county with a holding of 12,000 acres at the time of his death. (Courtesy Ava Wilson.)

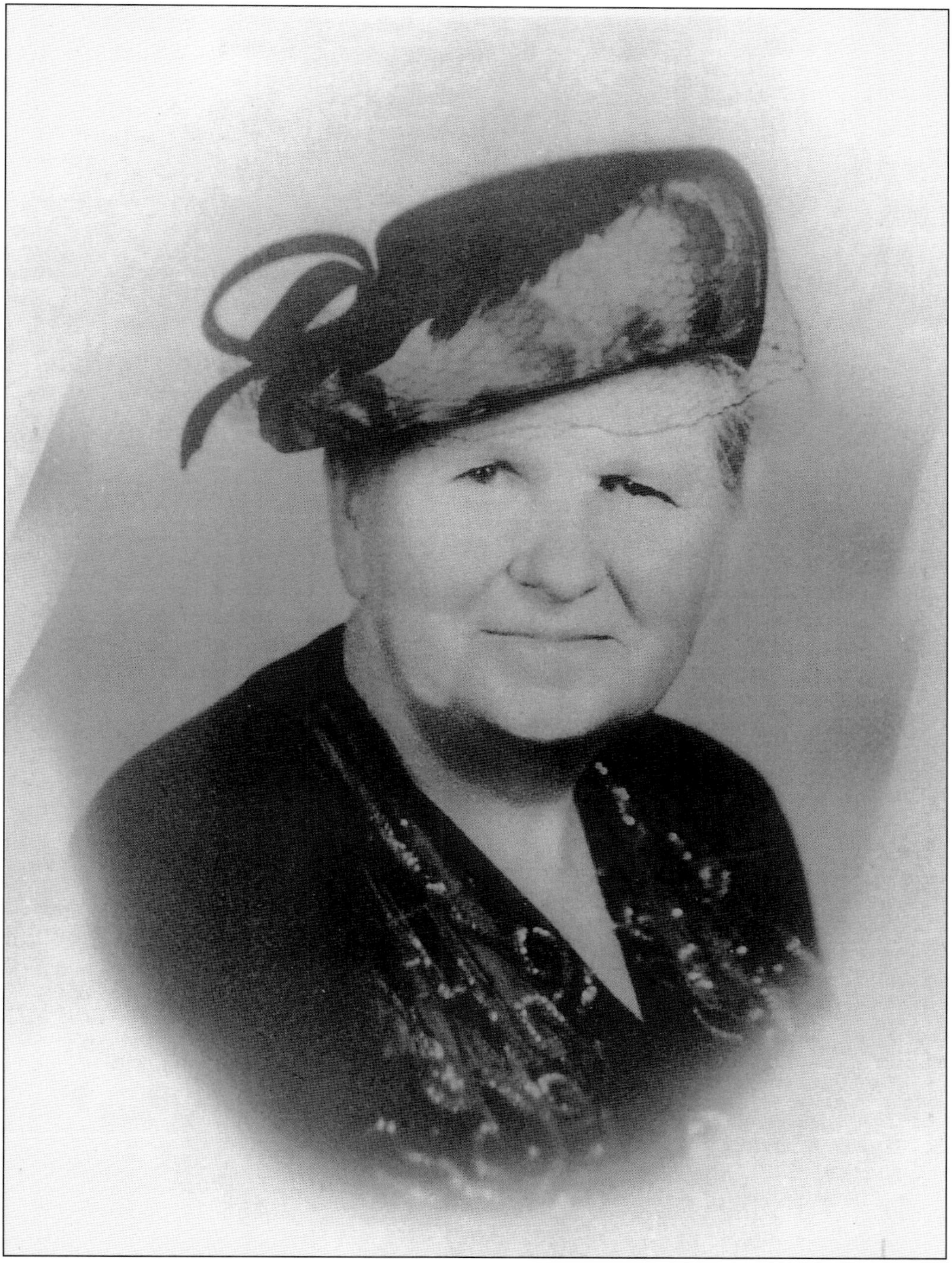

Serving as Wakulla County's first juvenile probation officer from 1926 to 1960, Florence Page Nesmith (1879–1969), with help from judges W. May Walker and A.L. Porter, created the Wakulla County Welfare Association in 1946. Through this organization, Florrie Nesmith, along with her nephew B.F. Page Sr., provided aid and support to the county's neediest citizens for many years. Upon her retirement in 1960, Nesmith's daughter Bruce Nesmith Alford (1908–1994) took her place on the board and served until her death. (Courtesy author.)

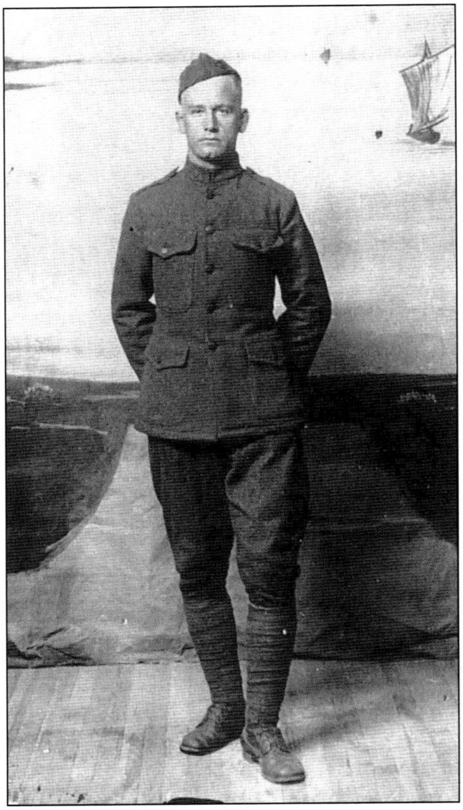

W.F. Robison Sr. (1895–1966) of Wakulla is pictured at the time of his service in World War I in 1917. In addition to serving as the county's legislative representative in 1935, Robison owned and operated two stores in Wakulla. (Courtesy Dr. W.F. Robison Jr.)

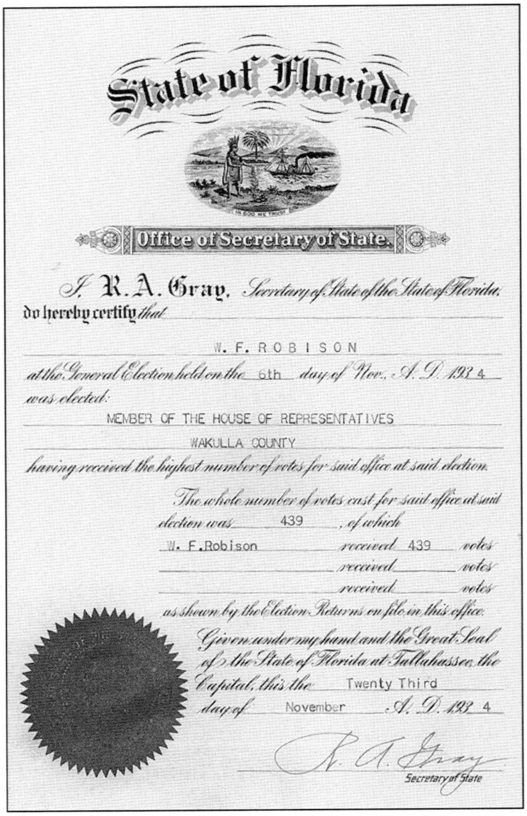

State of Florida

Office of Secretary of State.

I, R. A. Gray, Secretary of State of the State of Florida, do hereby certify that

W. F. ROBISON

at the General Election held on the 6th day of Nov. A. D. 1934 was elected:

MEMBER OF THE HOUSE OF REPRESENTATIVES

WAKULLA COUNTY

having received the highest number of votes for said office at said election.

The whole number of votes cast for said office at said election was 439, of which

W. F. Robison received 439 votes

received votes

received votes

as shown by the Election Returns on file in this office.

Given under my hand and the Great Seal of the State of Florida at Tallahassee, the Capital, this the Twenty Third day of November A. D. 1934

R. A. Gray

Secretary of State

This certificate was issued by Secretary of State R.A. Gray to W.F. Robison upon his election as Wakulla County representative in 1934. Robison was unanimously elected with a total of 439 votes. (Courtesy Dr. W.F. Robison Jr.)

Moving to Wakulla in 1914, George Kinsey (1882–1957) farmed and gathered lime rock for over 30 years. Kinsey's farm contained an unusually large amount of the rock, which he quarried and sold for as little as 33¢ a ton. In a 1947 interview, Kinsey estimated that over the previous 30 years he had gathered and sold 13 million pounds of lime rock by hand. He is pictured here with his wife, Maggie (1885–1953), in the late 1940s. (Courtesy Betty Reeves.)

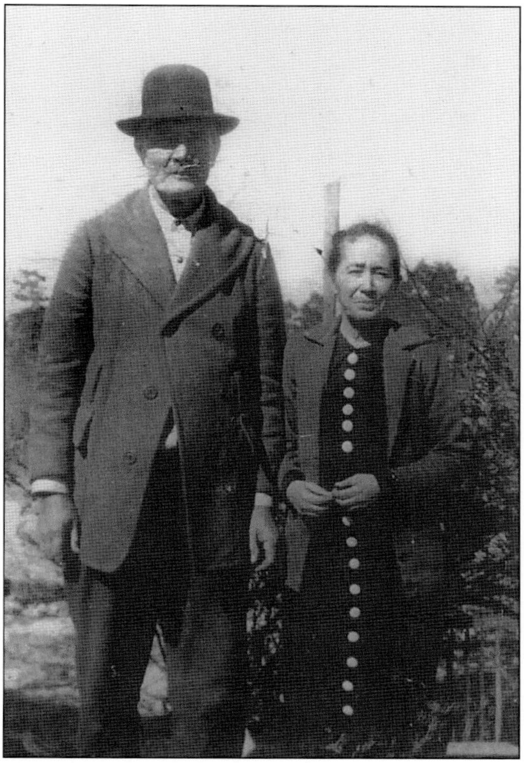

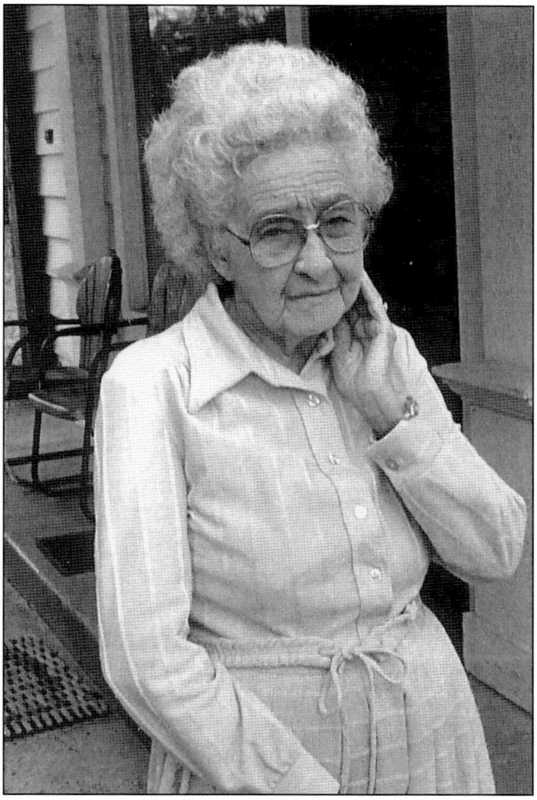

Born in 1898, Virginia Godwin Branch moved to the county with her family in 1901, traveling by ox cart. After brief stays in area communities such as Fig Tree, Vereen, Myrtlewood, and Juanita, Branch finally settled in Wakulla with her husband in 1945. A registered member of the Lumbee American Indian tribe, Virginia Branch, at the age of 103, remains one of Wakulla's most respected citizens. (Courtesy Betty Reeves)

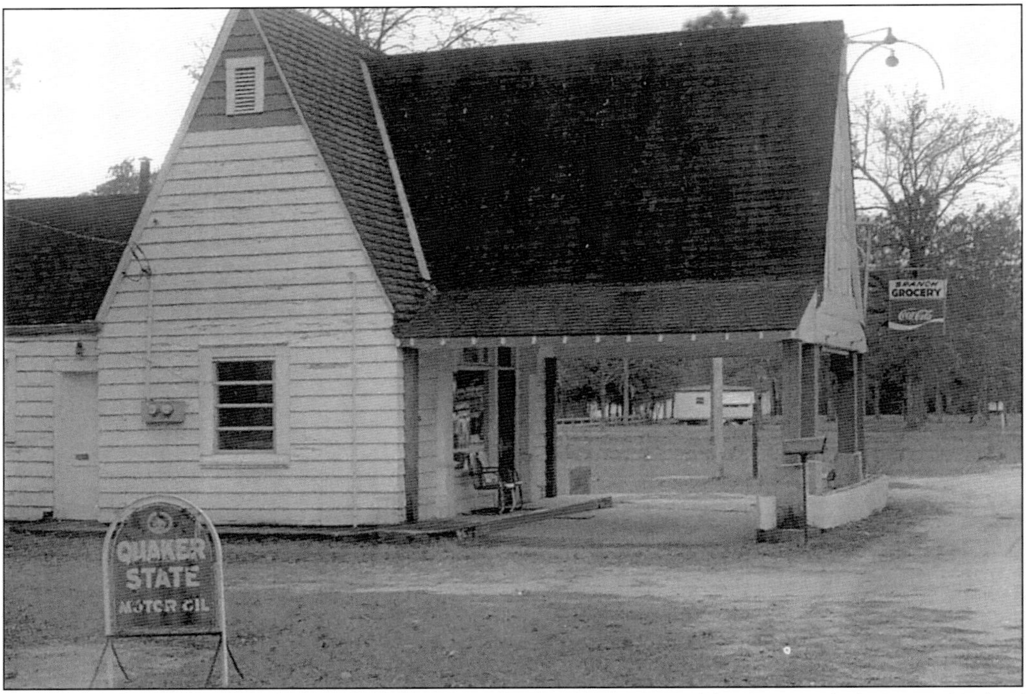

Built in 1938 by the Pure Oil Company, this store was operated by Joe Nails (1898–1993) of Wakulla until 1945 when it was taken over by William Wiley Branch (1892–1975) who ran it until 1960. Its operation was then turned over to his wife, Virginia Branch, who ran Branch Grocery until her retirement in 1985. (Courtesy Betty Reeves.)

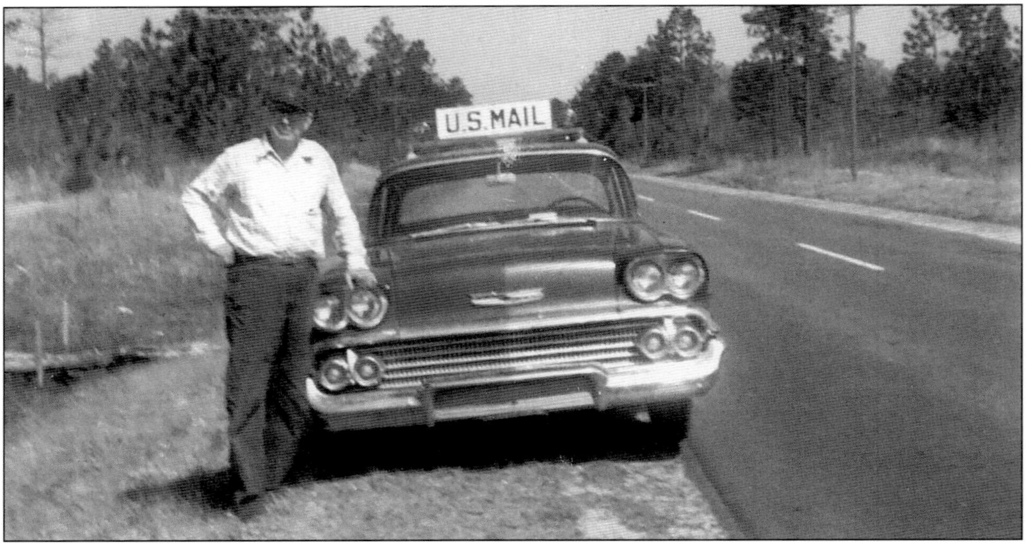

A familiar sight throughout the eastern part of the county, B.F. Page Sr. (1901–1964) is seen here on his rural route in 1960. A letter carrier for 42 years, Page also served as president of the county welfare association for 11 years and as county chairman of the Red Cross. Instrumental in revitalizing the county chamber of commerce he served both as president, vice president, and secretary/treasurer for ten years. Elected president of the Florida Rural Letter Carriers Association in 1957, he helped introduce many bills in the state legislature that improved conditions for rural carriers throughout the state. (Courtesy Peggy Page.)

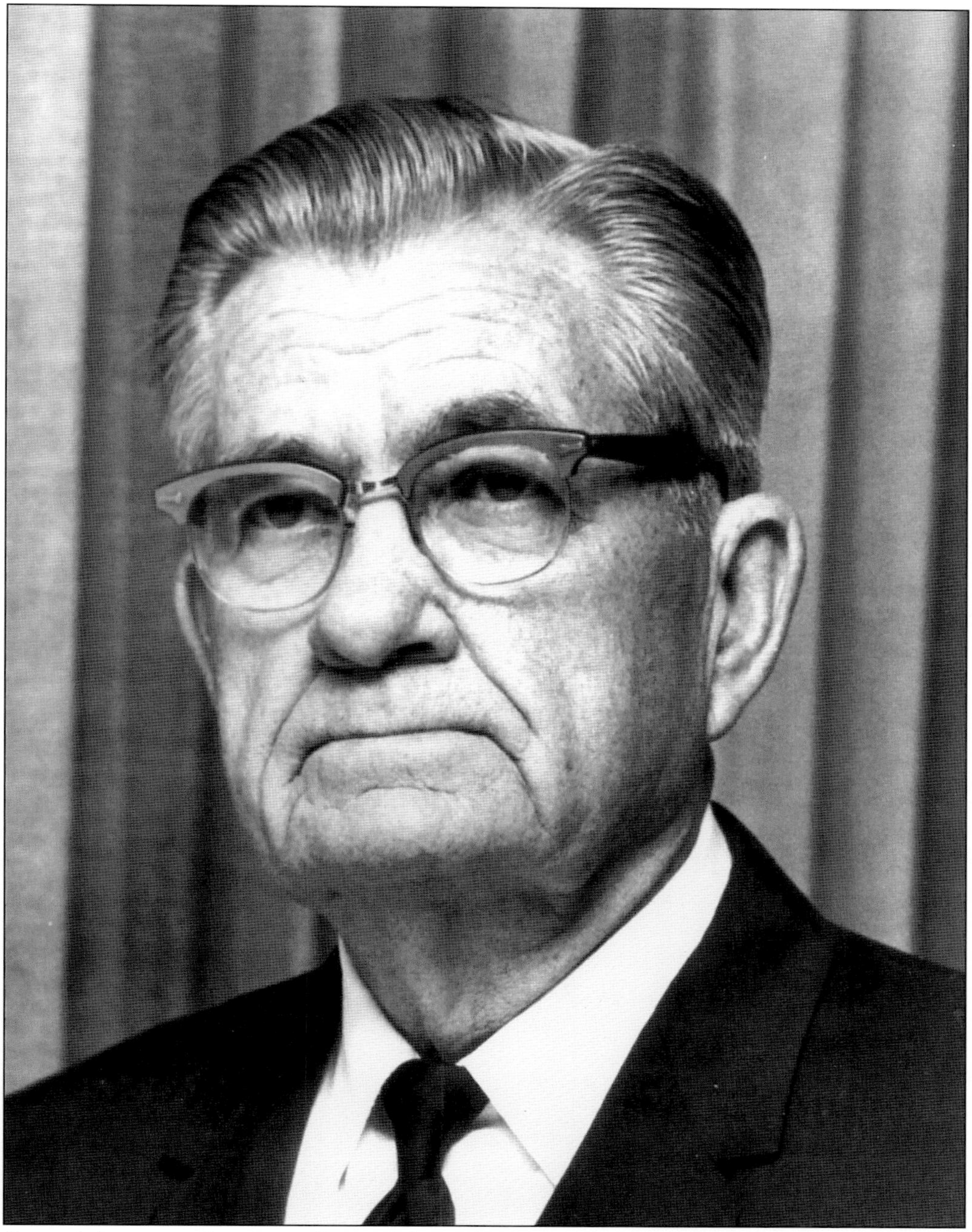

One of the county's most influential lawmakers was George A. Nesmith (1904–1992) of Wakulla, who served four terms in the state legislature between 1943 and 1953. In addition to securing funds necessary to build the county's courthouse, jail, and health unit, Nesmith was also responsible for having many county roads paved for the first time. His most significant contribution was saving the county from insolvency in 1942 through negotiations with Gov. Spessard Holland. Nesmith also had an impact on state government by being the first to introduce a bill that required full financial disclosure for state politicians, as well as a state-wide civil service bill offering job protection to state workers. He was recognized by the press as one of the state's most effective legislators in the 1940s. (Courtesy author.)

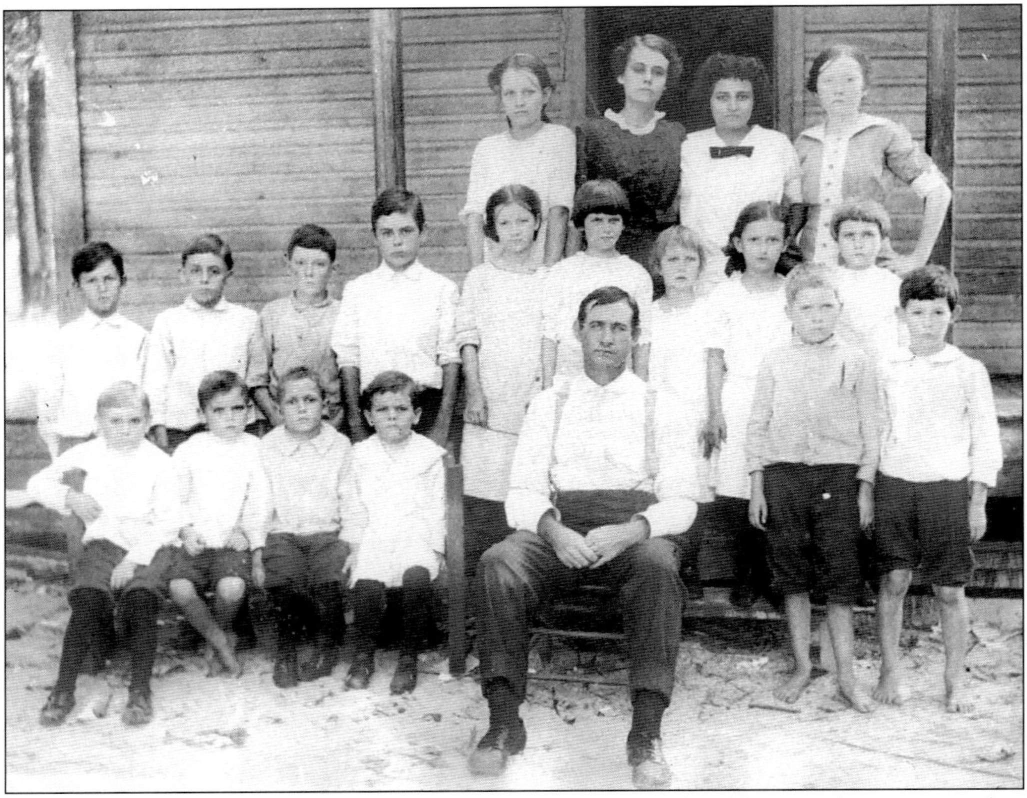

The Class of 1914 is shown in front of Wakulla's one-room school house. The man seated in front is Professor Luter. (Courtesy author.)

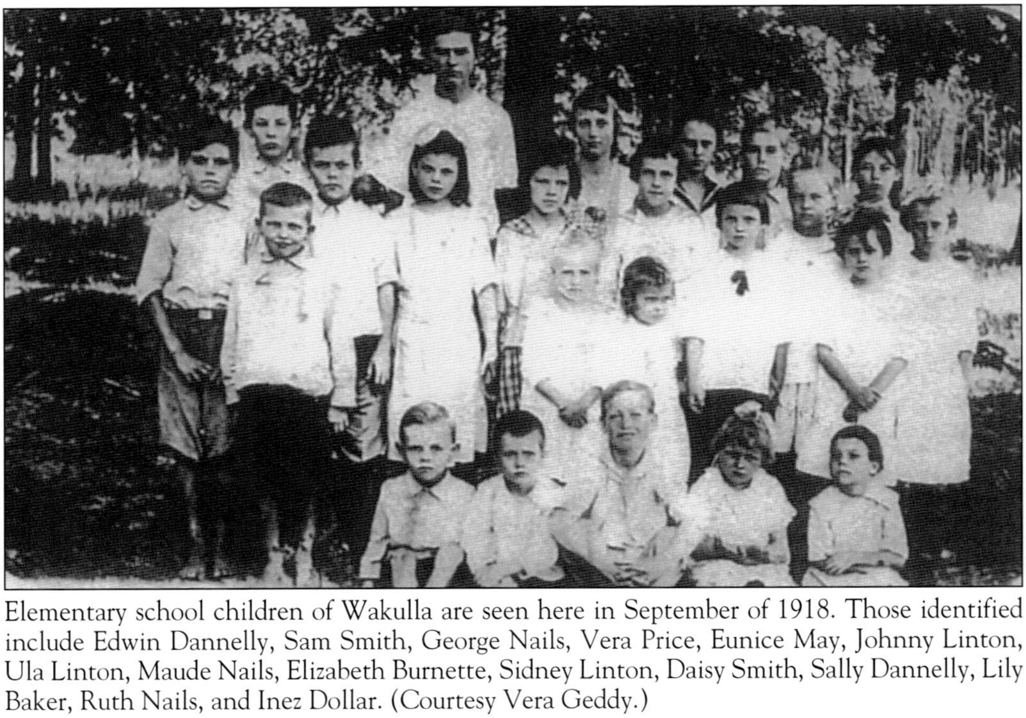

Elementary school children of Wakulla are seen here in September of 1918. Those identified include Edwin Dannelly, Sam Smith, George Nails, Vera Price, Eunice May, Johnny Linton, Ula Linton, Maude Nails, Elizabeth Burnette, Sidney Linton, Daisy Smith, Sally Dannelly, Lily Baker, Ruth Nails, and Inez Dollar. (Courtesy Vera Geddy.)

Alice Page Robison (1902–1994) served as Wakulla's postmistress from 1925 until the post office was closed in 1955. She is seen here sorting the mail in the 1940s. (Courtesy Dr. W.F. Robison Jr.)

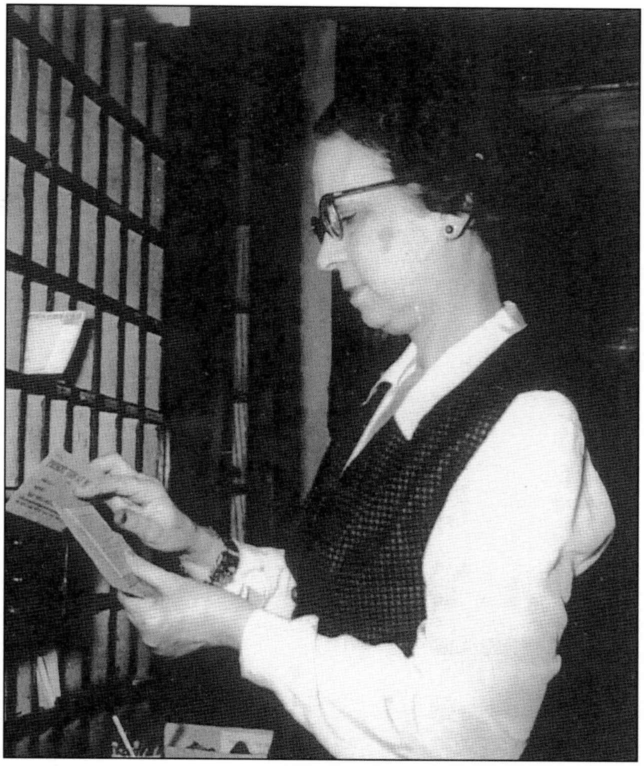

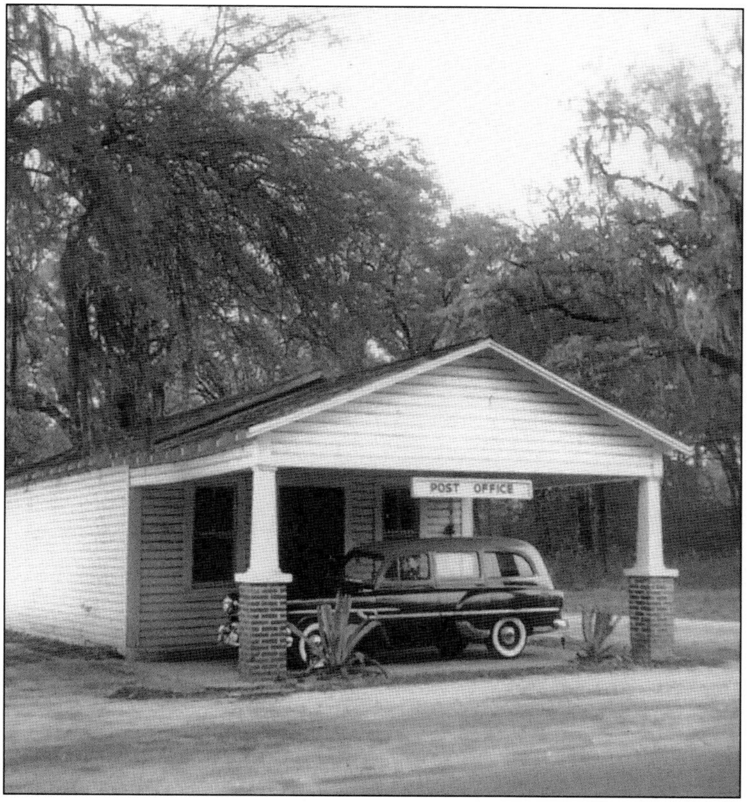

Constructed in 1938, this building served as Wakulla's post office until it was closed by the U.S. Postal Service in 1955. (Courtesy Dr. W.F. Robison Jr.)

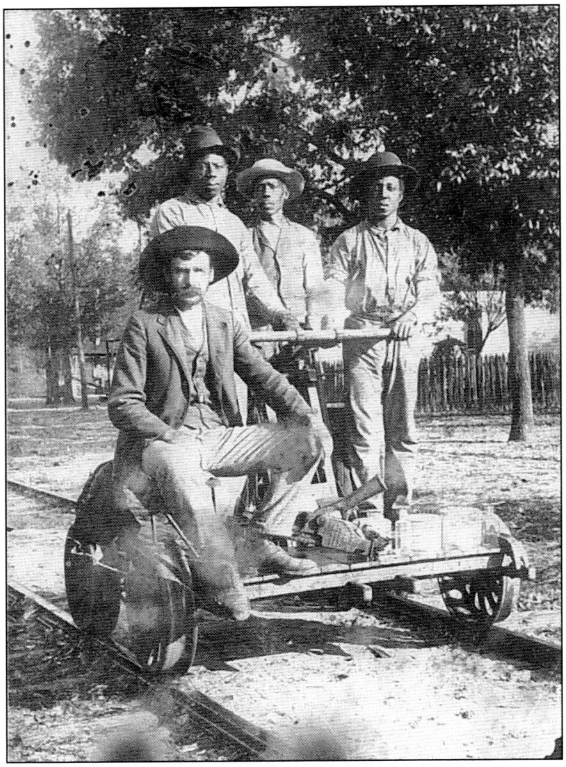

Pictured here are section foreman Francis Keightly Howard (1874–1961) and his crew on the St. Marks railroad. This photo was taken in Wakulla in 1915. From left to right are Howard (seated), James Ewing, Bill Jackson, and Agrippa Thompson. Howard worked for the railroad for 40 years before retiring in 1939. (Courtesy Dr. W.F. Robison Jr.)

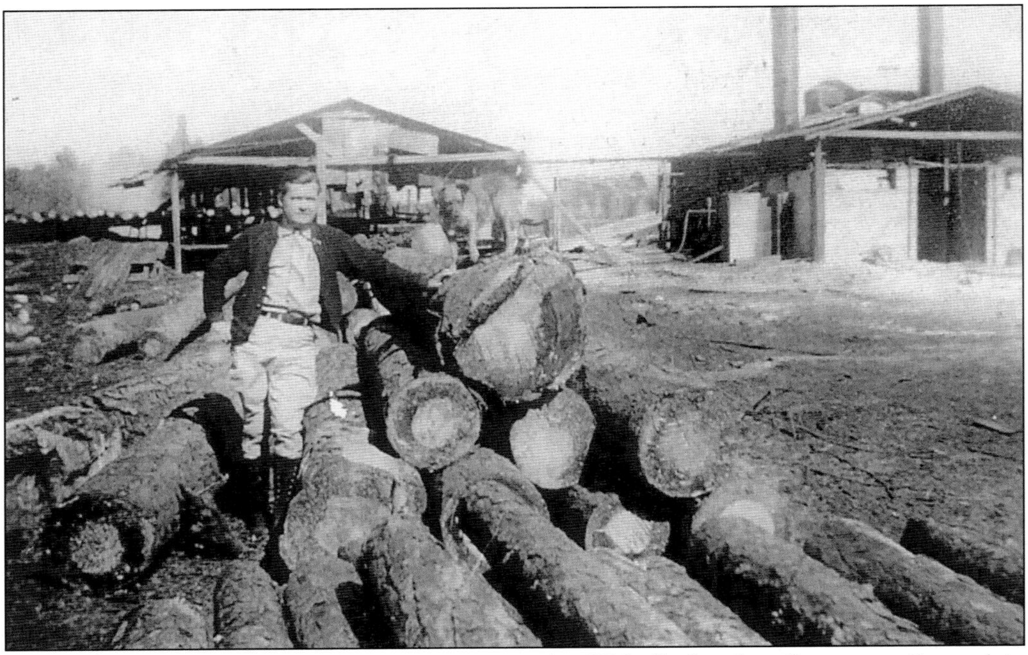

Wakulla's largest employer for many years was the Wakulla Lumber Company. Opened in 1929 as Reed Lumber Company by H.N. Reed of Macon, Georgia, the mill was purchased in 1937 by Kelly Smith and re-named Wakulla Lumber Company. George Nesmith, who bought the mill from Smith in 1945, is seen here in the early 1940s. The mill was closed in 1949. (Courtesy author.)

Employing as many as 50 men to operate a saw, planer mill, and dry kiln, Wakulla Lumber Company logged, cut, dried, planed, and stacked the timber before shipping it out by train. Mill hand Jonas Jackson is seen here in 1941 driving the tractor used to haul logs for cutting. (Courtesy author.)

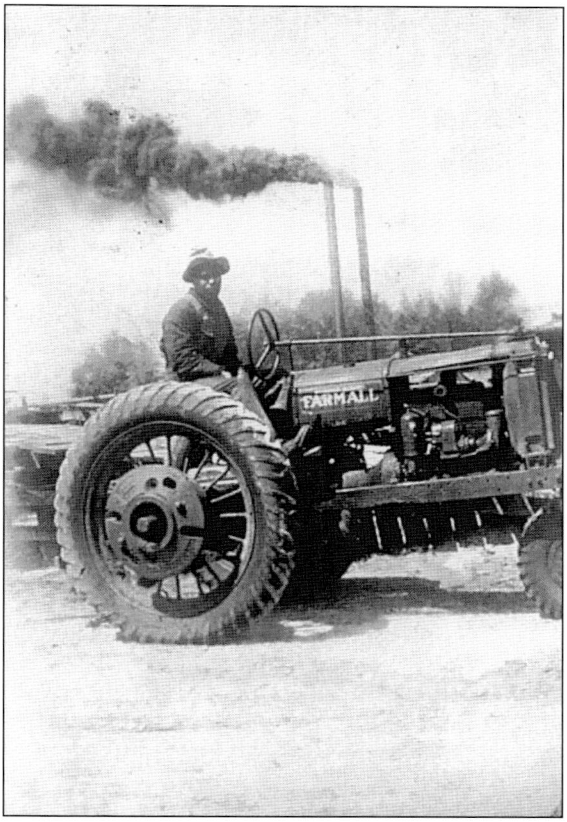

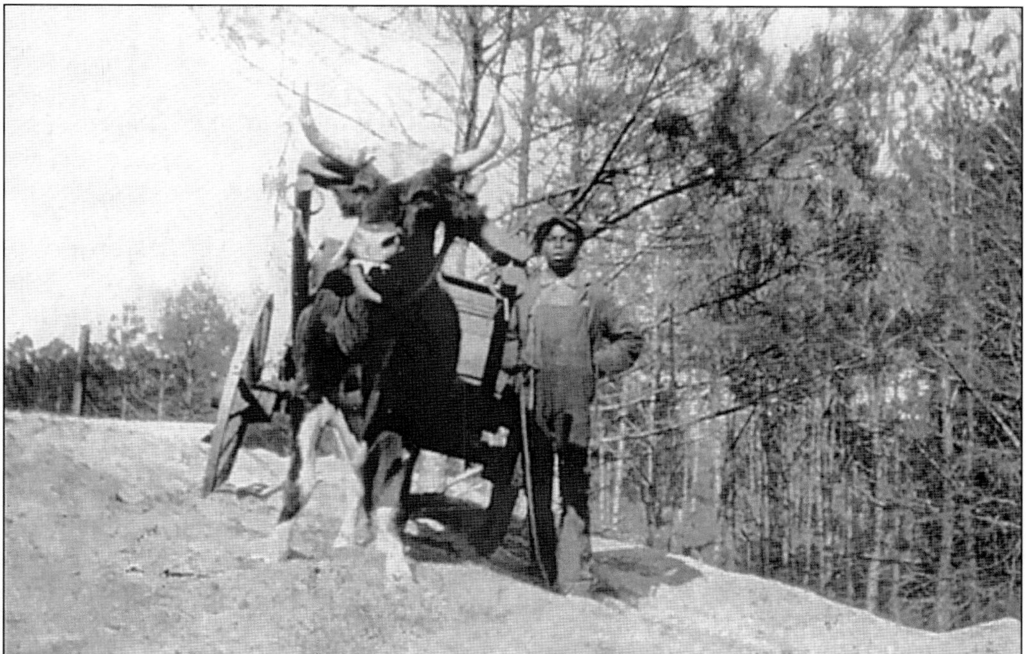

Tons of sawdust were generated by the mill. Here a young boy stands atop a huge sawdust pile with the oxcart used for hauling. (Courtesy author.)

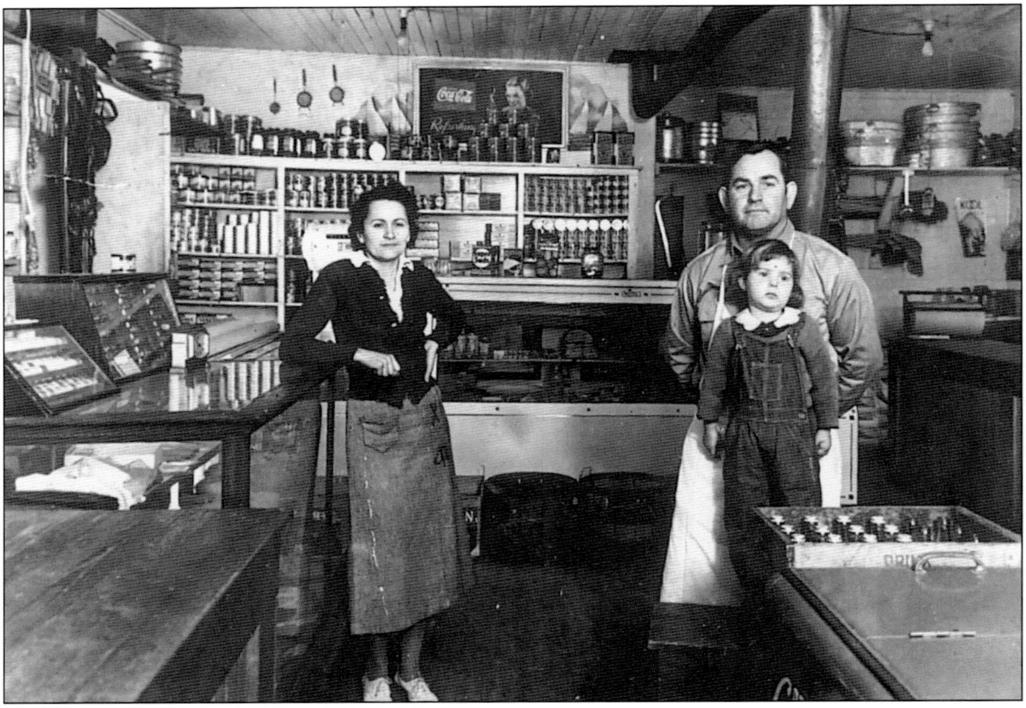

Bennie Rogers (1902–1987) moved to Wakulla in 1933 as mill foreman at the Reed Lumber Company. Rogers is seen here in the late 1930s with Vela Hughes and his daughter Sara Rogers in the small store he operated in the mill's old commissary. Rogers operated several stores in Wakulla in later years. (Courtesy Sara Ruryk.)

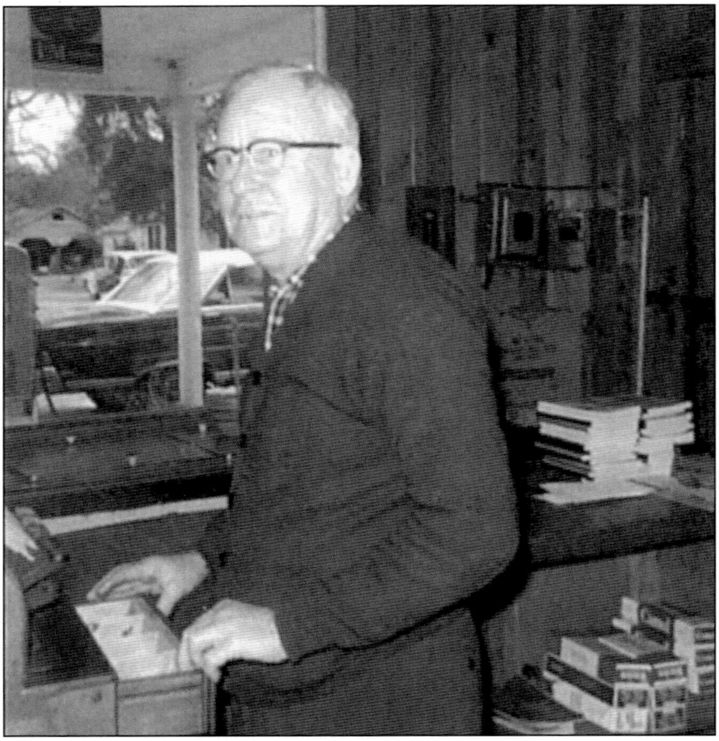

A native of Ozark, Alabama, William Hagler (1897–1974) operated a small store and café in Wakulla that was known for its huge hand-dipped ice cream cones. Hagler is pictured inside his store in the late 1960s. (Courtesy Thelma Jernigan.)

Eight

Wakulla Beach and Hyde Park

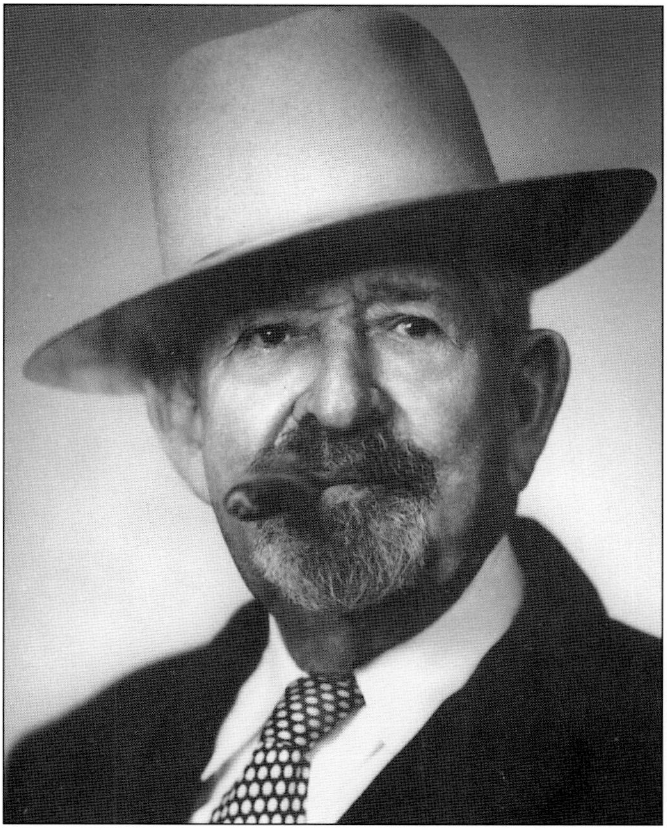

Henry N. Walker Sr. (1868–1958) was a prominent citizen of Wakulla County. Owner and operator of the *Wakulla Times* for ten years, Walker was also a school teacher, merchant, cattle rancher, and organizer of the Wakulla Home Guard during the Spanish-American War. In addition, he served as sheriff (1896–1901), clerk of the court (1905–1909), and four terms as senator of the fifth district (1925, 1927, 1937, 1939), where he worked to create a modern highway system in Florida. He also developed the Wakulla Beach coastal resort. (Courtesy Florida Photographic Collection.)

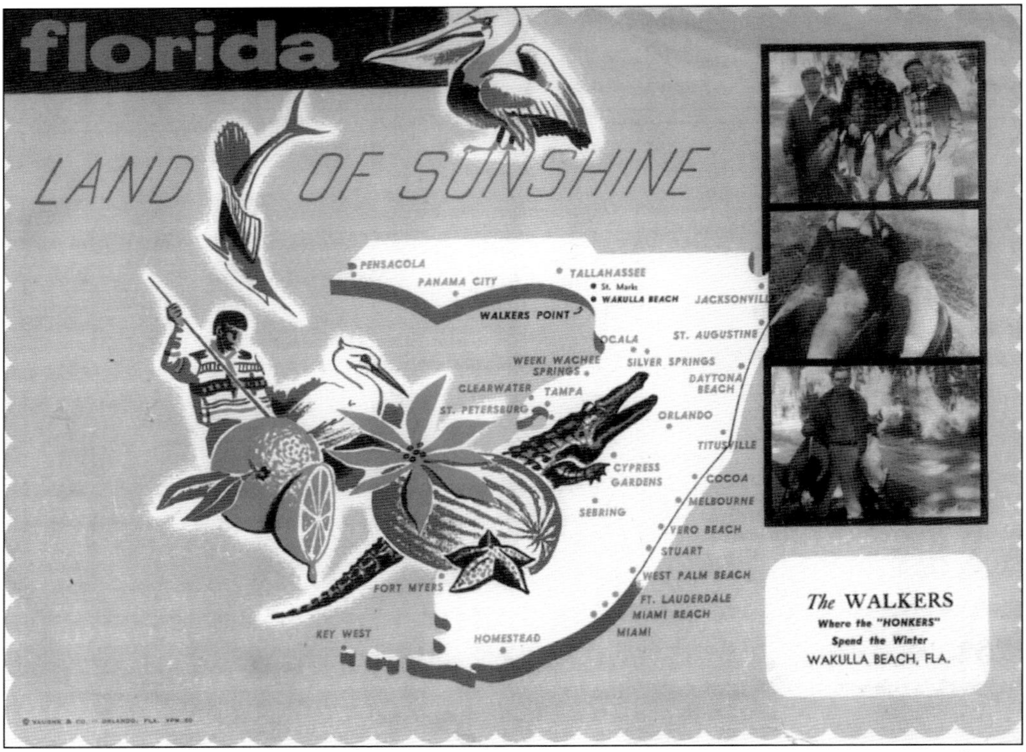

Wakulla Beach, also referred to as East Goose Creek, was a popular tourist and hunting resort developed and run by the Walker family. A series of three hotels were built there beginning in 1915, featuring the area's abundant hunting and fishing opportunities. Wakulla Beach enjoyed a great reputation as a goose and duck hunters' paradise. (Courtesy Daisy Petty.)

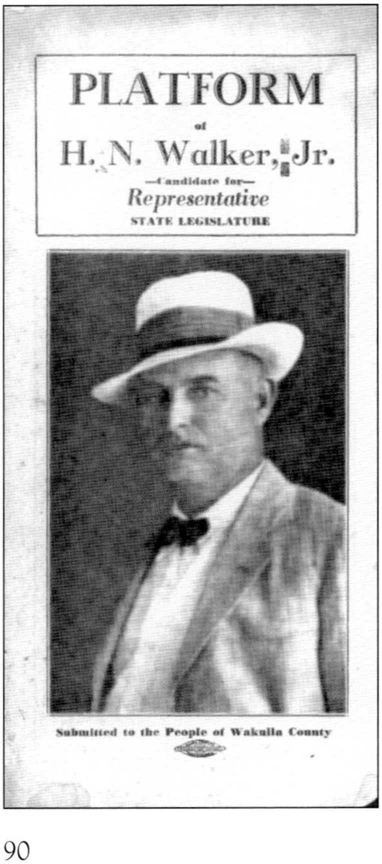

Henry N. "Hal" Walker Jr. (1892–1931) of Wakulla Beach operated a commercial fishing business in St. Marks. Elected as the county's representative in 1930, he pledged to abolish the poll tax, and improve county roads and public schools. Walker died suddenly at the end of the 1931 session at the age of 39. (Courtesy Daisy Petty.)

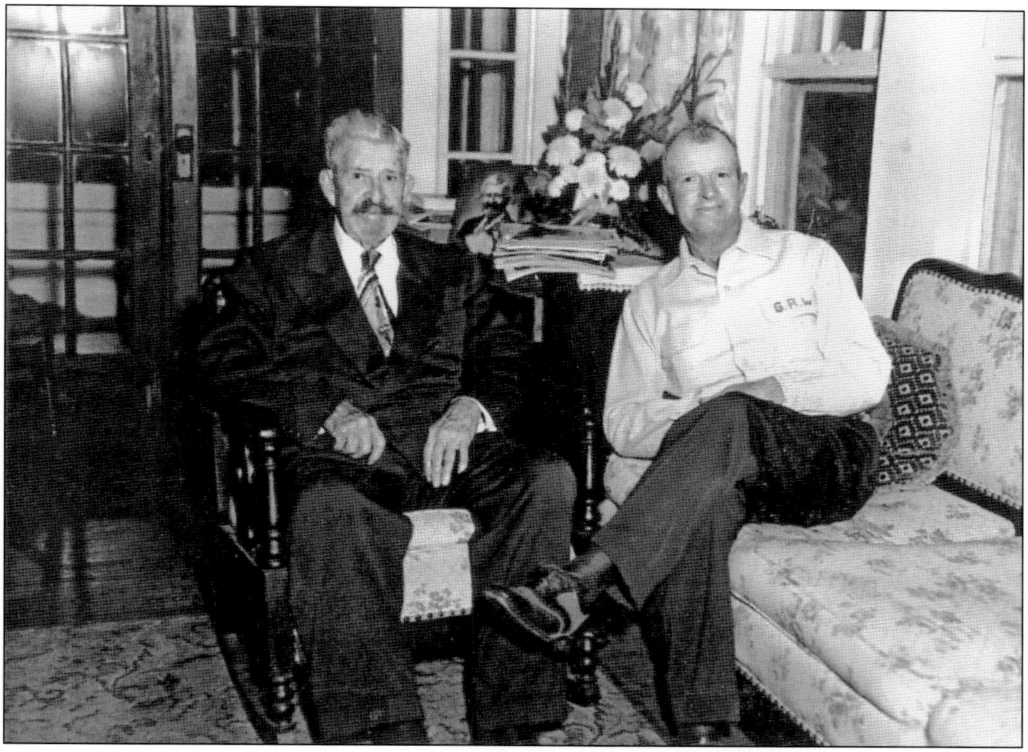

Senator Walker's son George R. Walker (1902–1972) managed his father's business interests at Wakulla Beach for many years. Pictured here with his father in the late 1950s, the younger Walker operated a number of private hunting clubs in addition to raising cattle. (Courtesy Daisy Petty.)

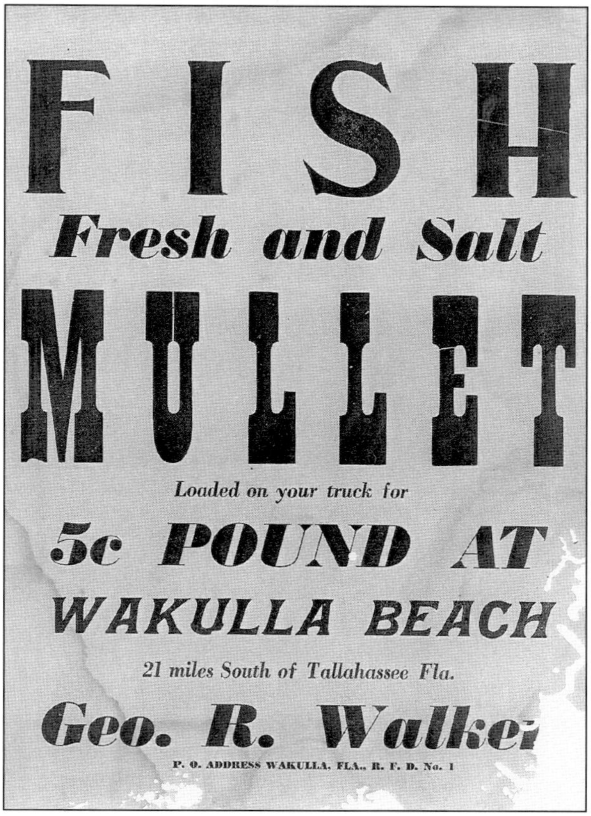

In addition to his other business concerns, George Walker also engaged in commercial fishing at Wakulla Beach and employed many men from the Hyde Park community. This handbill dates from the 1930s. (Courtesy Buddy Page.)

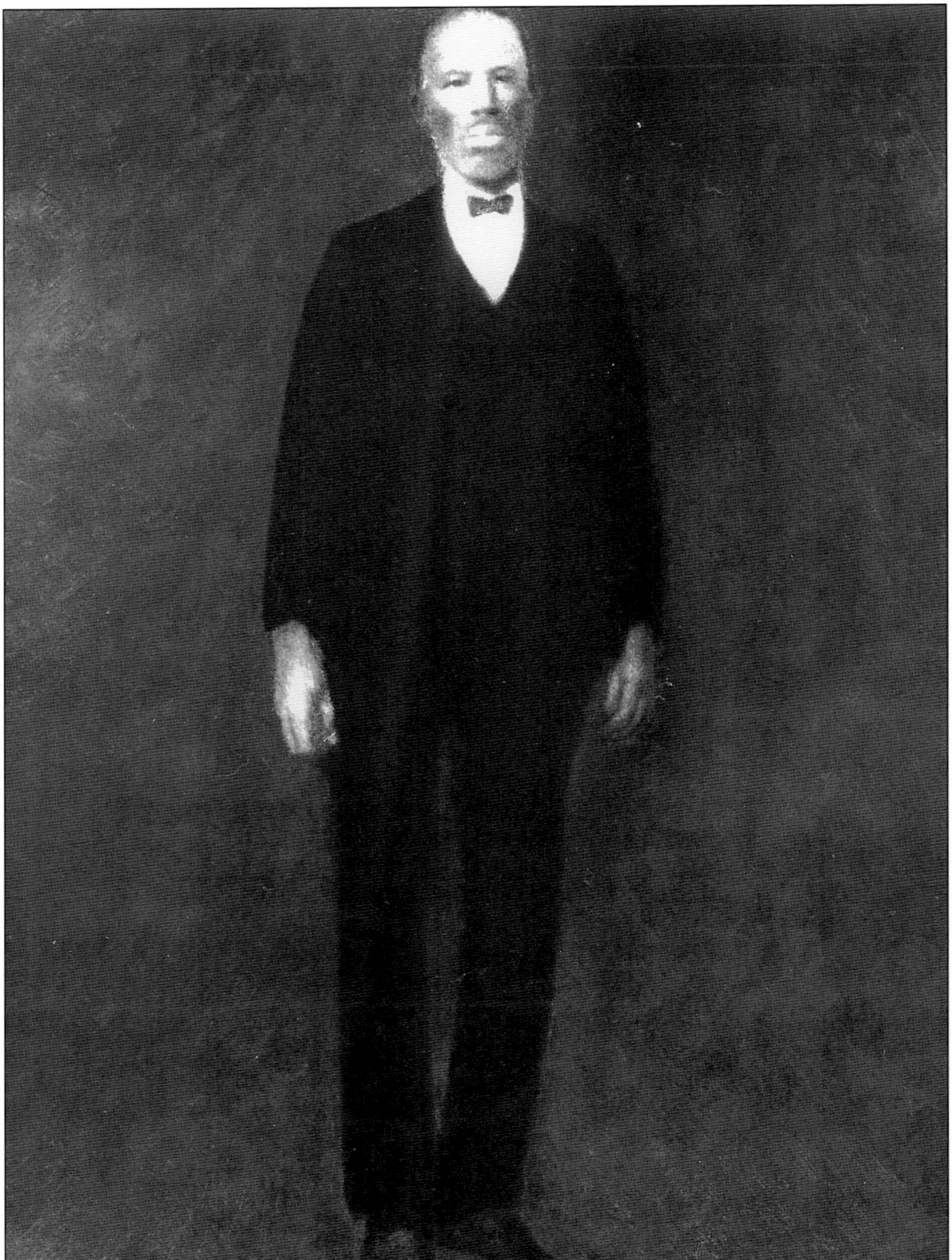

Andrew Joshua Hargrett Sr. (1879–1932) of Hyde Park was, for many years, the leading educator in the county's African-American community. Among his many accomplishments was the creation of the first school for grades one through eight for blacks in Hyde Park, where he served as principal for many years. Hargrett was also instrumental in creating the Shadeville School in 1909, which became the county's first high school for blacks in 1930. A lifelong advocate for education, Hargrett was one of the first to encourage teacher certification in the county. (Courtesy Garrett Lockley.)

Educator Delia Green Hargrett (1892–1964), the second wife of Andrew Hargrett Sr., taught not only in Wakulla County but in neighboring counties as well. After completing her studies at Florida A&M University, she operated a private school in her home for several years before teaching in the public schools. (Courtesy Garrett Lockley.)

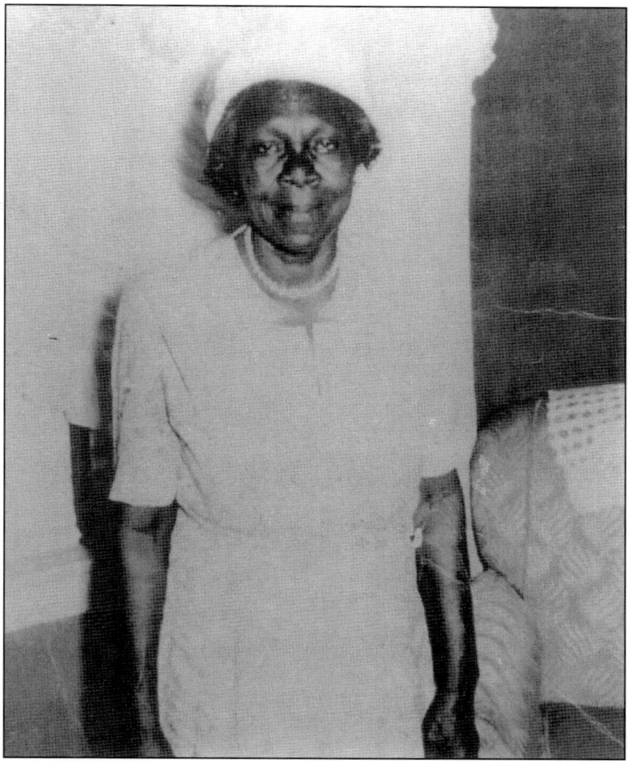

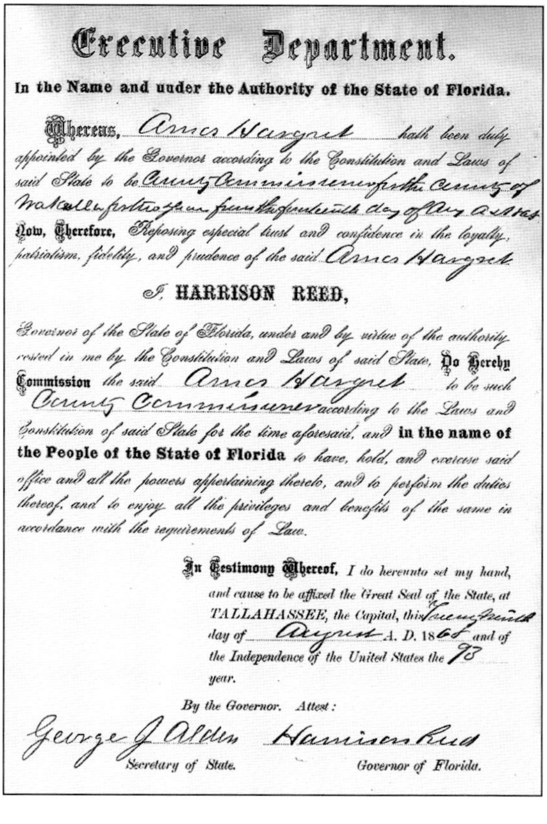

Executive Department.

In the Name and under the Authority of the State of Florida.

Whereas, Amos Hargret hath been duly appointed by the Governor according to the Constitution and Laws of said State to be County Commissioner for the County of Wakulla for two years from the fourteenth day of Aug A.D. [illegible]

Now, Therefore, Reposing especial trust and confidence in the loyalty, patriotism, fidelity, and prudence of the said Amos Hargret

I, **HARRISON REED,**

Governor of the State of Florida, under and by virtue of the authority vested in me by the Constitution and Laws of said State, **Do Hereby Commission** the said Amos Hargret to be such County Commissioner according to the Laws and Constitution of said State for the time aforesaid, and **in the name of the People of the State of Florida** to have, hold, and exercise said office and all the powers appertaining thereto, and to perform the duties thereof, and to enjoy all the privileges and benefits of the same in accordance with the requirements of Law.

In Testimony Whereof, I do hereunto set my hand, and cause to be affixed the Great Seal of the State, at TALLAHASSEE, the Capital, this twenty-[illegible] day of August A.D. 1868 and of the Independence of the United States the 93 year.

By the Governor. Attest:

George J. Alden — Secretary of State.

Harrison Reed — Governor of Florida.

Born a slave in 1833, Amos Hargrett Sr. was one of the county's leading citizens during the Reconstruction era. Appointed as a county commissioner in 1868 by Gov. Harrison Reed, Hargrett also served as a justice of the peace from 1876 to 1877, served as a delegate to the state's constitutional convention in 1885, and also served as postmaster of St. Marks from 1892 to 1894. (Courtesy Florida Photographic Collection.)

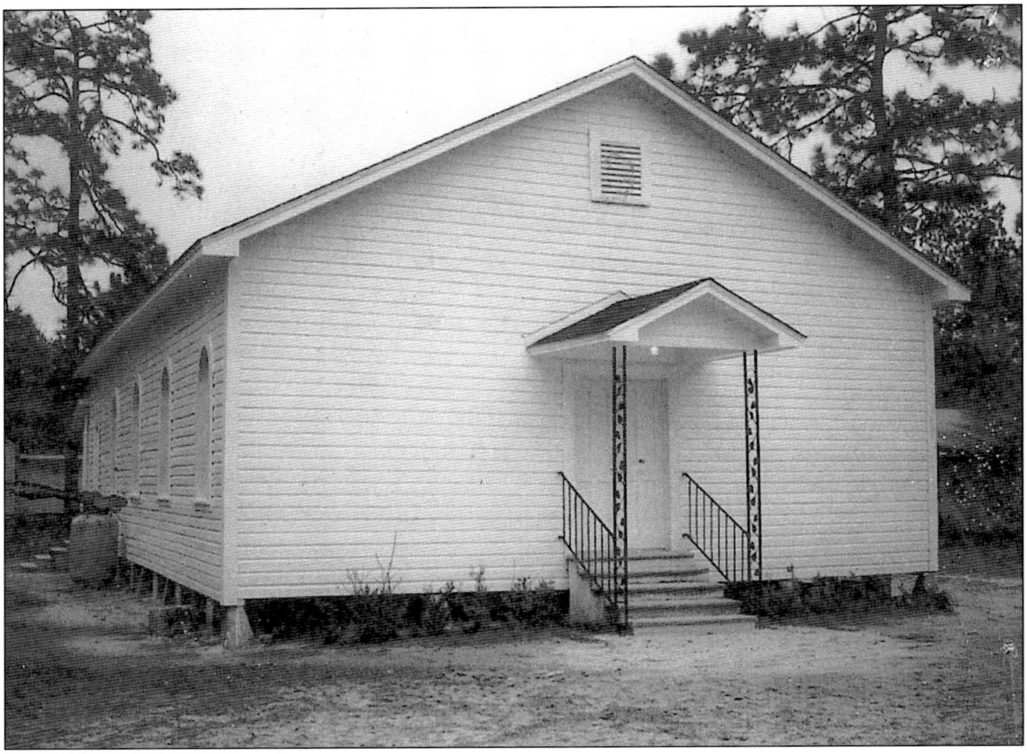

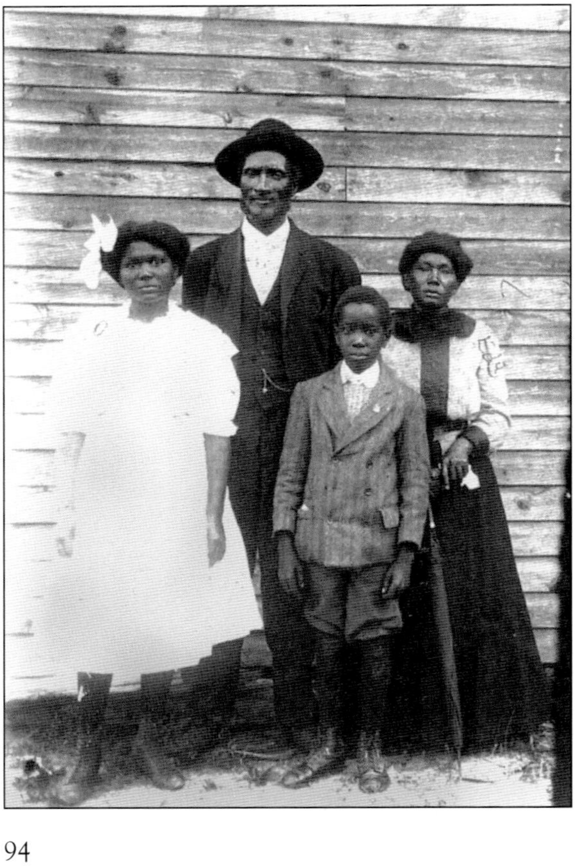

The center of the Hyde Park community is the Thessalonia Missionary Baptist Church, founded in 1889 by Amos Hargrett Sr. In addition to worship services, the church has also hosted public school classes, graduation exercises, and home extension classes. The church is seen here before it was remodeled in the 1980s. (Courtesy Mae Williams.)

One of the first families to settle in the Hyde Park community was the Triplett family. James Triplett poses with his children, Ollie, Obediah, and Louiza, in this c. 1907 photograph. (Courtesy Mary Triplett Jackson.)

Nine

Wakulla Springs

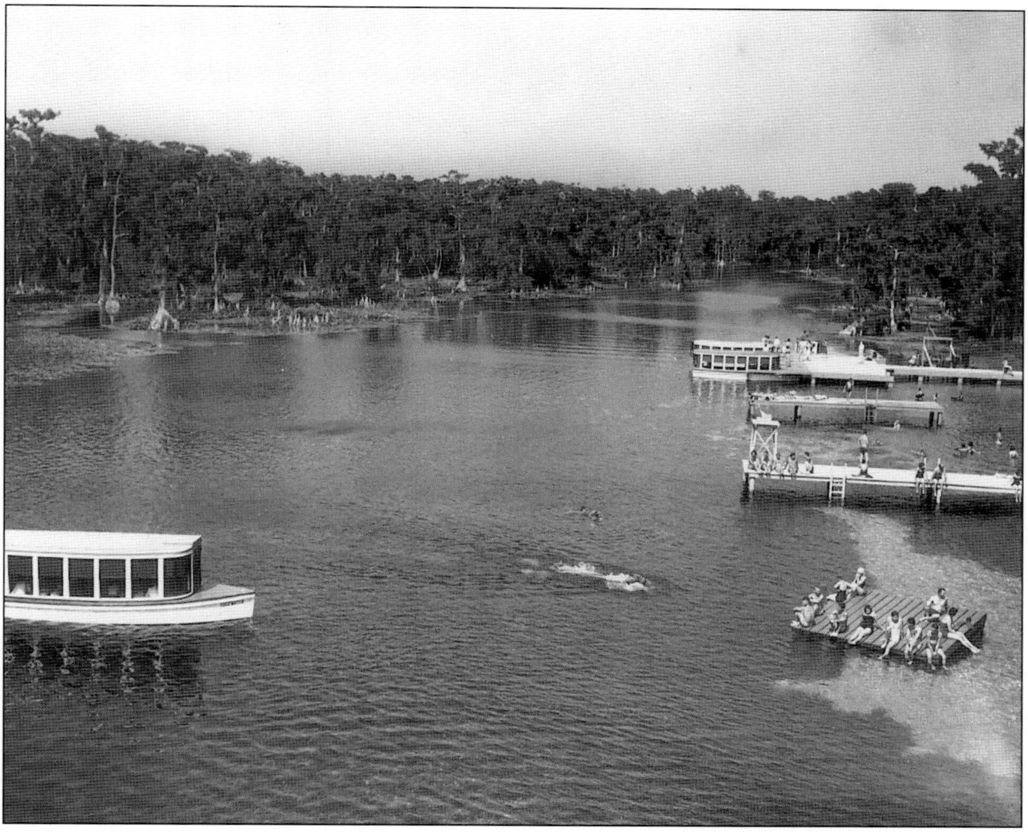

Producing an average of 183 million gallons of crystal-clear water each day, Wakulla Springs has attracted visitors from as early as the Paleoindian period (12,000–9,500 B.C.). In more recent times, Wakulla Springs has served as one of the state's most popular tourist attractions and the focal point of Wakulla County. Seen here is the Springs pool as it looked in the 1940s. (Courtesy Wakulla Springs.)

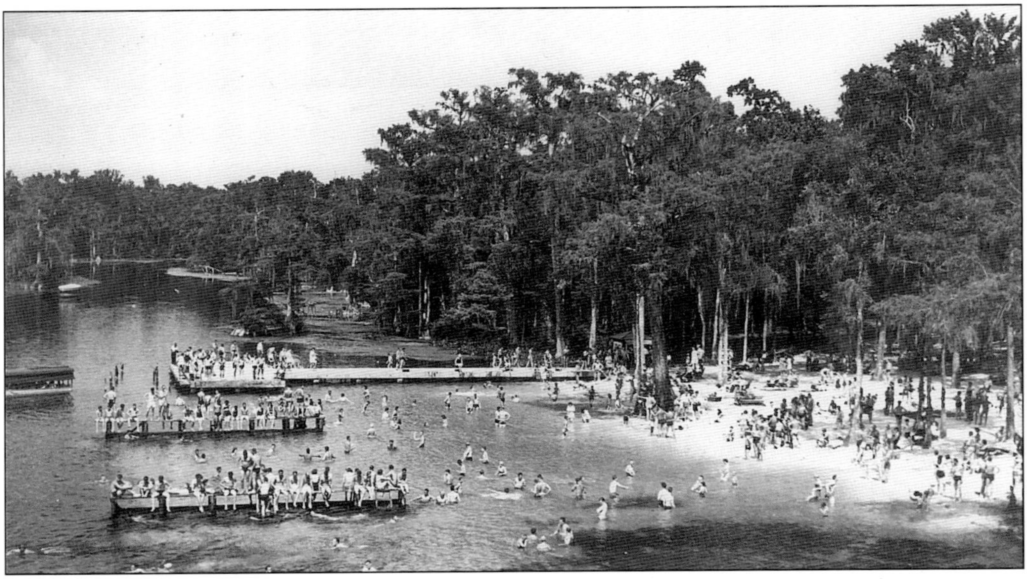

In 1931, George T. Christie, who owned Wakulla Springs from 1925 to 1934, sought to promote its tourist potential by introducing a glass-bottom boat, a diving tower, and a large pier for swimmers, seen here in the 1940s. (Courtesy Wakulla Springs.)

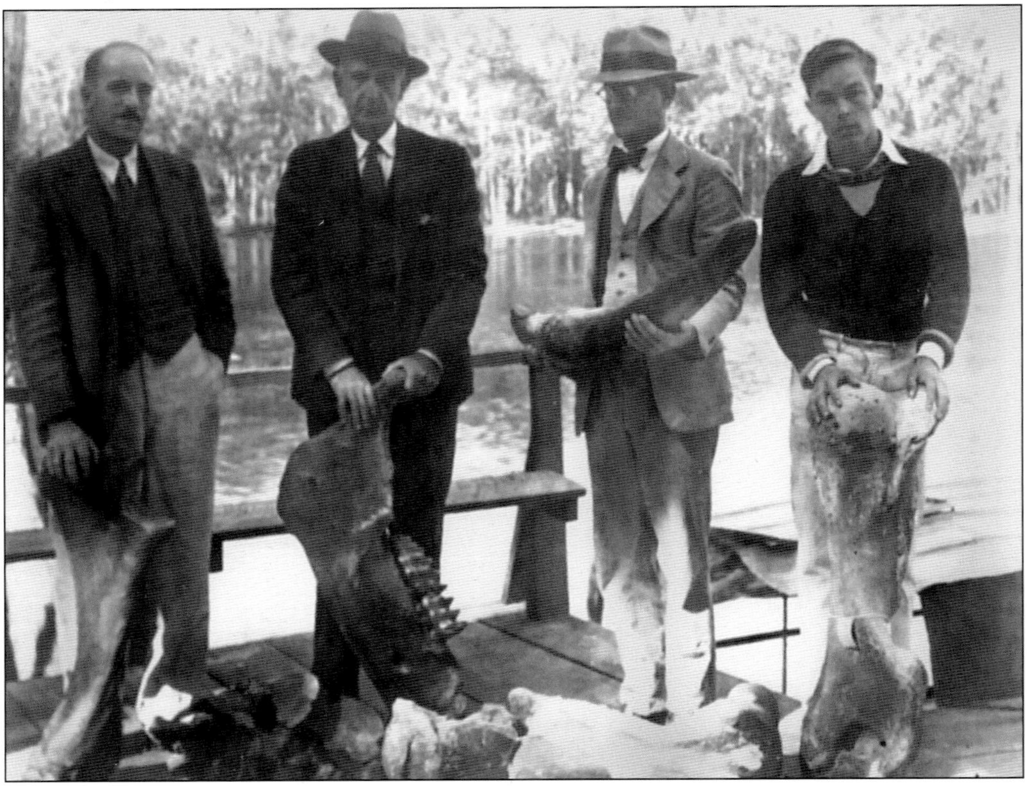

In August of 1930, a team from the Florida Geological Survey, led by State Geologist Dr. Herman Gunter, removed the bones of a mastodon from Wakulla Springs. Seen here, from left to right, with portions of the recovery are George Christie, Dr. Herman Gunter, Gerald Ponton, and James Clarence Simpson. (Courtesy Florida Photographic Collection.)

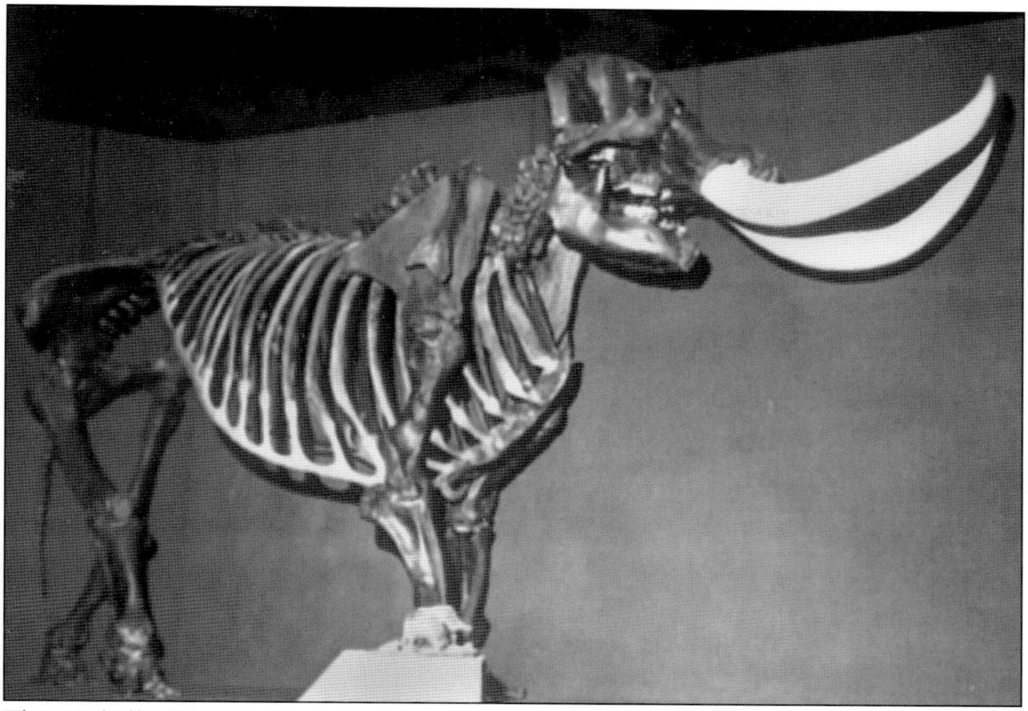

The Wakulla Mastodon, which dates from the Pleistocene Epoch (between 10 and 30 thousand years ago), was the first nearly complete mastodon skeleton recovered in Florida. It is currently displayed in the Museum of Florida History in Tallahassee. (Courtesy Florida Photographic Collection.)

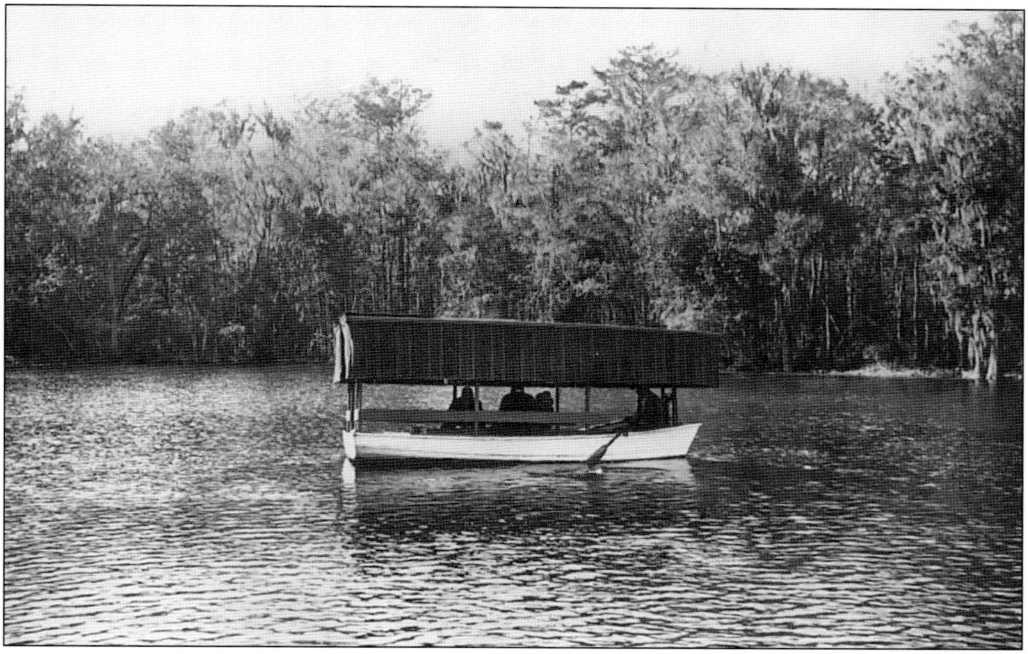

First introduced by Springs owner George Christie in 1931, the glass-bottom boat has long been a favorite attraction. In the early days, boatmen would row the boats over the pool of the Spring by hand, as seen here in the 1940s. (Courtesy Florida Photographic Collection.)

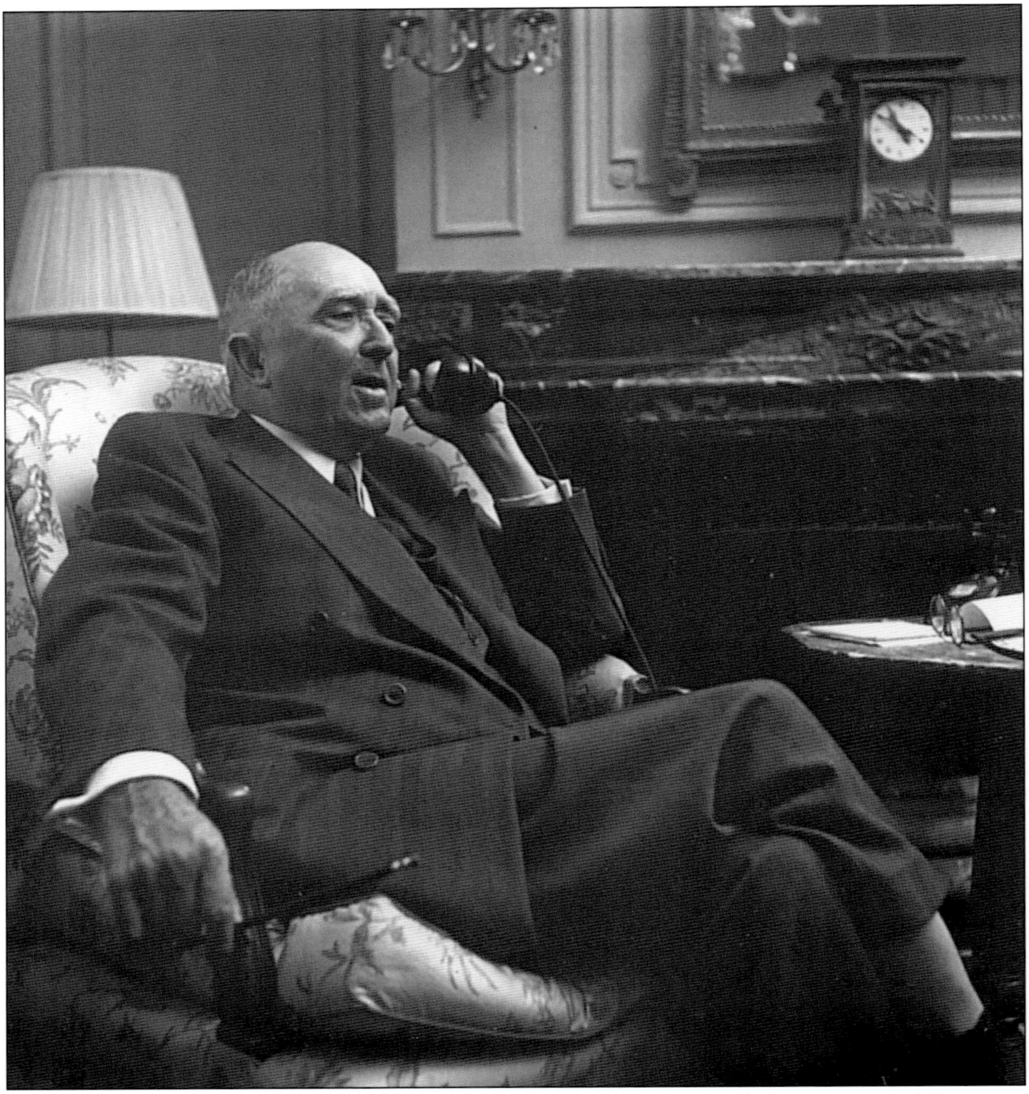

It is impossible to think of Wakulla Springs without remembering the controversial legacy of Florida business tycoon Edward Ball (1888–1981), who purchased the area in 1934. Opened to the public in 1937, the Wakulla Springs lodge was used by Ball as a private retreat where he entertained the rich and famous. While working to preserve and protect the area from commercial exploitation, he occasionally took actions that angered area environmentalists. Today, Wakulla Springs retains much of its original beauty due to Ball's work. (Courtesy Florida Photographic Collection.)

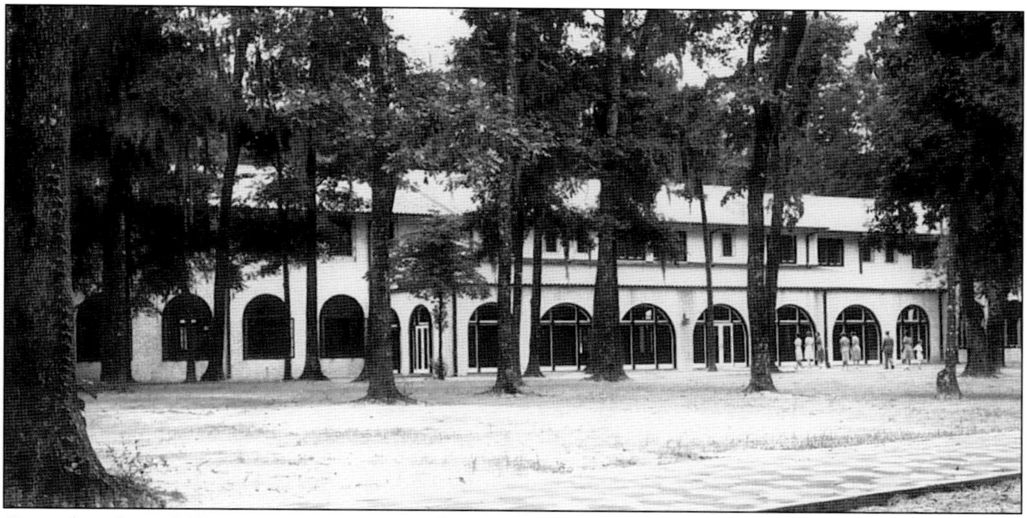

Completed in 1937 at a cost in excess of $75,000, the Wakulla Springs Lodge is an architectural masterpiece designed by Ed Ball that incorporates both Spanish-Moorish and art deco motifs. Hand-wrought iron, marble, local cypress, and hand-made ceramic tiles are featured throughout the 27-room hotel, which includes a large lobby, dining room, and snack bar. The lodge is listed on the National Register of Historic Places. (Courtesy Wakulla Springs.)

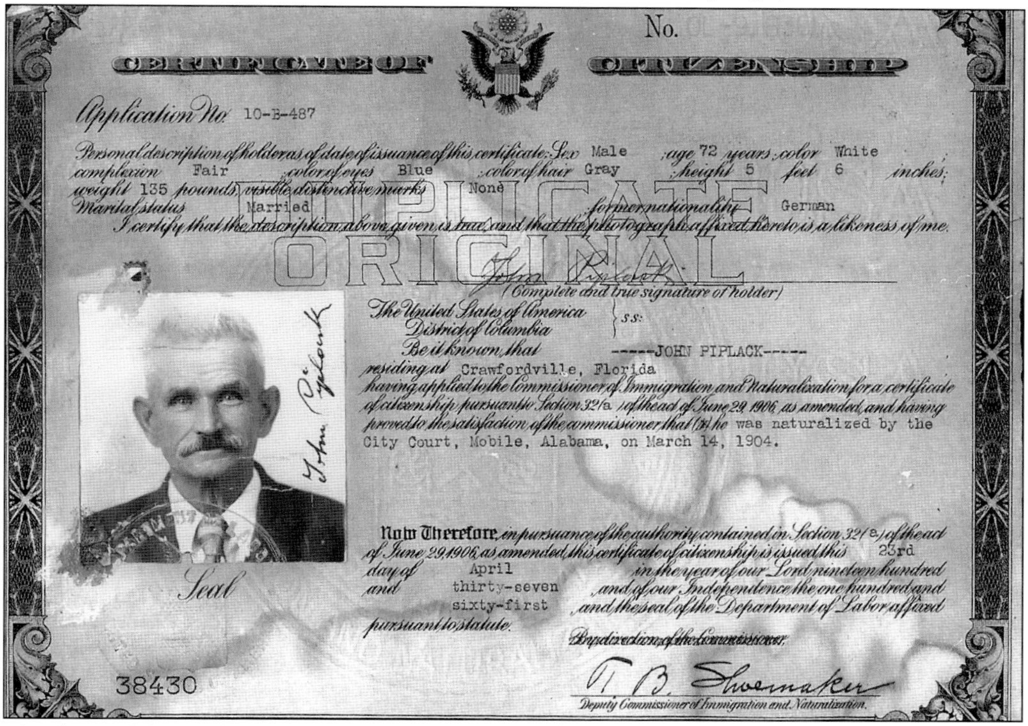

No.

CERTIFICATE OF CITIZENSHIP

Application No. 10-E-487

Personal description of holder as of date of issuance of this certificate: Sex Male ; age 72 years; color White complexion Fair color of eyes Blue color of hair Gray height 5 feet 6 inches; weight 135 pounds; visible distinctive marks None

Marital status Married former nationality German

I certify that the description above given is true, and that the photograph affixed hereto is a likeness of me.

DUPLICATE ORIGINAL

John Piplack
(Complete and true signature of holder)

The United States of America
District of Columbia } ss:

Be it known, that -----JOHN PIPLACK-----
residing at Crawfordville, Florida
having applied to the Commissioner of Immigration and Naturalization for a certificate of citizenship pursuant to Section 32(a) of the act of June 29, 1906, as amended, and having proved to the satisfaction of the commissioner that (s)he was naturalized by the City Court, Mobile, Alabama, on March 14, 1904.

Now Therefore, in pursuance of the authority contained in Section 32(a) of the act of June 29, 1906, as amended, this certificate of citizenship is issued this 23rd day of April in the year of our Lord nineteen hundred and thirty-seven, and of our Independence the one hundred and sixty-first, and the seal of the Department of Labor affixed pursuant to statute.

Seal

By direction of the Commissioner,

T. B. Shoemaker
Deputy Commissioner of Immigration and Naturalization.

38430

The beautiful murals that can be seen on the lodge's cypress ceiling were painted by John Piplack (1864–1951). Born in Germany, Piplack moved to Shadeville in the 1920s and earned his living as a house painter. Employed by Ed Ball during the construction of the lodge in 1935–1936, Piplack designed and painted the murals, incorporating suggestions from Ball. In addition, he was an expert gardener, painted portraits, and is rumored to have worked on the staff of Kaiser Wilhelm I. (Courtesy Don Piplack.)

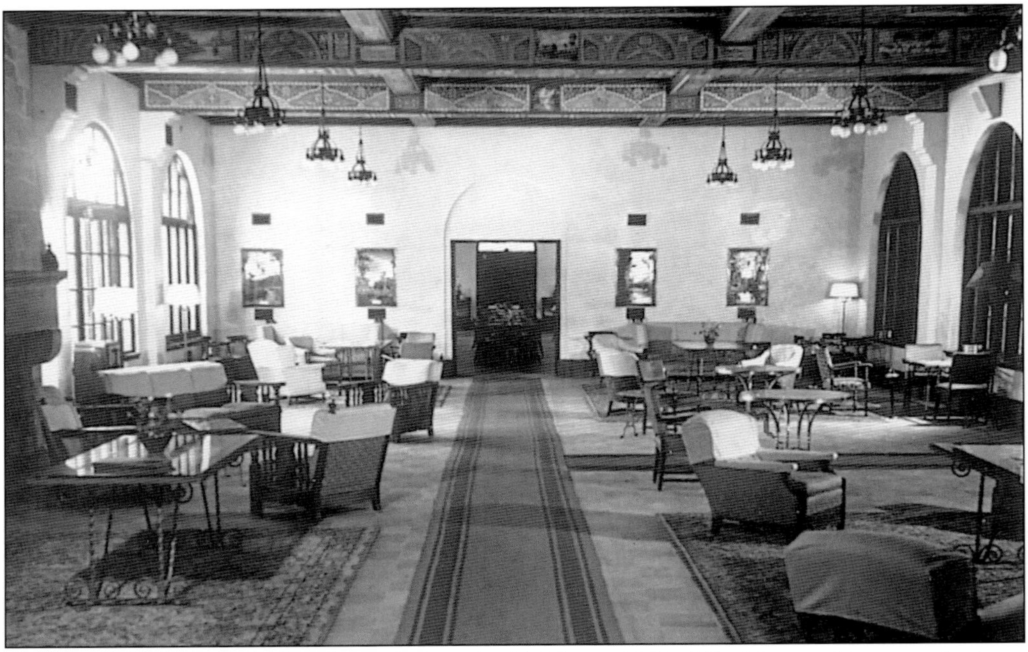

This interior view shows the elegantly furnished lobby in 1942. All of the marble, wrought iron, and woodwork was done on site. Note the Piplack murals on the 16-foot-high ceiling at the top of the photograph. (Courtesy Florida Photographic Collection.)

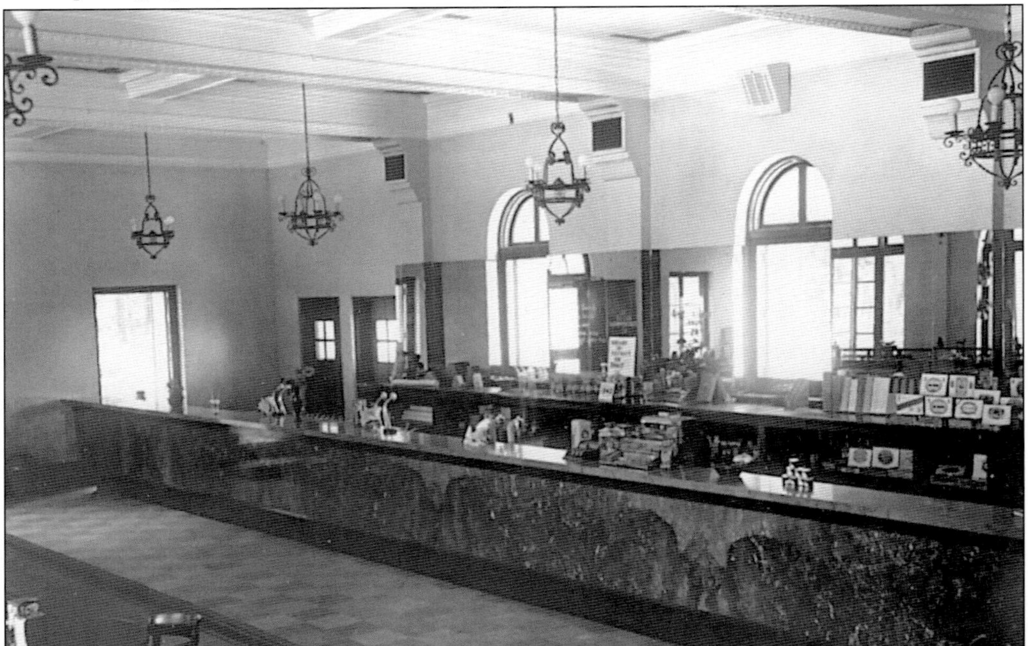

A view of the snack bar in 1942 highlights the book-cut marble counter and bar, which, at 70 feet, is the longest in the Southeast. Ed Ball was extremely proud of the marble's beauty, referring to it as his "butterfly collection" due to its distinctive grain pattern. The countertop was cut from one huge piece of marble specially quarried in Tennessee to Ball's exact standards. (Courtesy Florida Photographic Collection.)

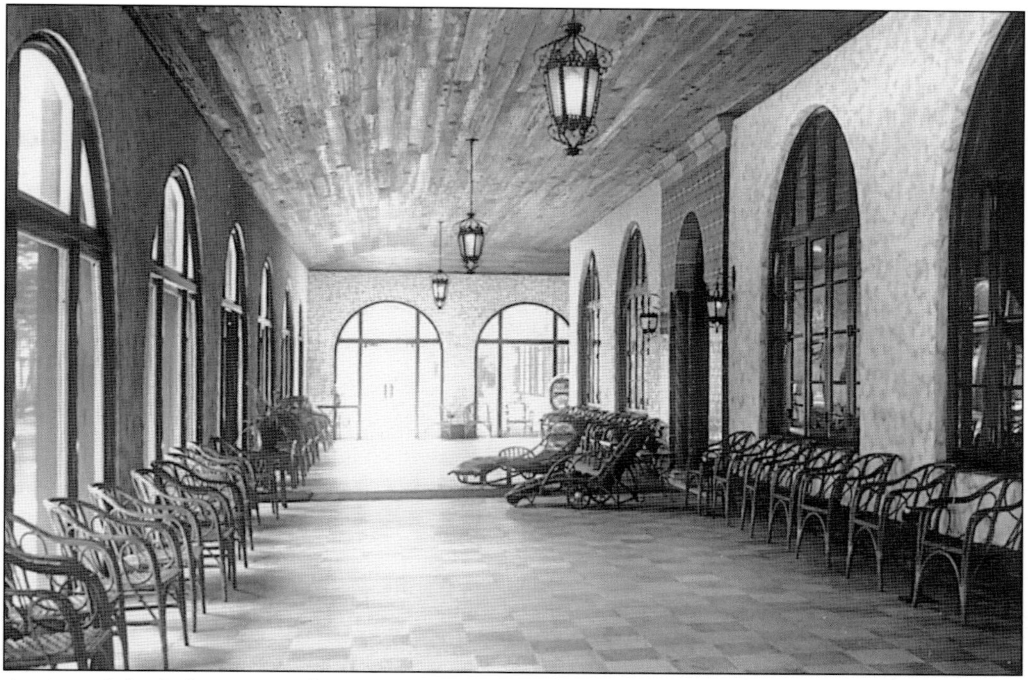

A view of the lodge terrace features its native "pecky" cypress ceiling. Painted a light blue and then sanded, the cypress knots were highlighted in beautiful relief. The imported ceramic tile lobby entrance can be seen at right. (Courtesy Florida Photographic Collection.)

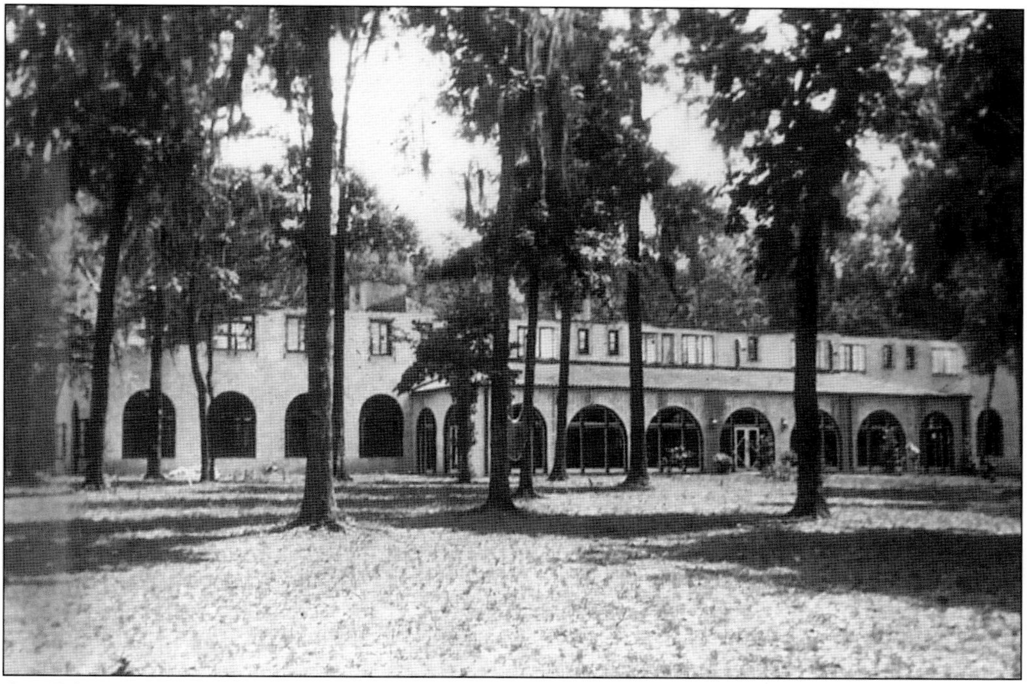

On February 23, 1943, the lodge's roof was destroyed by fire. In order to prevent a similar occurrence, Ball custom ordered a pre-fabricated roof made of concrete and steel from New York. The large, numbered panels were shipped down by rail and installed in their proper order. (Courtesy Florida Photographic Collection.)

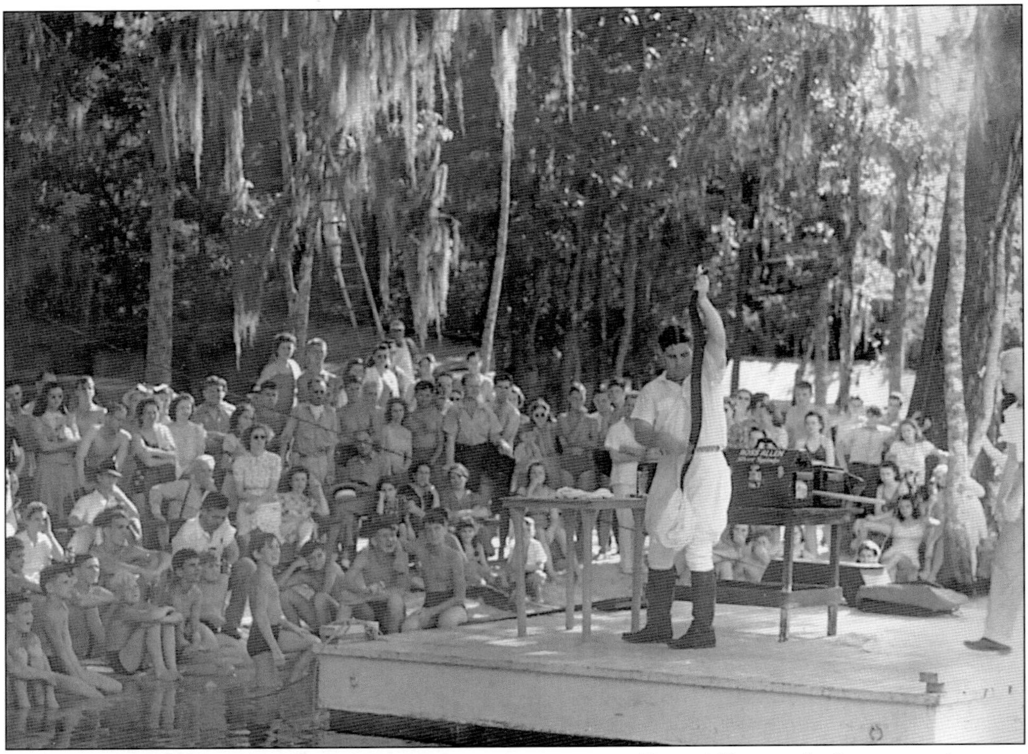

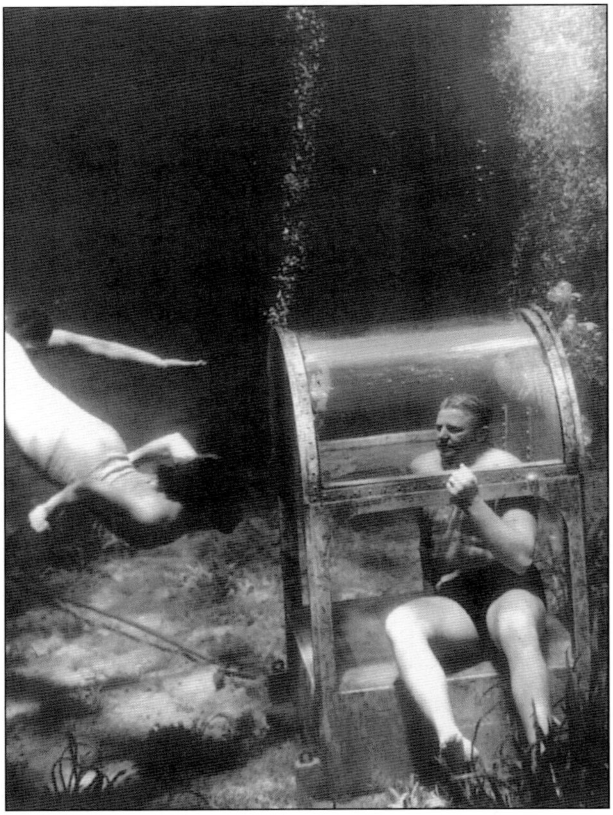

Ross Allen made frequent trips to Wakulla Springs to collect specimens for his Florida Reptile Institute at Silver Springs in Ocala. While visiting he would perform demonstrations such as the one seen here in the 1940s. (Courtesy Florida Photographic Collection.)

Newton Perry (1909–1987), general manager from 1941 to 1947, did much to promote the Springs throughout his tenure. In addition to training U.S. Navy frogmen during the war, Perry was responsible for bringing MGM Studios to the area to film two Tarzan movies, for which he served as coordinator and stuntman. Perry is seen here in a breathing station he developed to aid members of his underwater swimming shows. After leaving Wakulla Springs, Perry moved south and developed Weeki Wachee Springs. (Courtesy Wakulla Springs.)

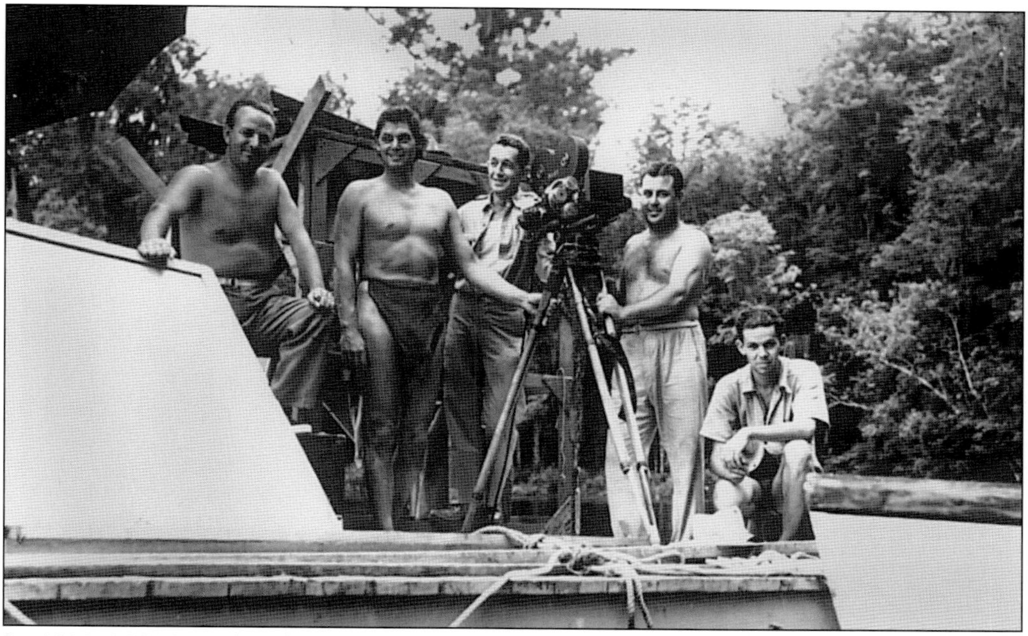

In 1941, MGM Studios brought their cameras to Wakulla Springs to film *Tarzan's Secret Adventure*, starring Johnny Weismuller and Maureen O'Sullivan. In 1942, scenes for *Tarzan's New York Adventure* were filmed here. Weissmuller, second from left, is seen here with members of a camera crew in 1941. (Courtesy Florida Photographic Collection.)

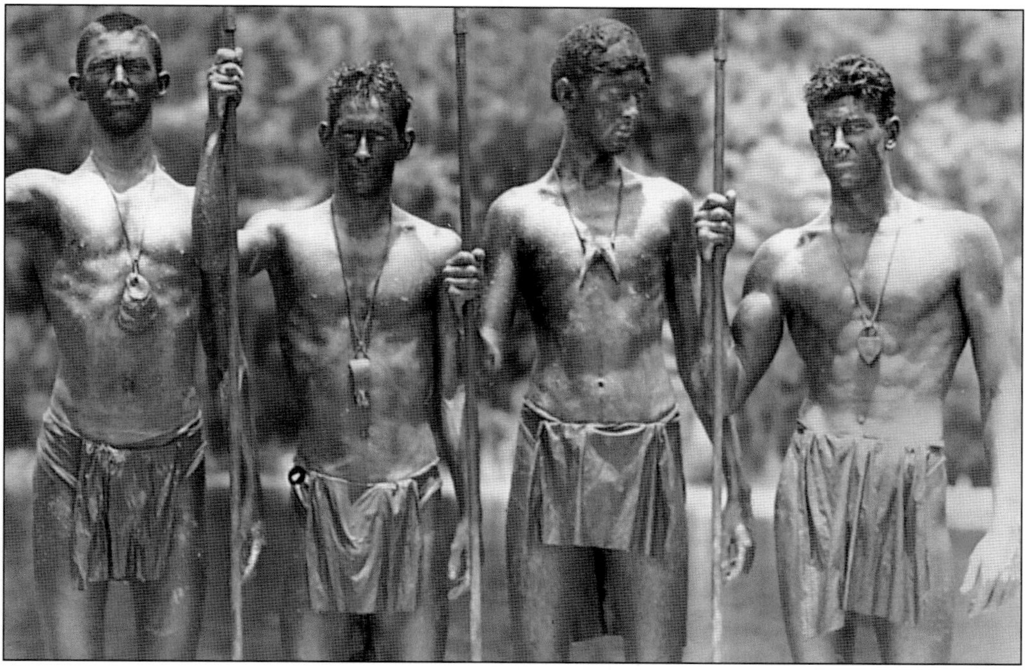

Many local residents were hired to perform stunts and act as doubles during the filming of *Tarzan's Secret Adventure*, having been recruited by Newton Perry. Perry himself also performed stunts and served as a swimming coach. Seen here, from left to right, are Joe Holton, Jack Trawick, Mac Withers, and Jack Yaeger Jr., area schoolboys portraying jungle "savages." (Courtesy Florida Photographic Collection.)

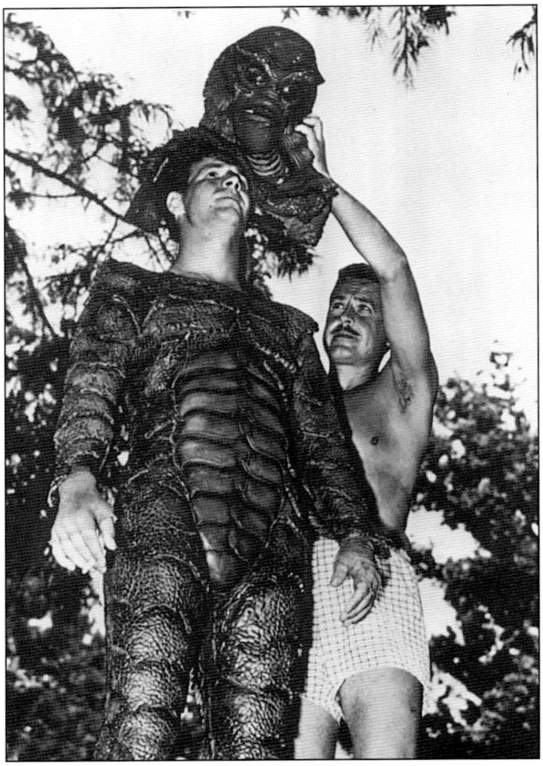

In 1954, Universal Studios used the Springs to film *The Creature from the Black Lagoon*. Tallahassee resident Ricou Browning, shown here being helped into his costume, performed the underwater stunts as the Creature. (Courtesy Florida Photographic Collection.)

Universal Studios returned to Wakulla Springs in 1977 to film underwater segments of its disaster film *Airport '77*. Local divers were hired to assist the filming, with actor Jack Lemmon spending several days at the lodge between shots. Divers are seen here working with the prop that was built for the shoot. (Courtesy Florida Photographic Collection.)

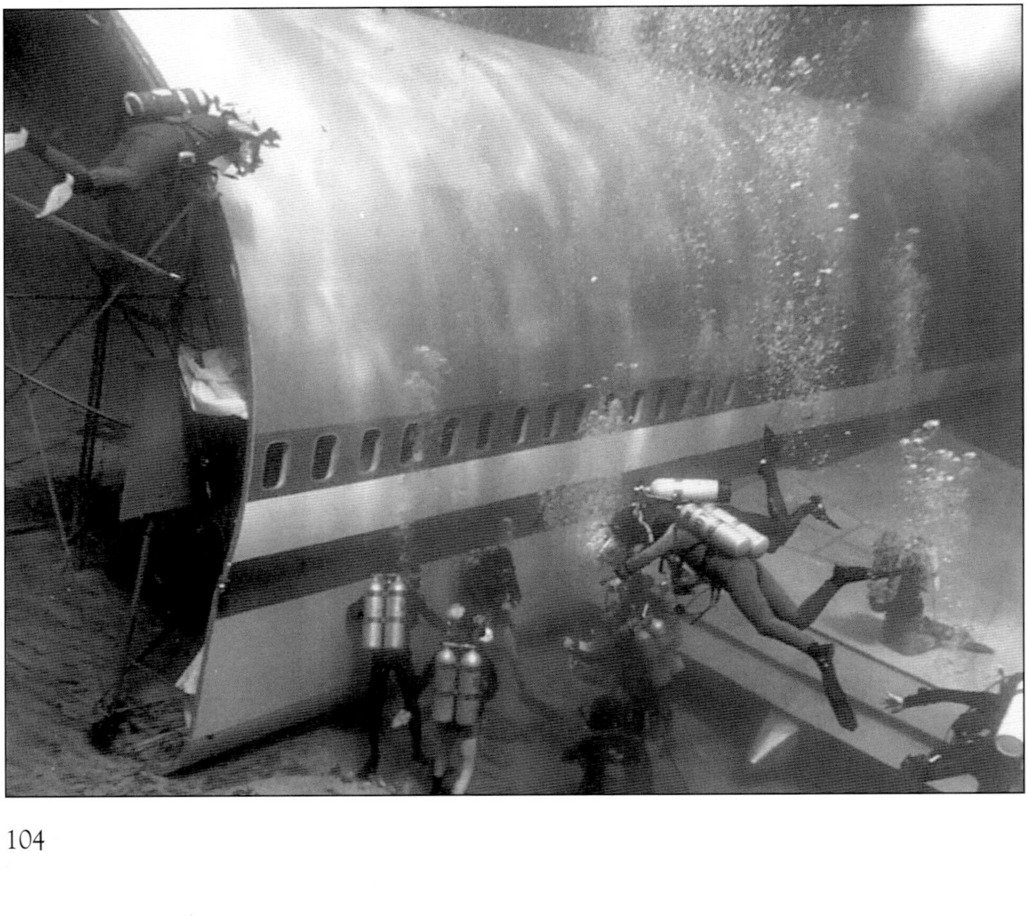

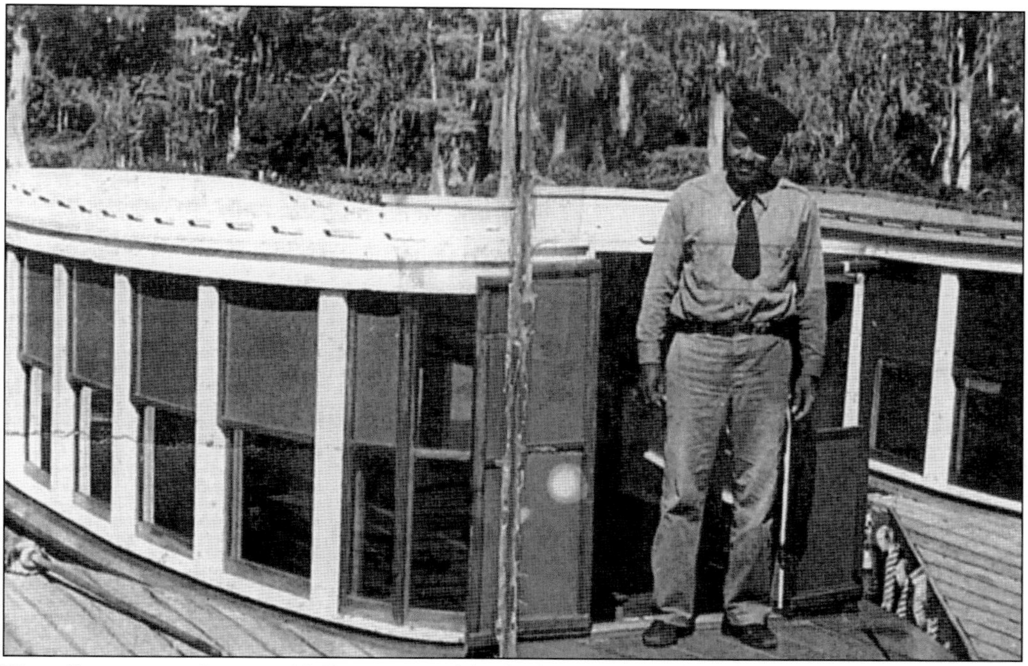

Tom Gavin, seen here in 1943, captained both the jungle and glass-bottom boat cruises from 1937 until his death in 1977. Hired with Luke Smith as the first cruise boatmen, Gavin used a distinctive "river chant" to entertain his passengers. Four generations of the Gavin family have worked at the Springs, with Don Gavin of Shadeville now in his 25th year as a boat captain. (Courtesy Ruth Williams.)

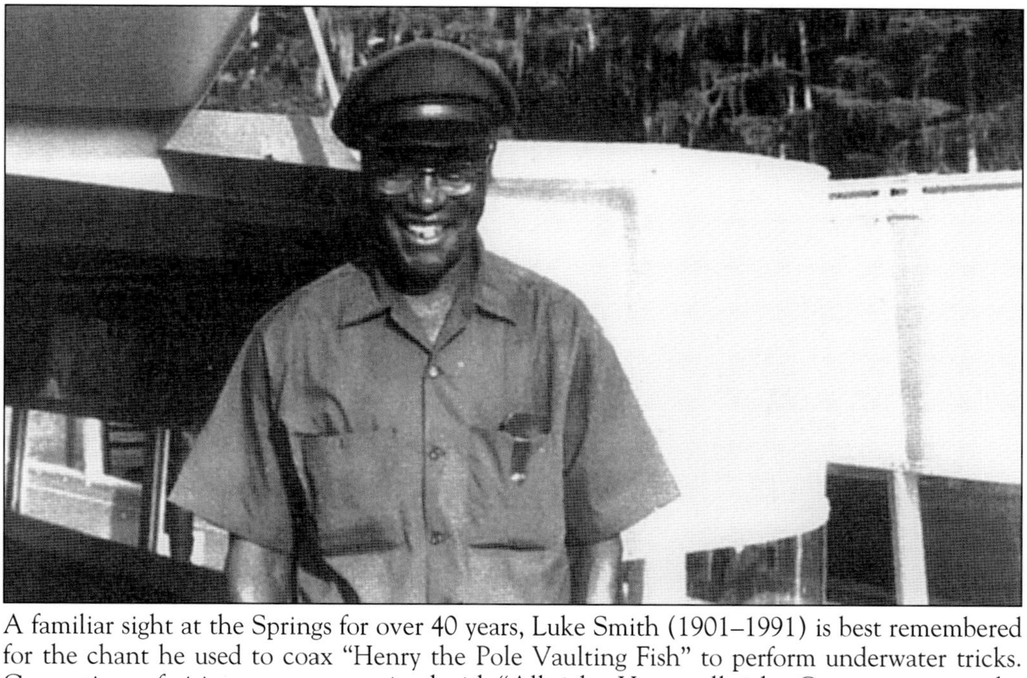

A familiar sight at the Springs for over 40 years, Luke Smith (1901–1991) is best remembered for the chant he used to coax "Henry the Pole Vaulting Fish" to perform underwater tricks. Generations of visitors were entertained with "All right, Henry, all right. Come meet us at the pole. Wake up now, I call you. You heard what I say—come on and get across this here pole." Four generations of Smith's family have worked at Wakulla Springs. (Courtesy author.)

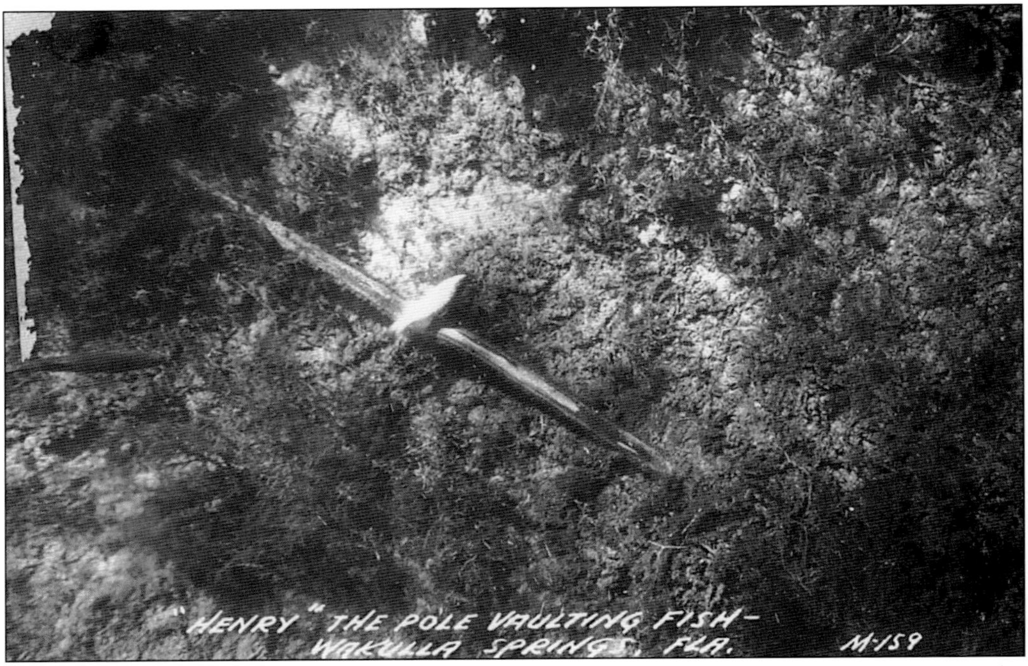

A special treat for those taking the glass-bottom boat ride was watching Henry jump the cypress pole some 25 feet below the surface. Henry and a long line of his descendants have been performing this trick for over 60 years now. (Courtesy Florida Photographic Collection.)

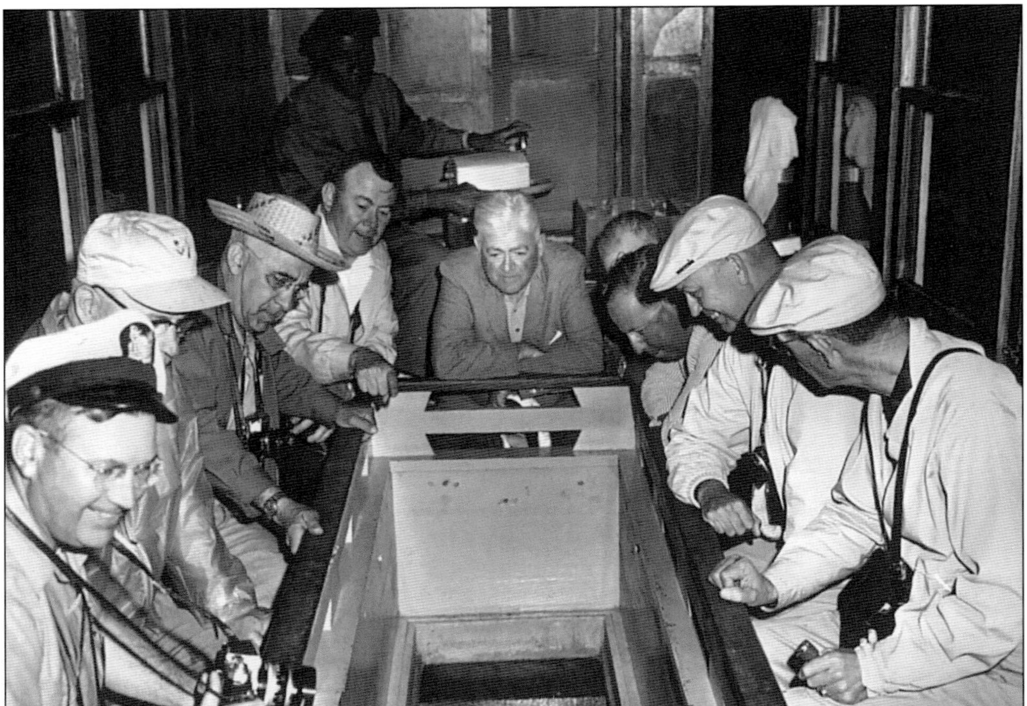

In later years motorized boats were introduced. Boatman Luke Smith conducts a glass-bottom boat tour in the 1950s. (Courtesy Florida Photographic Collection.)

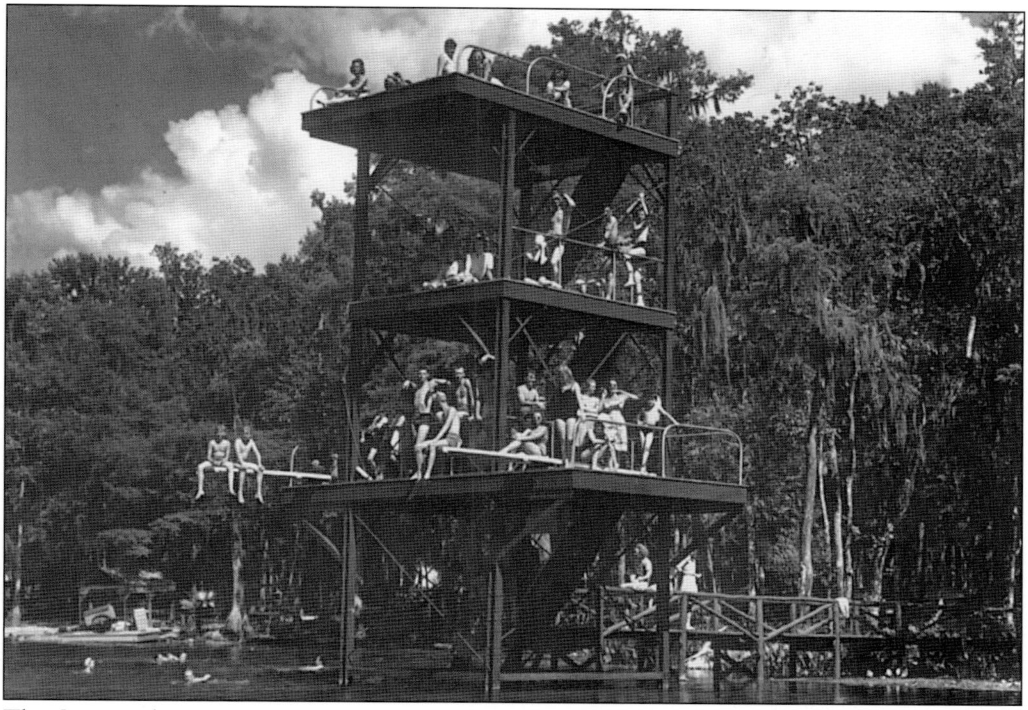

The Springs diving tower is seen here as it appeared in the 1950s. At 33 and 1/3 feet tall, the tower was used during the war to train soldiers how to disembark a ship. During filming of the Tarzan movies, a special platform was added raising the tower to 50 feet and allowing Johnny Weismuller to perform spectacular dives. (Courtesy Florida Photographic Collection.)

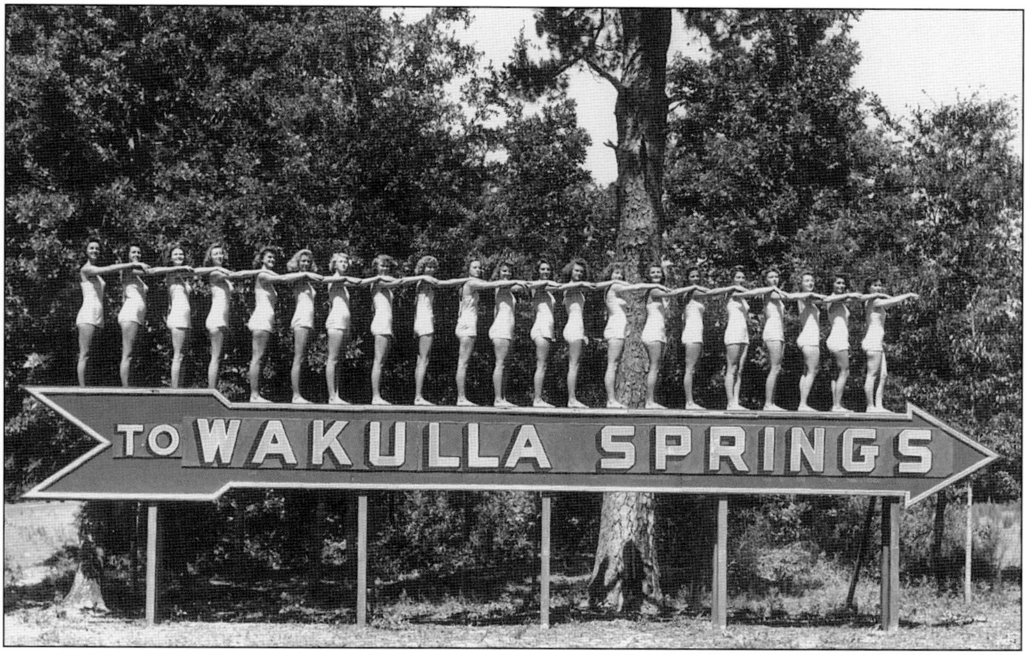

Members of the Florida State College for Women synchronized swimming team, the Tarpon Club, pose here in the 1940s. The club would often perform at the Springs. (Courtesy Wakulla Springs.)

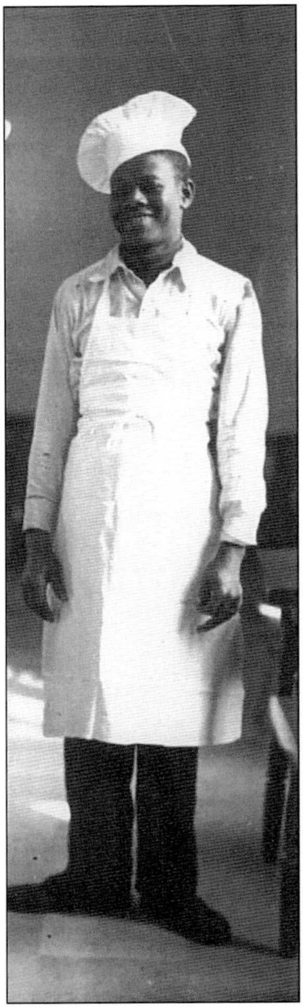

Tommie Lee Lewis first began working at Wakulla Springs in 1935 by helping with the construction of the lodge. He later became head chef and coordinator of the kitchen staff, retiring in 1981 after 46 years of service. He is seen here in the 1940s. (Courtesy Frenchie Lewis.)

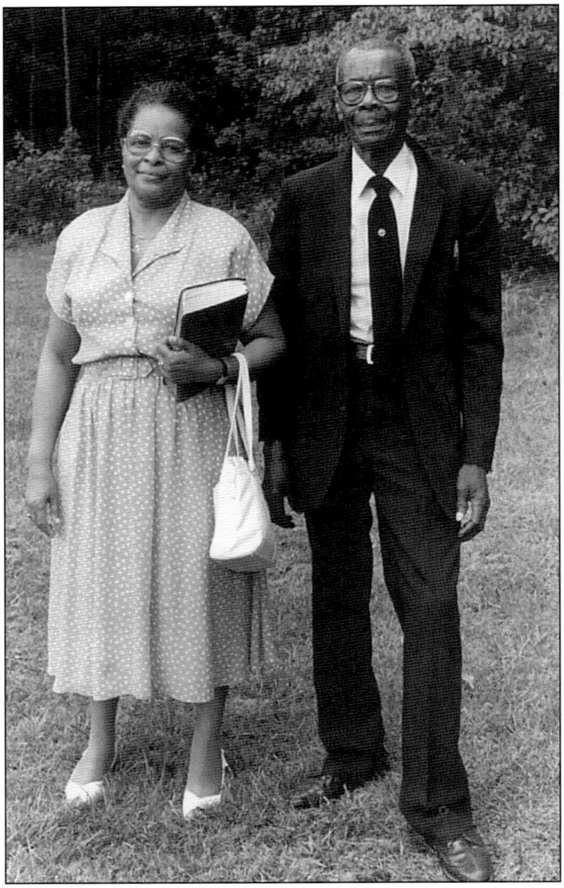

Frenchie Roberts Lewis began working at the Springs in 1955. In 1962 she became head waitress of the dining room, a position she held until her retirement in 1997. Three generations of the Lewis family have worked at the Springs. She is seen here with her husband, Tommie Lee Lewis. (Courtesy Frenchie Lewis.)

John "J.D." Harvey started working at Wakulla Springs in 1960 when he was 13 years old. From 1975 to 1983 he was assistant manager, and from 1983 until his retirement in 1991 he was director of marketing and sales. He is seen here with "Freedom" who was brought to the Springs as a cub in 1981; she lived there until 1985. Freedom now resides at Homosassa Springs. (Courtesy John D. Harvey.)

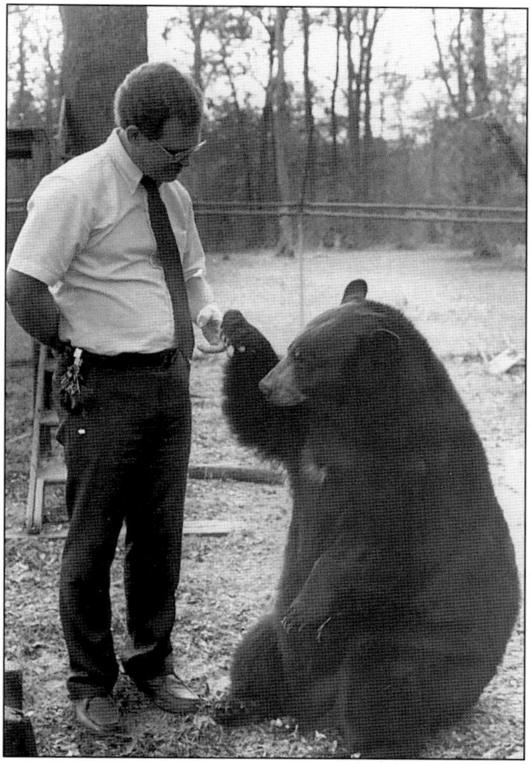

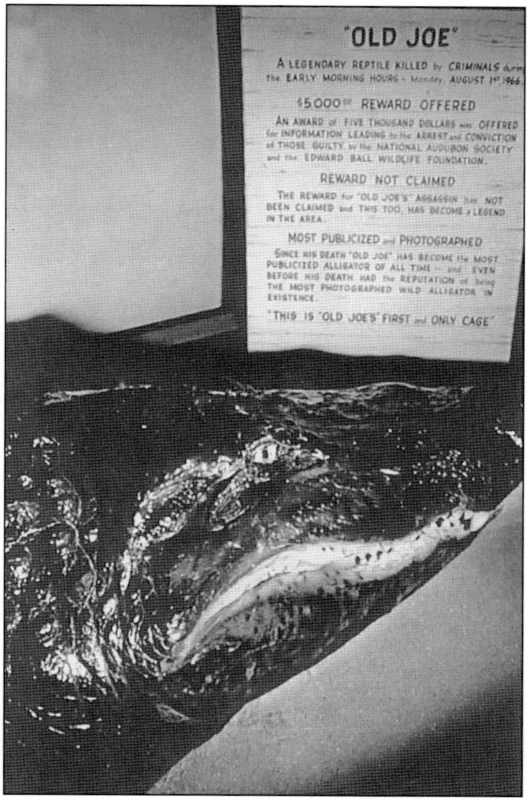

"Old Joe," the 11-foot-long, 650-pound alligator known as "the most photographed wild alligator in existence," was killed by poachers on August 1, 1966. He was estimated to have been 200 years old at the time of his death. For years, Old Joe could always be seen from the boats sunbathing in his favorite spot. His preserved remains are displayed in the lodge lobby. (Courtesy Wakulla Springs.)

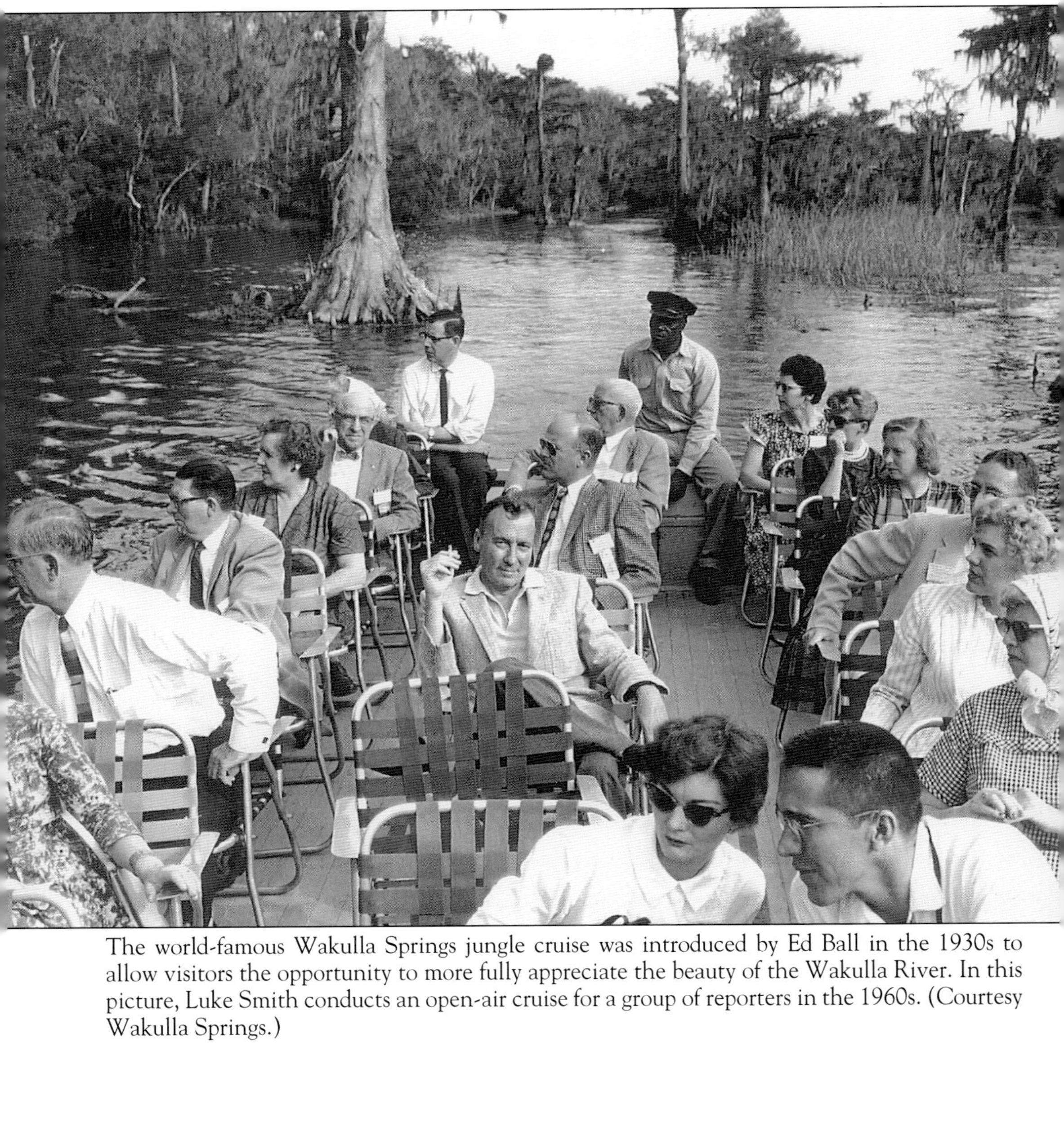

The world-famous Wakulla Springs jungle cruise was introduced by Ed Ball in the 1930s to allow visitors the opportunity to more fully appreciate the beauty of the Wakulla River. In this picture, Luke Smith conducts an open-air cruise for a group of reporters in the 1960s. (Courtesy Wakulla Springs.)

Ten

Around the County

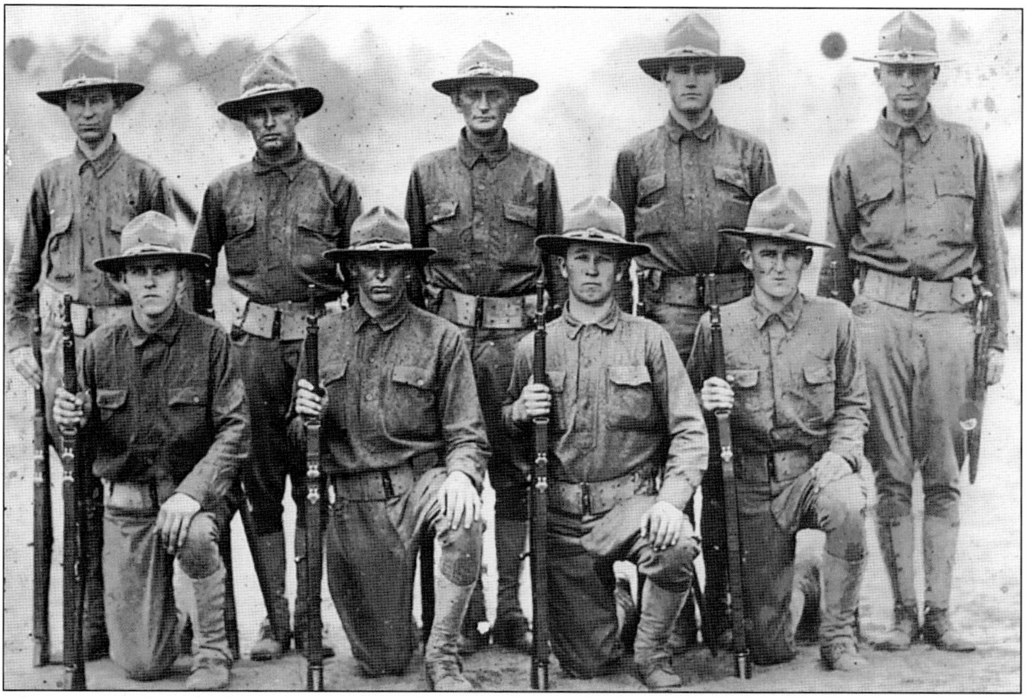

This group of Wakulla volunteers during World War I, from left to right, includes (front row) Henry Daniel McLeod, Lige Hogan, Charles Roberts, and Clarence Morrison; (back row) Roscoe Grant, Hal Walker, Cal Revell, Eli McKenzie, and Eddie Lawhon. (Courtesy Florida Photographic Collection.)

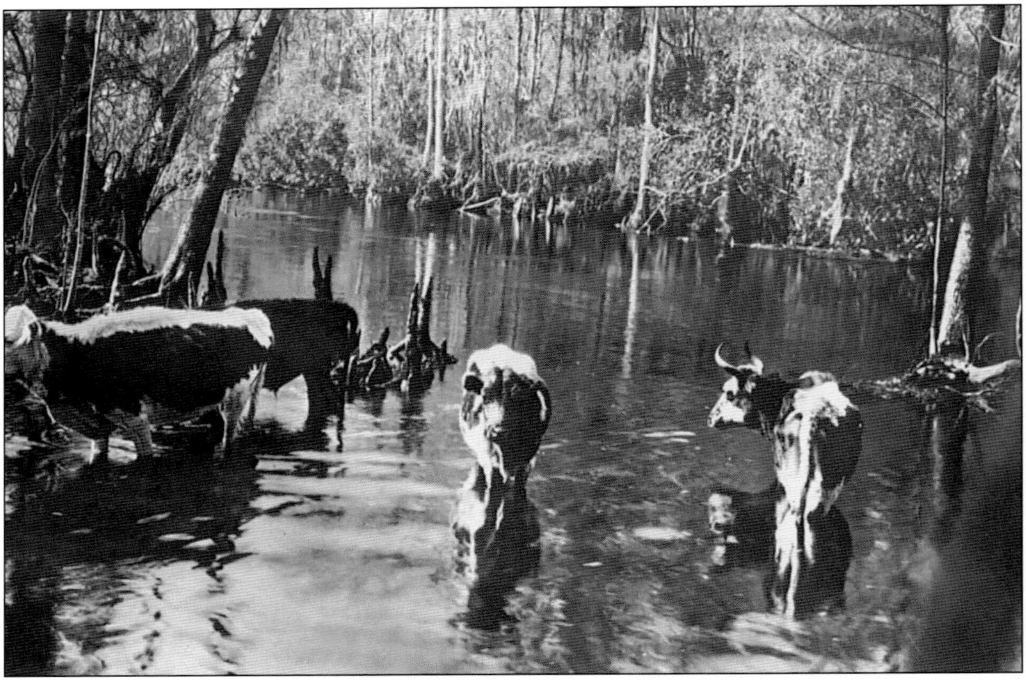

Prior to the passage in 1949 of the state-wide livestock fencing law, it was not uncommon to see cows grazing in the Wakulla River. In the winter, when food was scarce, the cows would dive under water to feed on the river grass. (Courtesy Florida Photographic Collection.)

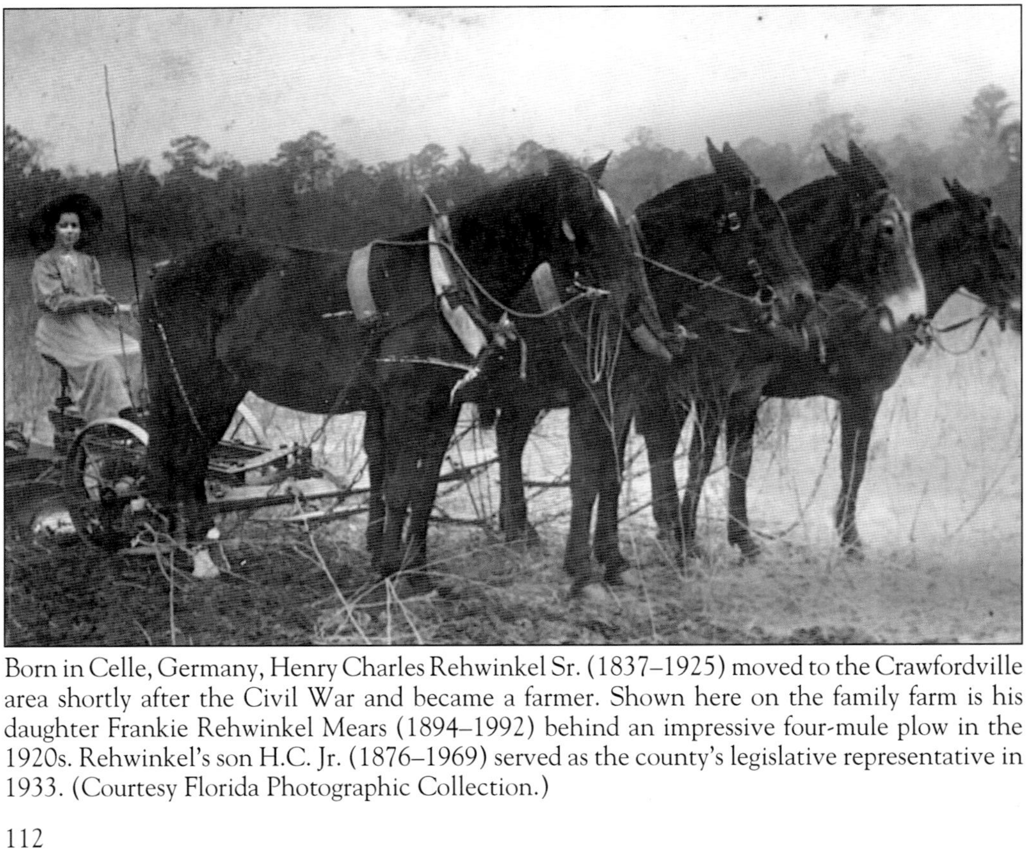

Born in Celle, Germany, Henry Charles Rehwinkel Sr. (1837–1925) moved to the Crawfordville area shortly after the Civil War and became a farmer. Shown here on the family farm is his daughter Frankie Rehwinkel Mears (1894–1992) behind an impressive four-mule plow in the 1920s. Rehwinkel's son H.C. Jr. (1876–1969) served as the county's legislative representative in 1933. (Courtesy Florida Photographic Collection.)

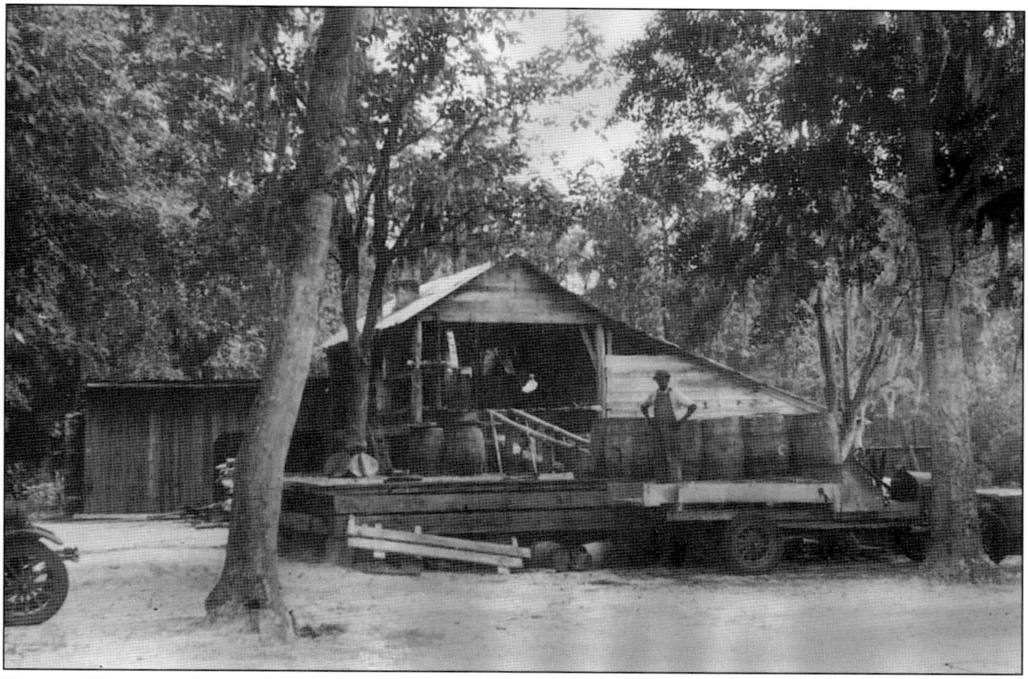

Pictured here in the mid-1920s is the turpentine still on the Wakulla River owned by George Russ and Newton Culbreath. Raw turpentine was distilled here and in similar camps around the county. (Courtesy Florida Photographic Collection.)

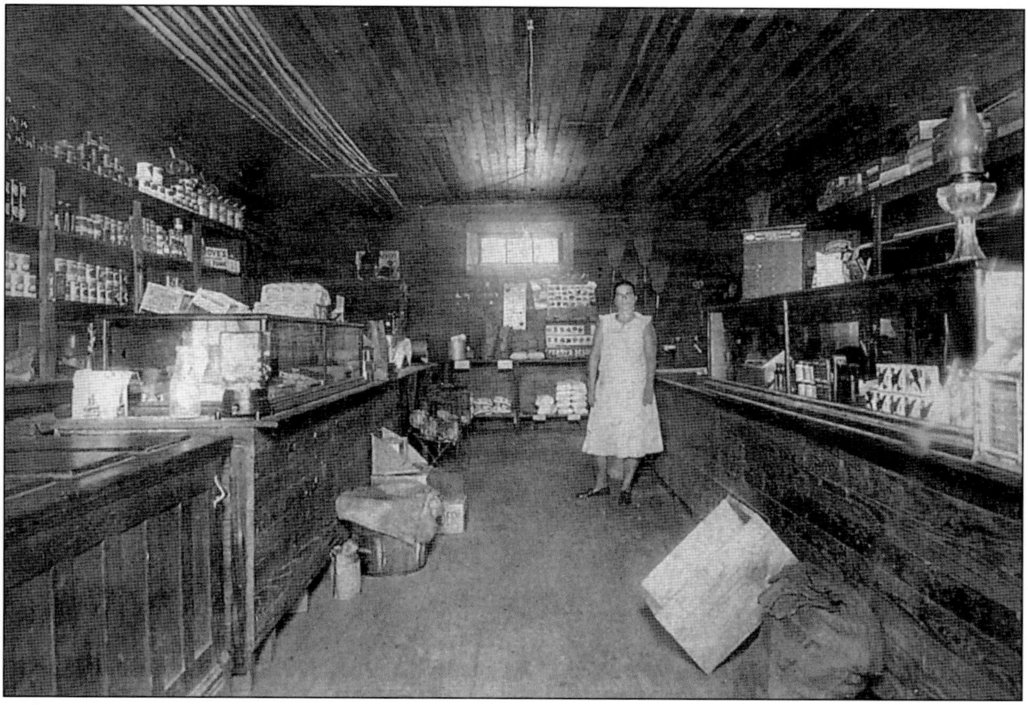

Adjacent to the Culbreath still was this commissary where workers would purchase food and sundries. The commissary was managed by Joe Nails (1898–1993) and his wife, Elva Brown Nails (1901–1984), pictured here in 1930. (Courtesy Dr. W.F. Robison Jr.)

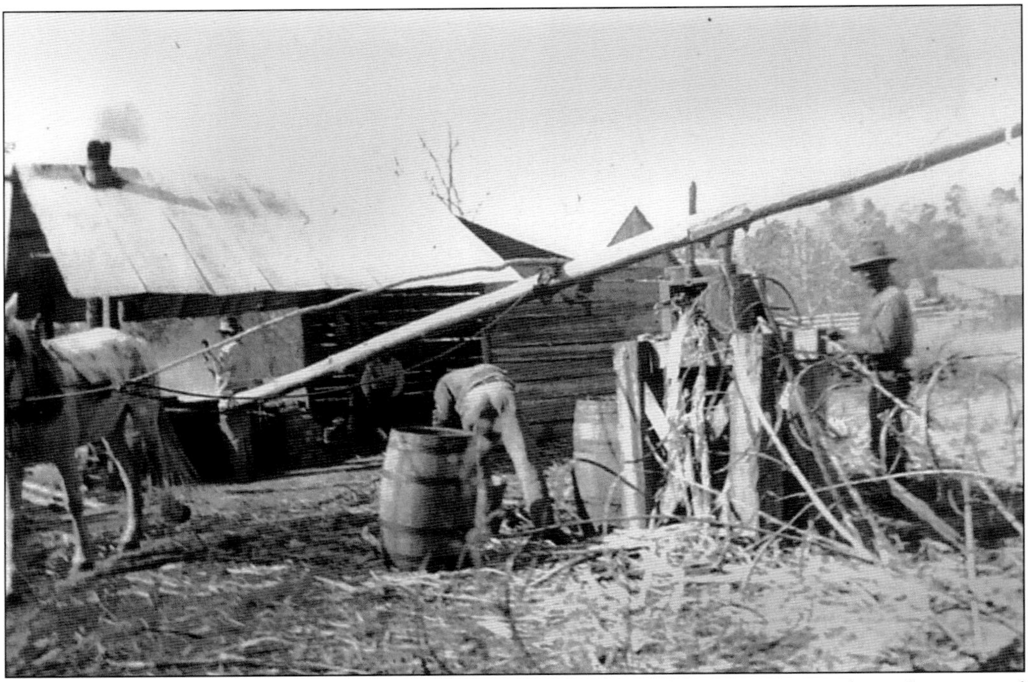

Syrup-making was a common occurrence on county farms for many years. A mule-powered cane grinder is seen here in the 1930s on the farm of Riley Americus Harvey (1888–1957). (Courtesy Marylou Carter.)

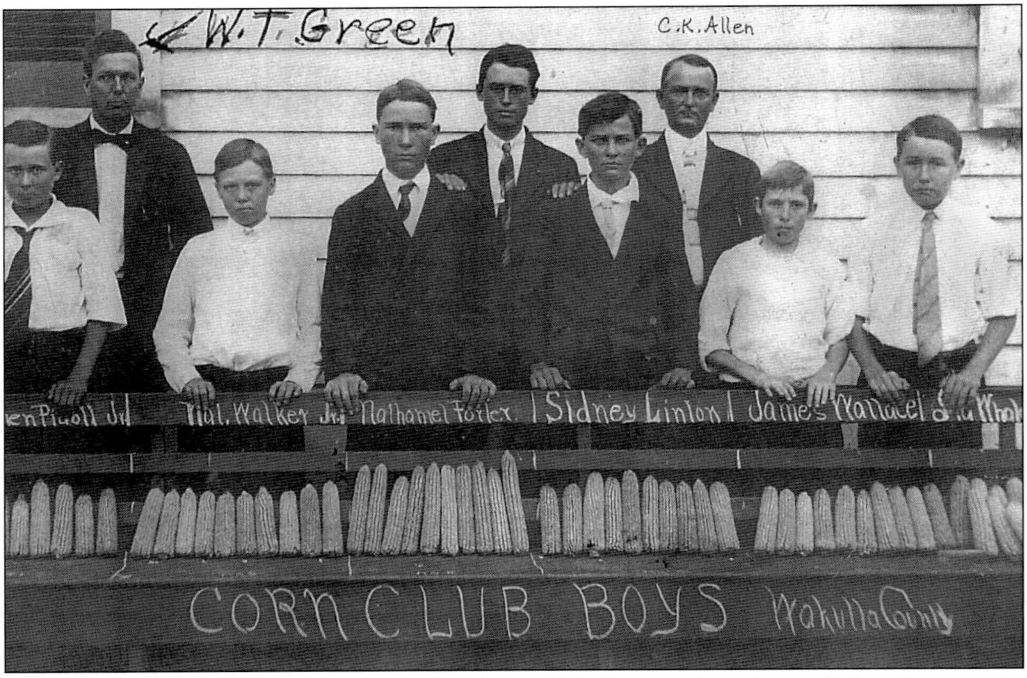

County agent W.T. Green poses with the Corn Club Boys as they show off their harvests in 1918. From left to right are Stephen Pigott Jr., W.T. Green, Nat Walker Jr., Nathaniel Porter, unidentified, Sidney Linton, School Superintendent C.K. Allen, James Wallace, and ? Whaley. (Courtesy Clarice Ward Taff.)

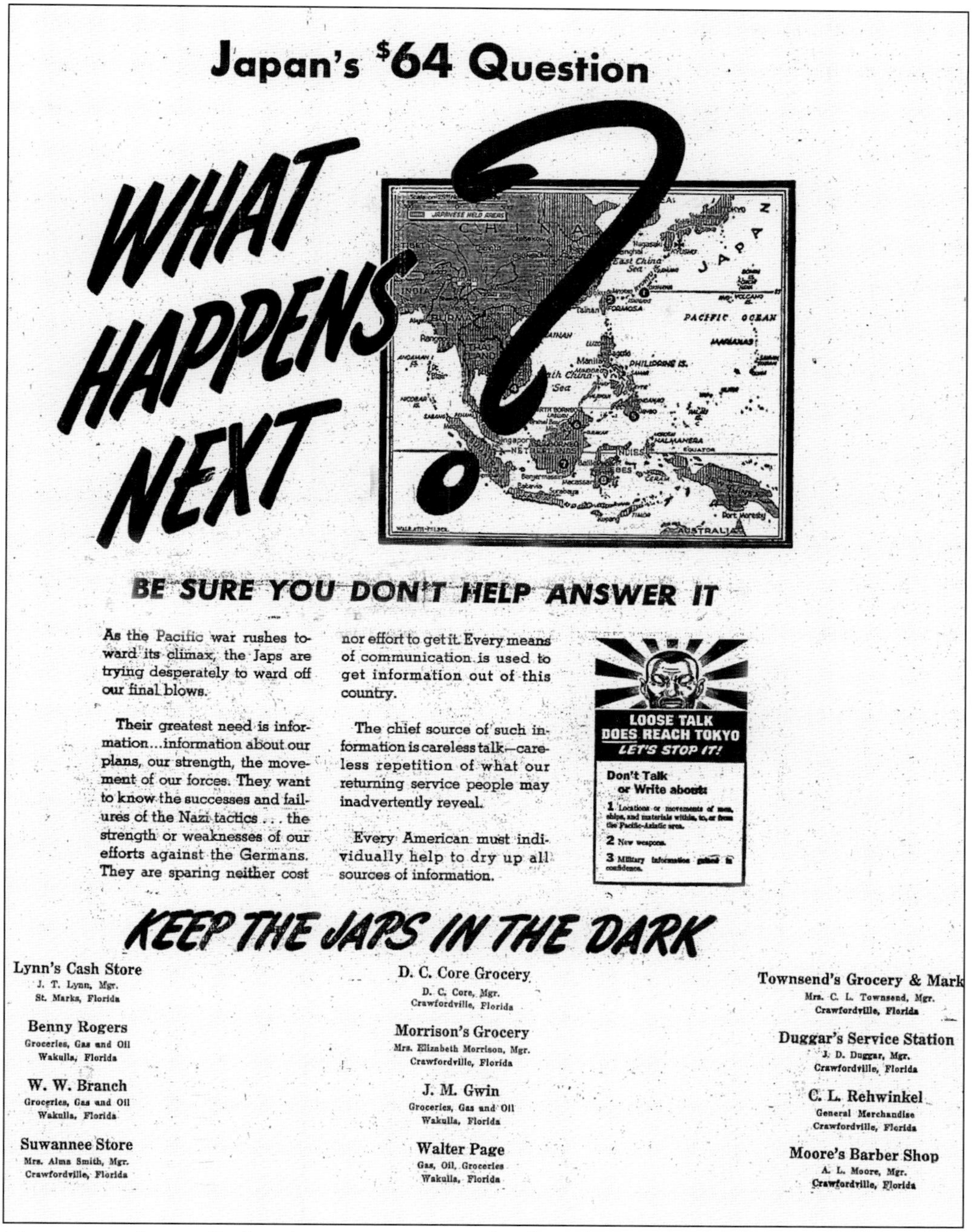

County merchants display their patriotism in this bit of wartime propaganda in the July 27, 1945 issue of the *Wakulla County News*. (Courtesy *Wakulla County News*.)

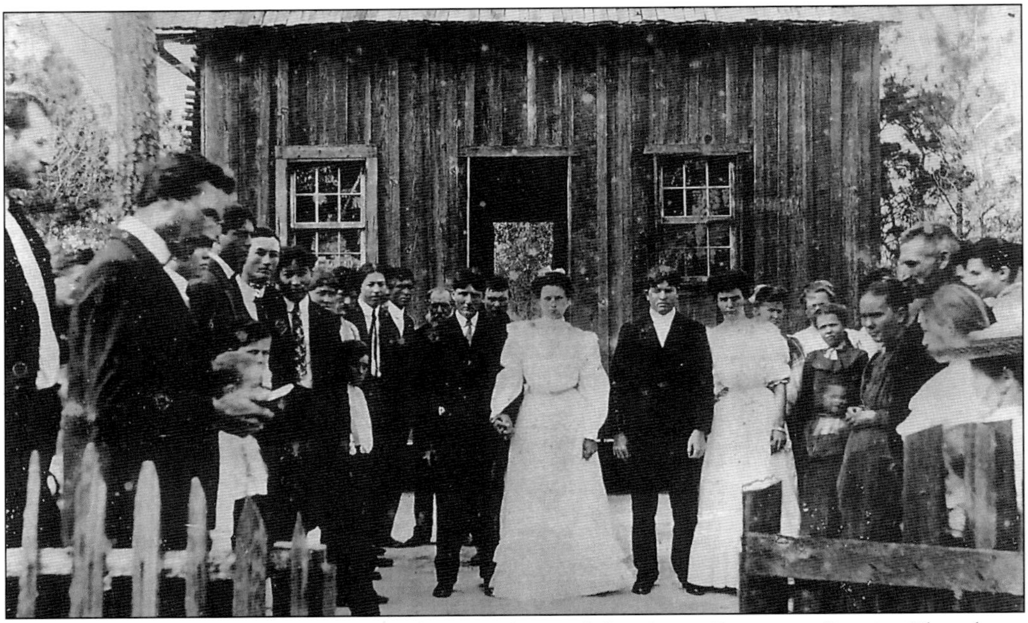

Members of a wedding party are seen here in front of the Arran Primitive Baptist Church on December 20, 1908. Unfortunately, the names of the couple in the center are not known. The couple on the right are identified as Riley Harvey (1888–1957) and Lily Anna Smith (1876–1923). Minister Joshua Spears is second from the left. (Courtesy Lily Jean Jordan.)

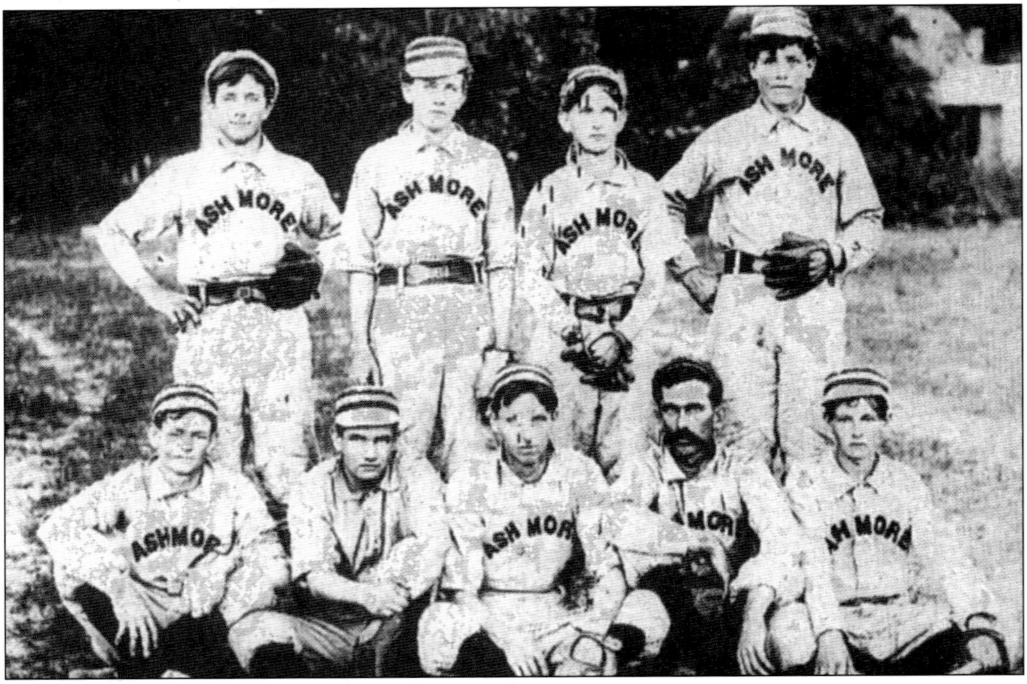

In the old days practically every community had its own baseball team. Traveling around the county, the teams would compete with each other on Saturday afternoons. Members of the Ashmore team in 1904, from left to right, are (front row) John Ashmore, Roy Hutchinson, Joe Gray, Busby Wynn, and Johnnie Winburn; (back row) Walter Durrance, Early Durrance, Arthur Tully, and Bernard Pigott. (Courtesy Freeman Ashmore.)

Born in 1908 in the Ashmore community, Freeman Ashmore has been a lifelong educator. Receiving his bachelor's degree from the University of Florida in 1932, Ashmore served as assistant principal at Crawfordville High School in 1935–1936 and as principal between 1937 and 1939. He later moved to Leon County, where he served as a principal from 1940 to 1964 and as Leon County superintendent of schools from 1964 to 1972. He received his master's from FSU in 1949. Ashmore is one of the county's most respected historians. (Courtesy Freeman Ashmore.)

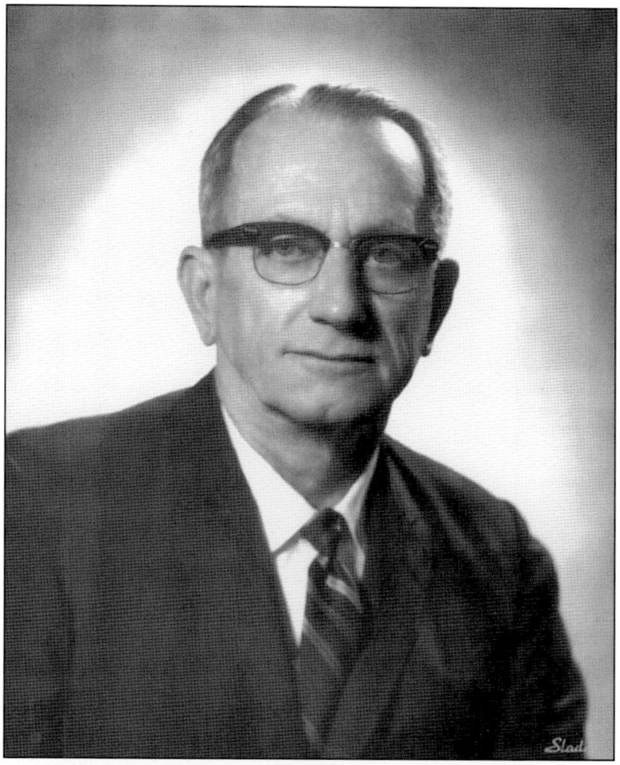

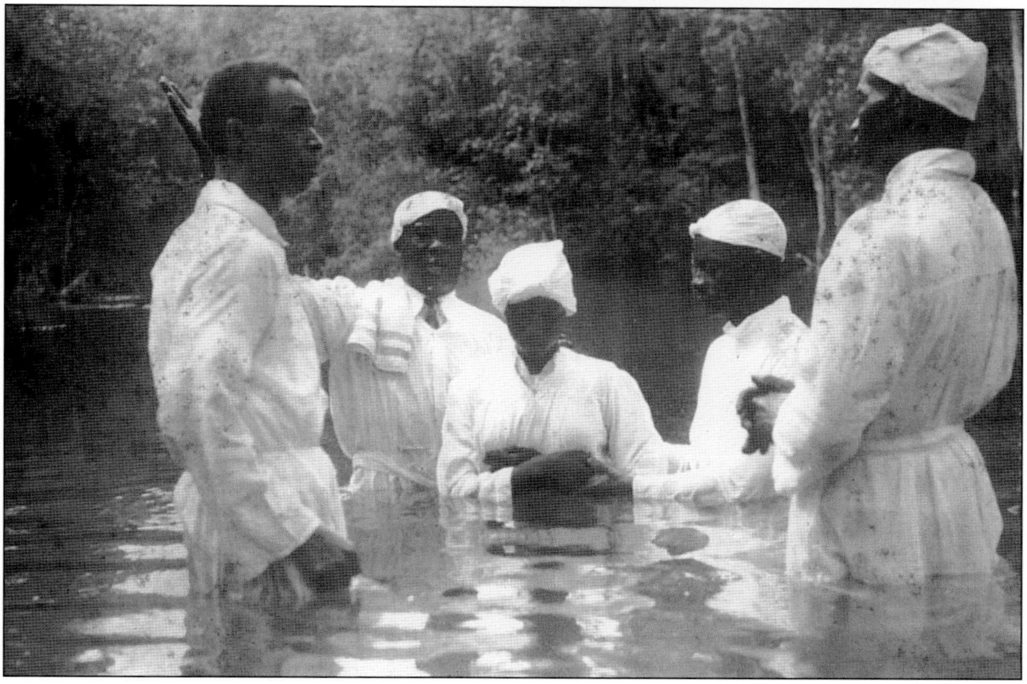

Members of the Mt. Olive Primitive Baptist Church are seen here conducting a baptismal ceremony in Barco Spring in the late 1940s. Members, from left to right, are Deacon Stacy Roberts, Rev. R.B. Ivery, unidentified, Deacon Willie Shingles, and Deacon Edward Thomas. (Courtesy Frenchie Lewis.)

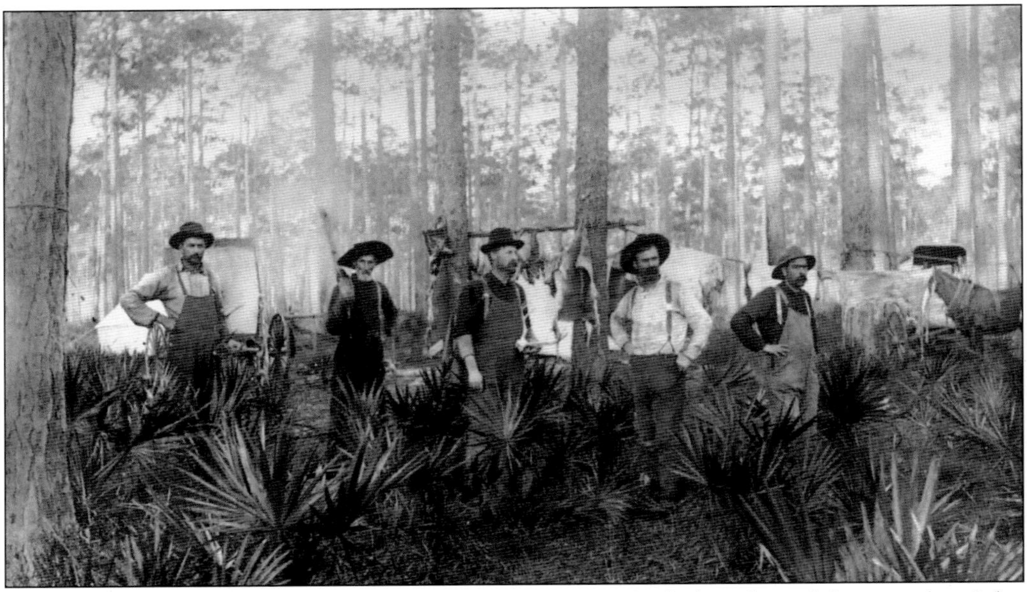

This successful 1928 hunting party in Gum Swamp includes, from left to right, John Edward Houston, Jimps Langston, Edward Sauls, Martin Sauls, and Gadsen Porkin. (Courtesy Houston Taff.)

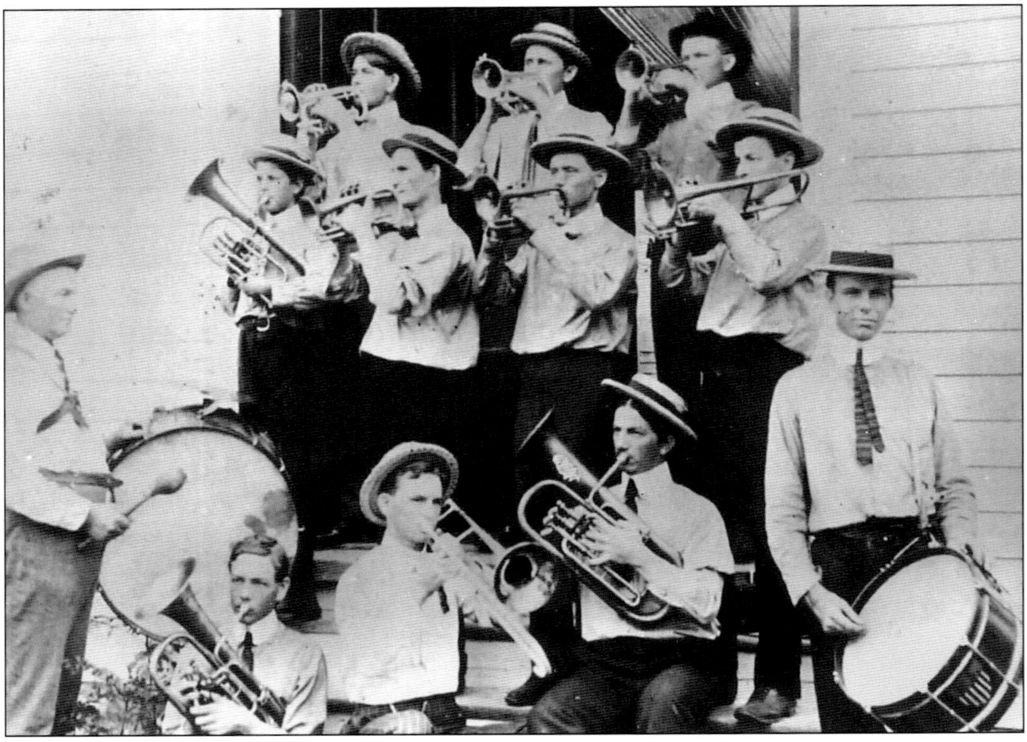

The Hilliardville Brass Band, pictured c. 1920, performed at baseball games and other functions around the county. From left to right are (front row) Frank Duval, A.R. Pearce, A.M. Tully, Wright Walker, and Sylvester Baker; (middle row) Ira Council, William Harvey, Gip Sheppard, and George Smith; (back row) Quintus Ashmore, C.D. Robinson, and Harry Pearce. (Courtesy Carol Allbritton.)

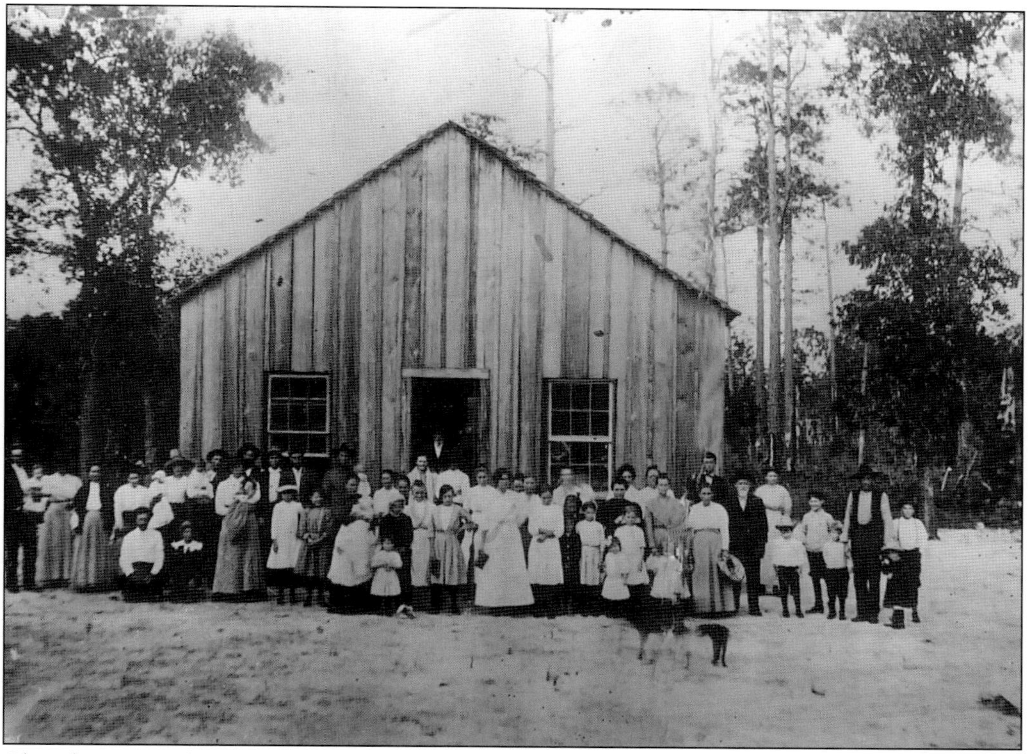

Church services for the Ivan community were held in the old Holiness Church, officiated by the "Lady Preacher of Ivan," who always dressed in white and carried a large black bible. She is seen here in 1911 in the center holding her bible. (Courtesy Johnnie McCallister.)

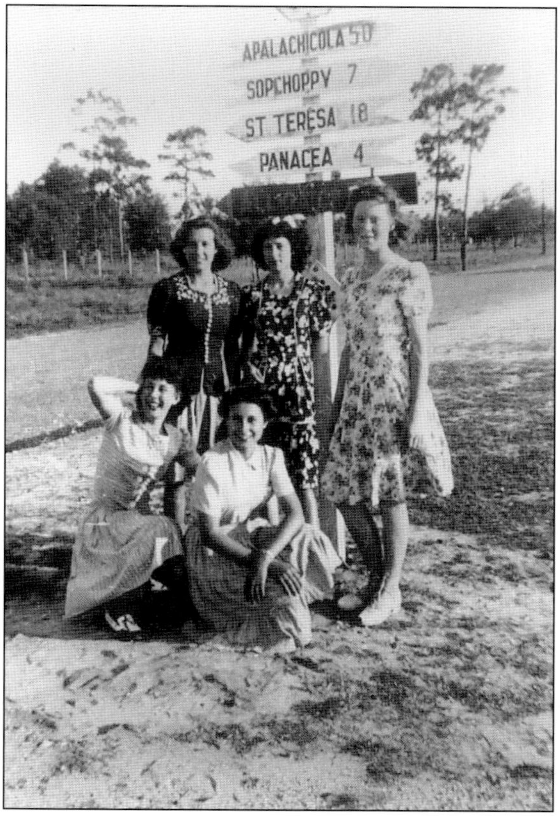

Friends pose by a road sign in Medart in the summer of 1943. They are, from left to right, (front row) Vonysea Sparkman Lee and Louise White Tucker; (back row) Wilhelmina White Morrison, Christine Locke Roberts, and Kathryn McLaughlin DeShirlia. (Courtesy Kathryn DeShirlia.)

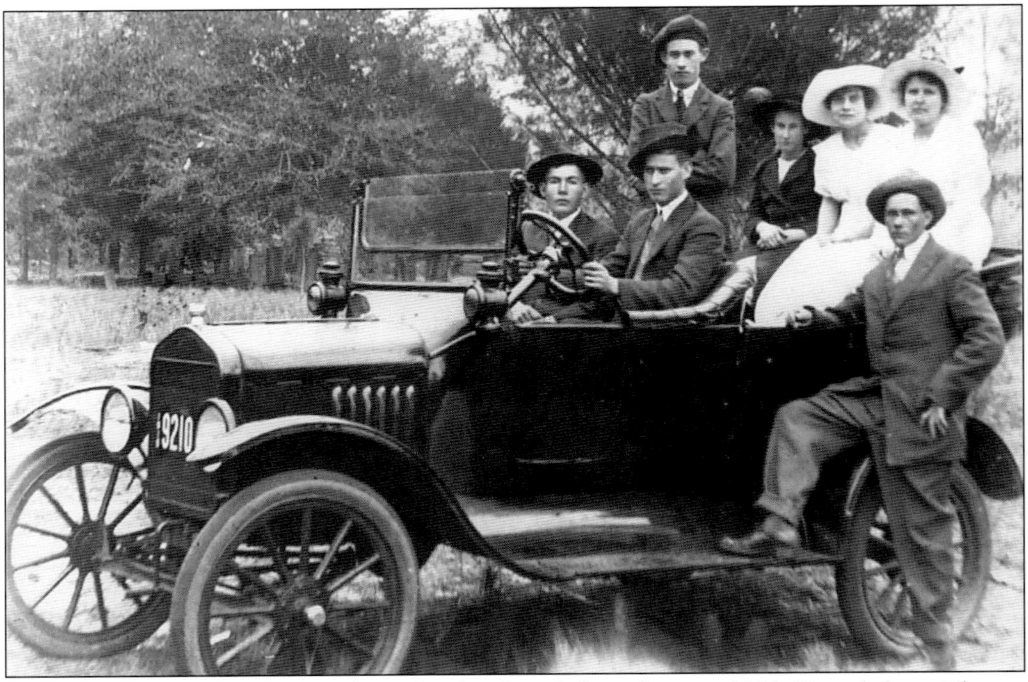

Tom Posey (1895–1970) of Medart takes his friends for a drive, c. 1921. From left to right are Austin Carraway, Tom Posey, Tom Harrell, ? Simmons, Maggie Simmons, Nolee Burge, and Carly Harrell. This photo was taken in the Sanborn community. (Courtesy Florida Photographic Collection.)

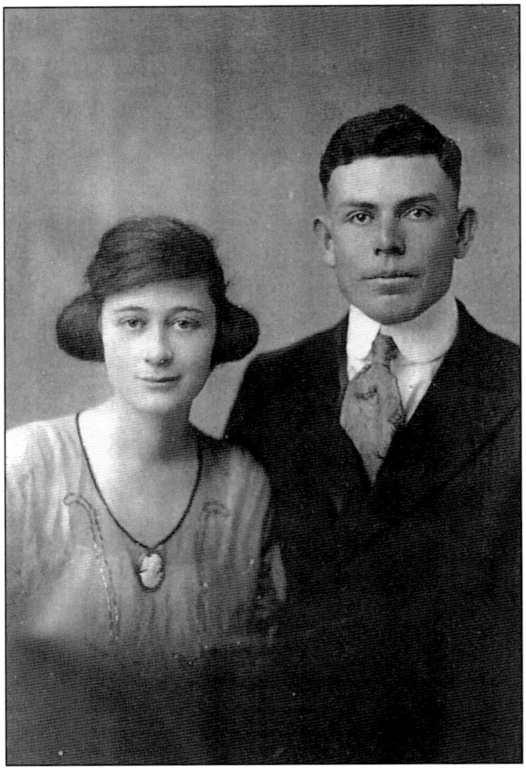

Jake Pigott (1894–1962) of Medart is pictured here with his new bride, Lucy Mosley Pigott (1896–1971), in 1921. A school teacher before serving in World War I, Mr. Pigott was elected county school superintendent in 1920, holding the position for 16 years. A columnist for the *Wakulla News* for many years he was voted Wakulla's Man of the Year in 1951. (Courtesy Earlene Pigott.)

Opened in 1920 by Bernard Pigott, Pigott's Store in Medart was originally a general merchandise store and later became a grocery store. Purchased from Jake Pigott in 1960, John Pigott Jr. re-opened the store as Pigott's Cash & Carry, a full-service hardware store and lumberyard. John's son Stephen Pigott continues to operate the business, which is now in its 81st year. (Courtesy Earlene Pigott.)

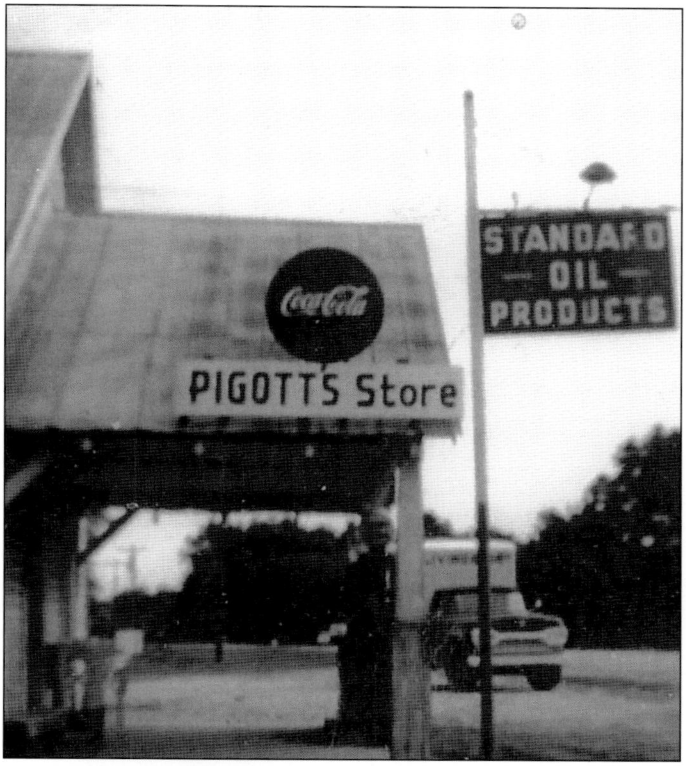

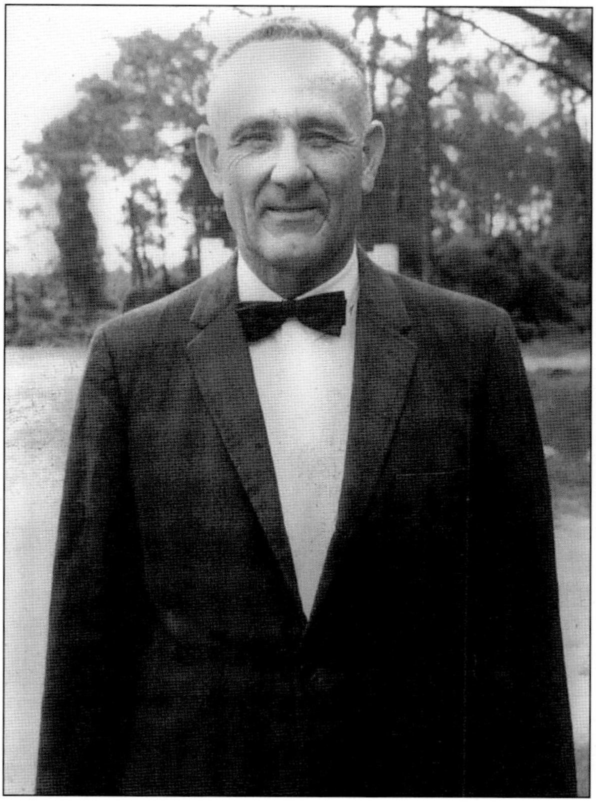

Ordained July 24, 1949, Emmett W. Whaley Sr., born in 1916 in Medart, is one of the county's most respected and active ministers. In addition to conducting more than 1,000 funeral services and over 50 revivals, Elder Whaley has pastored in six different primitive Baptist Churches throughout Wakulla. He and his wife, Celia Revell Whaley, are two of the county's most respected citizens. (Courtesy Celia Whaley.)

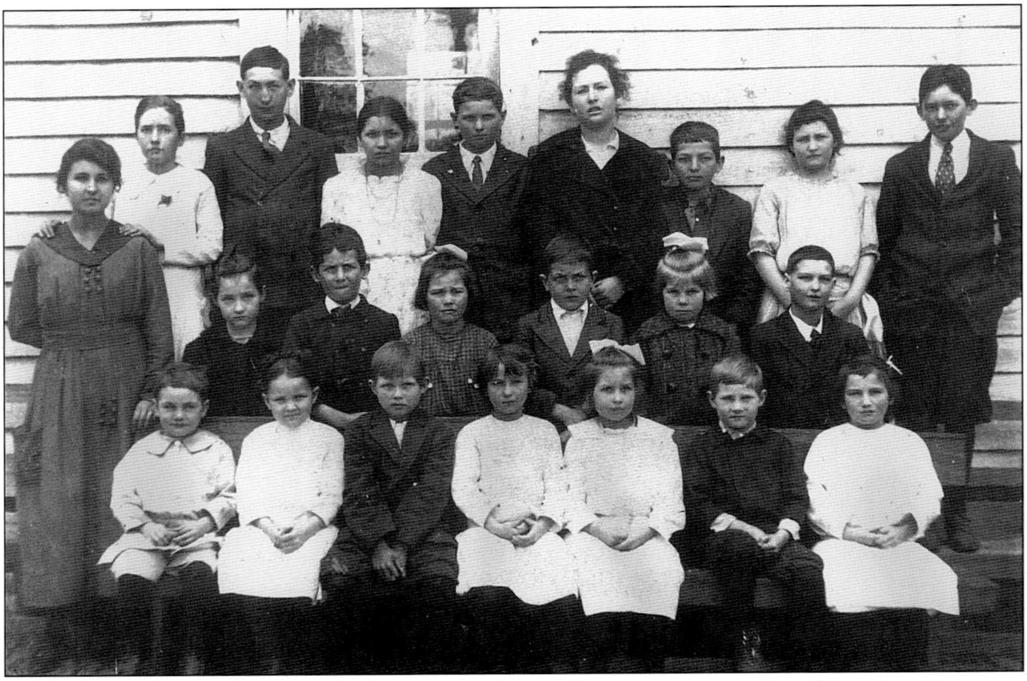

Children of the Revell, Barwick, Grimes, and Green families pose outside of the schoolhouse in the Old Park community in 1918. (Courtesy Celia Whaley.)

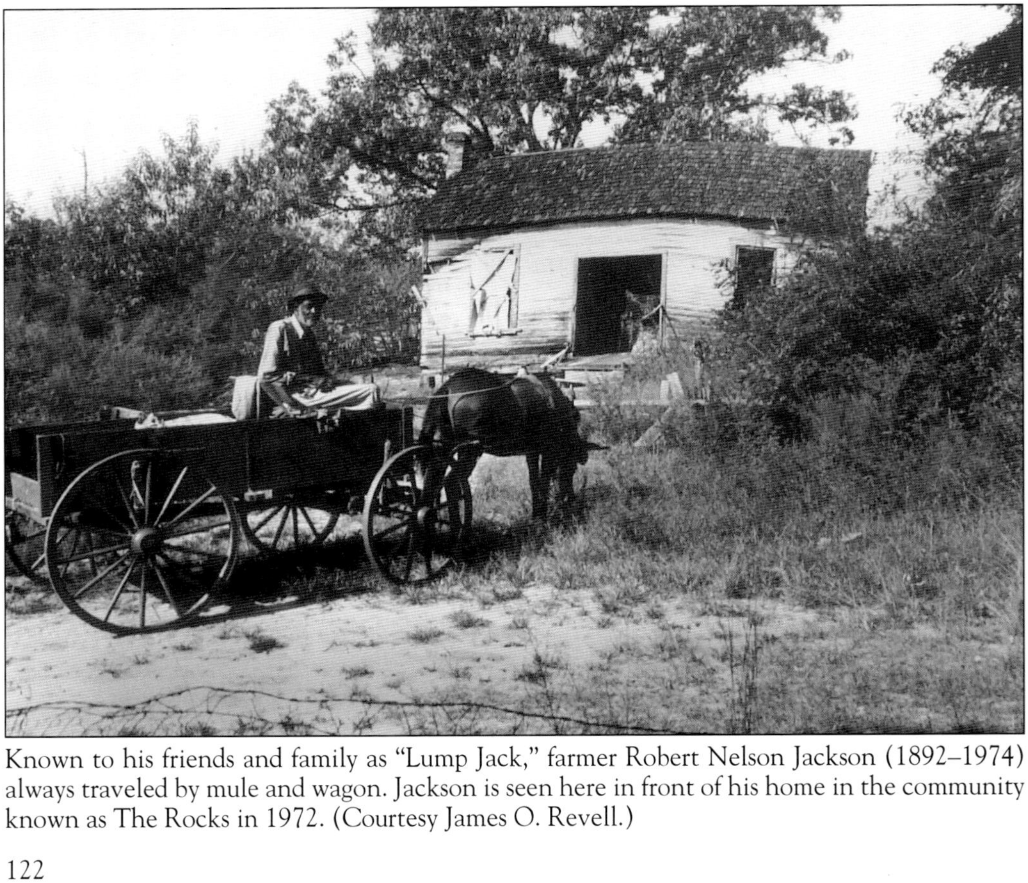

Known to his friends and family as "Lump Jack," farmer Robert Nelson Jackson (1892–1974) always traveled by mule and wagon. Jackson is seen here in front of his home in the community known as The Rocks in 1972. (Courtesy James O. Revell.)

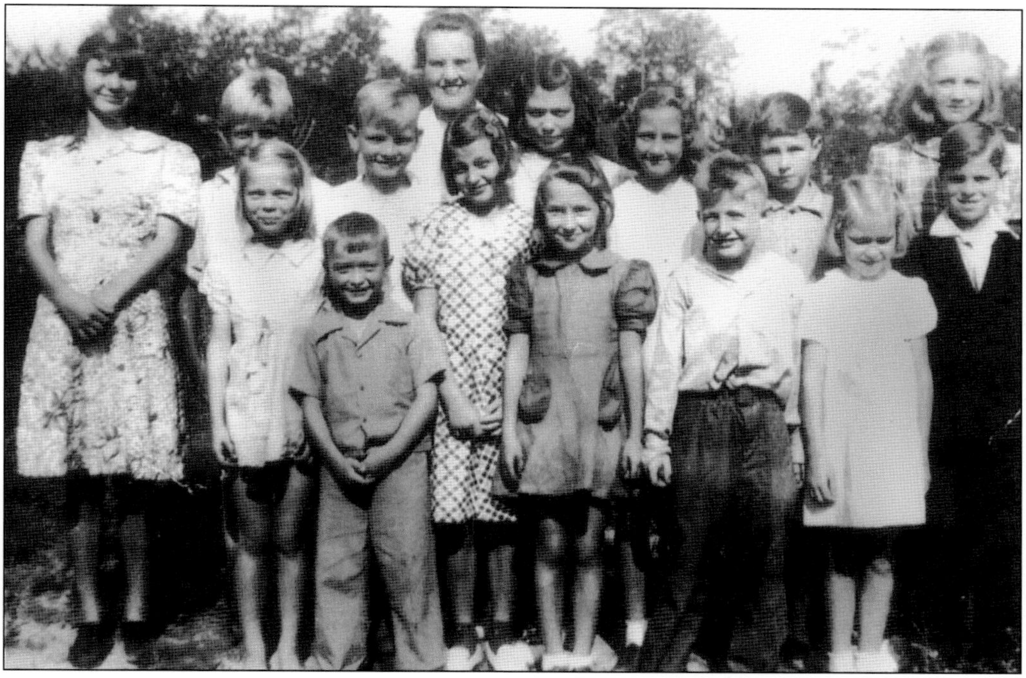

Seen here is the 1941–1942 class of the Smith Creek school. From left to right are (front row) Anna Jean Berry, Jimmy Langston, June Langston, Rochelle Aplin, P.L. Langston, Margie Chason, and Walton Langston; (back row) Evelyn Berry, Charles Berry, Lawrence Chason, Mrs. Agnes Cox, Janie Langston, Betty Mae Anderson, Roderick Tucker, and Elaine Langston. (Courtesy Ernie Cox.)

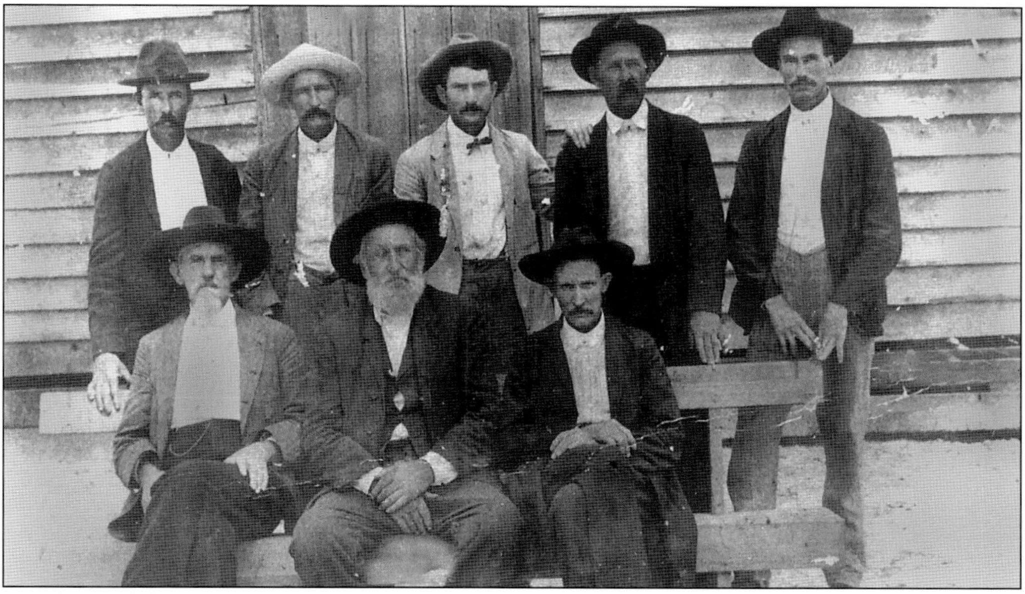

Members of the Primitive Baptist Association pose next to the old Beulah Church in Sink-of-the-Creek near Crawfordville, *c.* 1910. Members would serve in the county's churches on a rotation basis, preaching one weekend a month at each church. Pictured, from left to right, are (front row) R.J. Carraway, Stephen C. Revell, and J.M. Shepherd; (standing) S.C. Scarbourgh, G.H. Revell, W.D. Levy, Eli Russell, and F.J. Spears. (Courtesy Celia Whaley.)

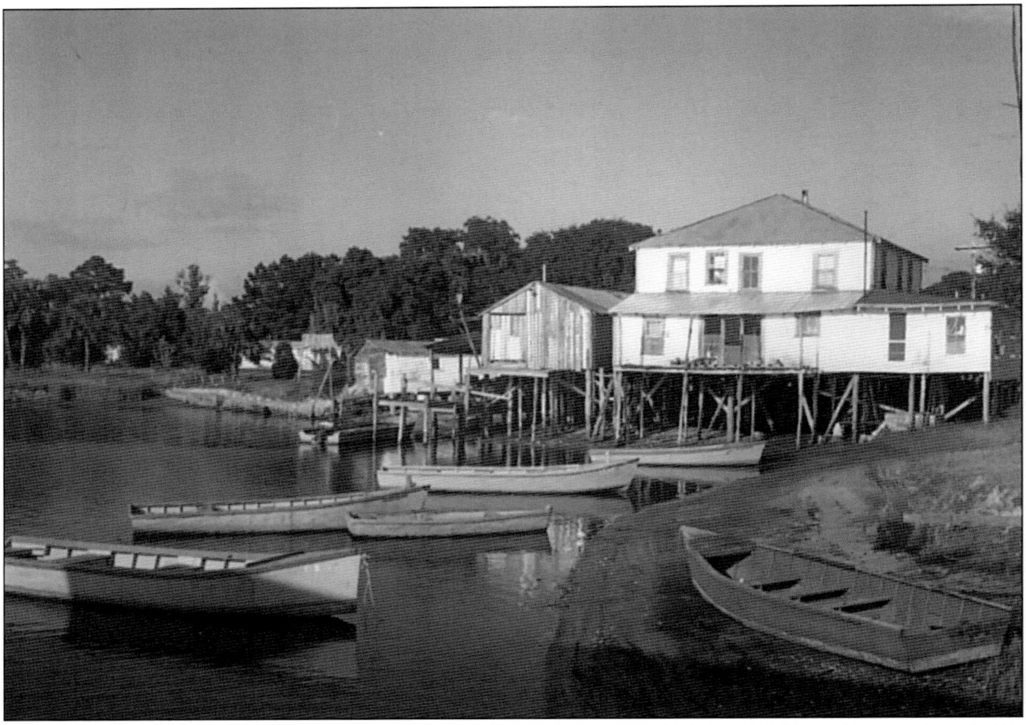

Having moved to Spring Creek in 1928, Willie Lee Spears (1909–1990) and his wife, Nellie Whaley Spears (1909–1976), worked in the seafood business for 50 years. Their large house, seen here on the right, has long been an area landmark. Spears and his son Lee also operated the West Goose Creek seine yard for many years, helping make the family name synonymous with Wakulla County seafood. (Courtesy Florida Photographic Collection.)

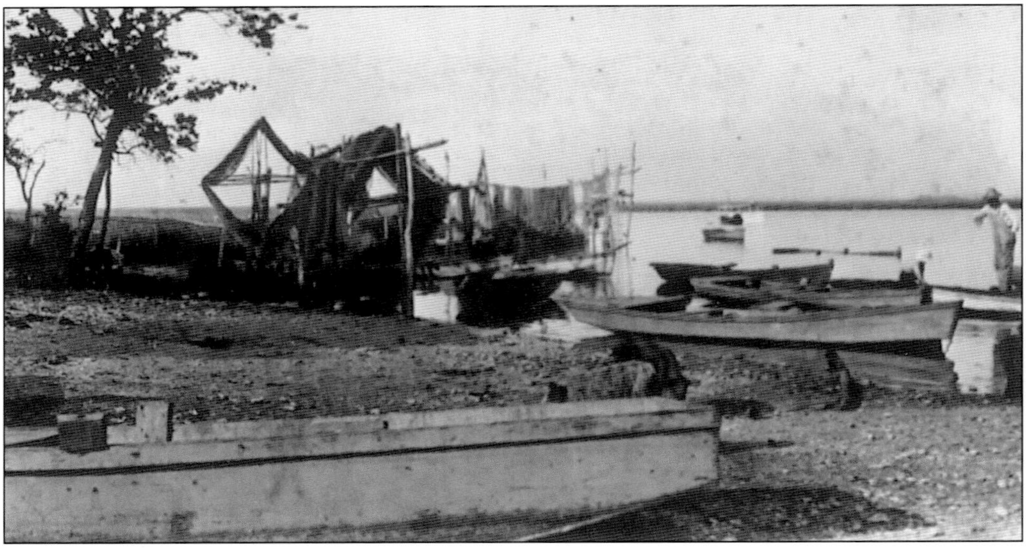

In this picture dated May 4, 1918, mullet nets can be seen drying on wooden racks at Spring Creek. Known primarily as one of the county's many fishing communities, Spring Creek is also home to one of the state's 27 first-magnitude springs. Wakulla has four such springs, named Kini Spring, River Sink Spring, Wakulla Spring, and the Spring Creek Spring, the largest number in the state. (Courtesy Florida Photographic Collection.)

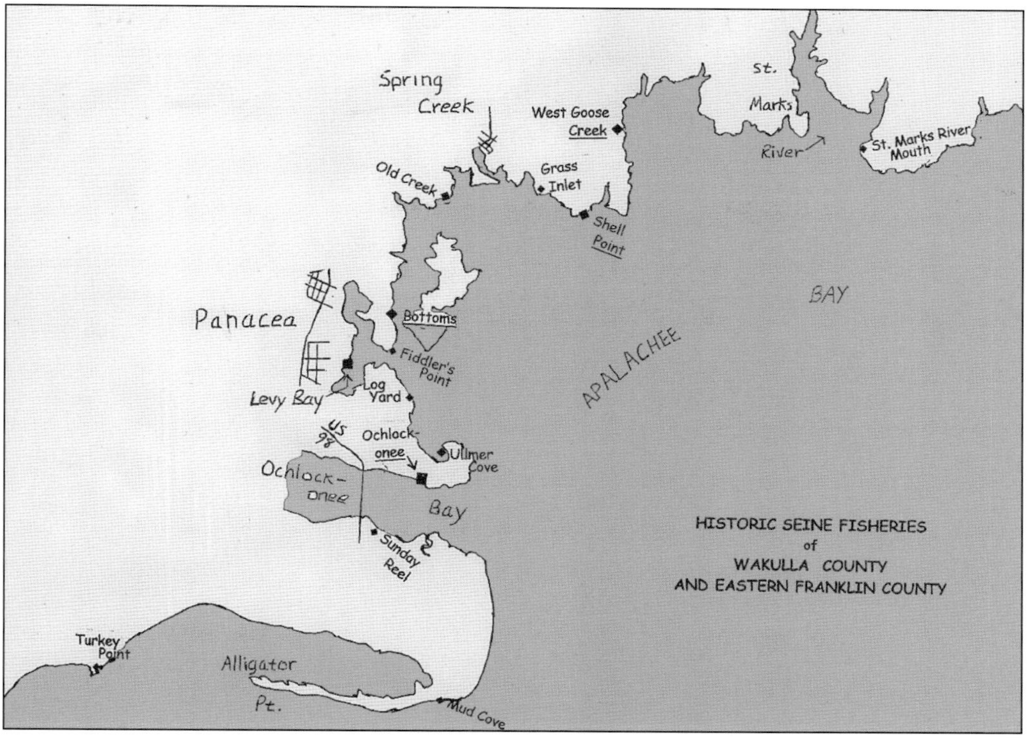

Commercial seining for black mullet has a long history in Wakulla County. This map shows the location of the various fisheries throughout the county that were operated each year during the mullet spawning or "run" season. (Courtesy David Roddenberry.)

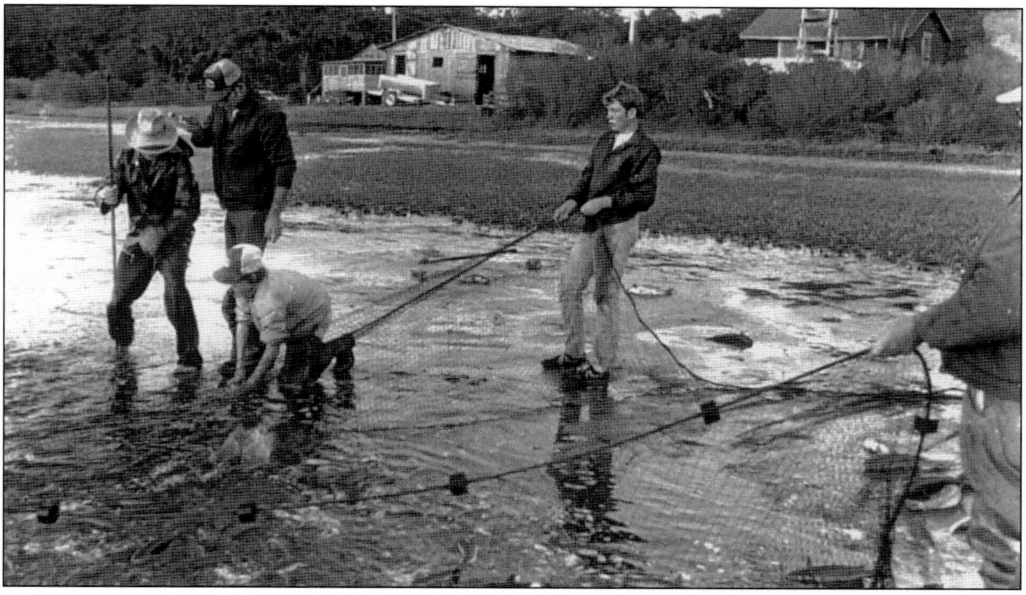

The most popular of the county's fisheries was the West Goose Creek seine yard. In operation before the Civil War and closed in 1987, the Goose Creek yard attracted customers from as far away as Georgia. In early days, farm families would travel to the yard by wagon, trading produce and cured meats for fresh mullet. In this photo from 1980, Lee Spears, at far left, and crew haul mullet ashore with a seine net. (Courtesy Maurice Raker.)

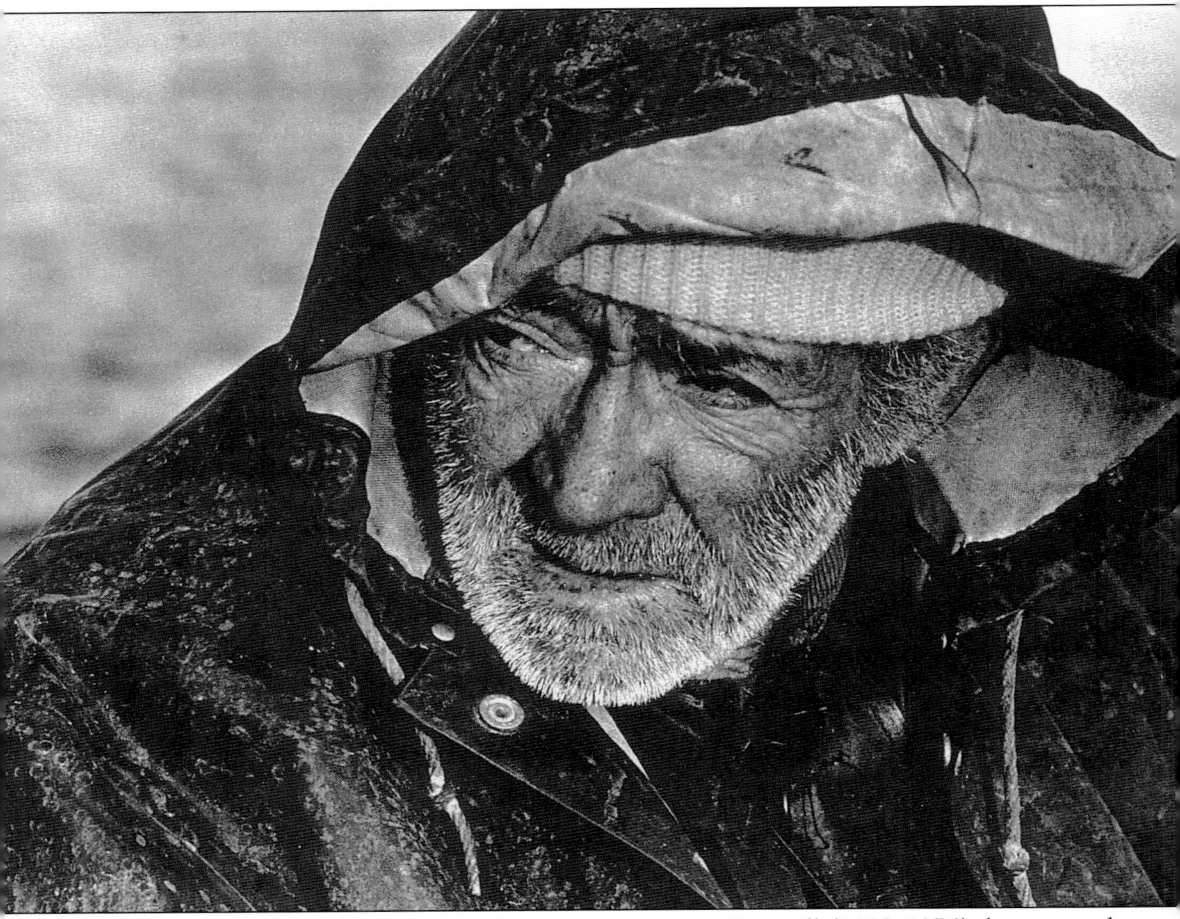

One of the county's most unique characters was Lamar Braswell (1903–1976), known as the Hermit of Shell Point. Braswell spent the last 35 years of his life aboard a small boat fishing and communing with nature along the coast. Moving briefly to Jacksonville in the 1940s to work in the shipyards, he grew tired of the crowds and hectic pace and walked back to Wakulla, never to leave again. While preferring a solitary existence, Braswell had countless friends who both loved and respected him. (Courtesy of George Kochaniec Jr.)

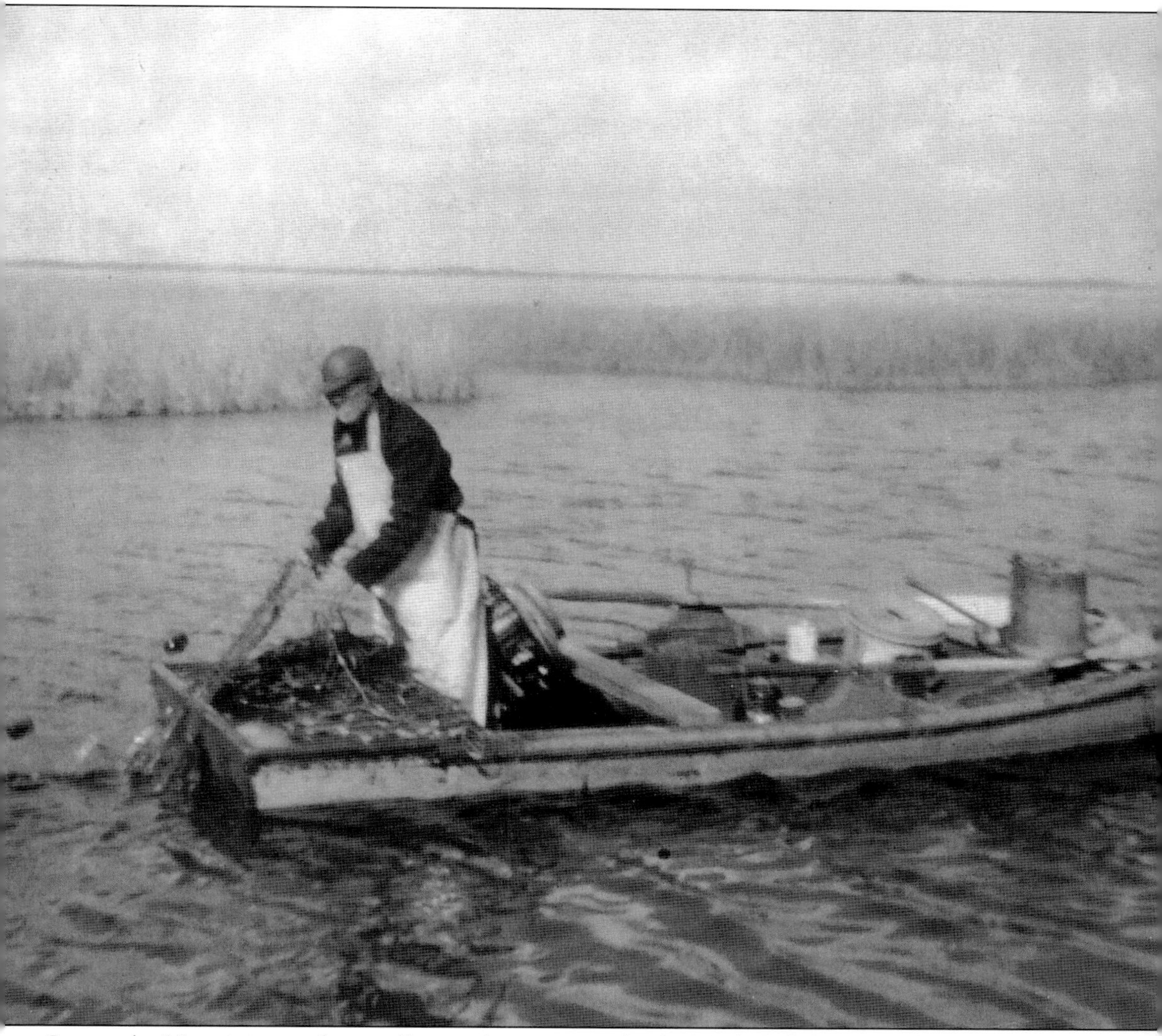

Lamar the Hermit is seen here collecting his net near the St. Marks lighthouse in the late 1950s in the small boat that contained all that he owned. Requiring only coffee, tobacco, and fish, he was for many years one of Wakulla County's most contented citizens. (Courtesy Peggy Page.)

SELECT BIBLIOGRAPHY

Gerrell Jr., Allen R. *The Civil War in and around St. Marks, Florida*. Privately published, 1991.

Gerrell, Pete. *The Illustrated History of the Naval Stores (Turpentine) Industry*. Crawfordville: SYP Publishing, 1998.

———. *Old Trees-The Illustrated History of Logging the Virgin Timber in the Virgin Timber in the Southeastern U.S.* Crawfordville: SYP Publishing, 2000.

Hann, John H. *Apalachee: The Land between the Rivers*. Gainesville: University Presses of Florida, 1988.

Morris, Allen. *Florida Place Names*. Sarasota: Pineapple Press, Inc., 1995.

Olds, Dorris L. *History and archaeology of Fort Saint Marks in Apalachee*. Master's thesis. Florida State University, 1962.

Paisley, Clifton L. *The Red Hills of Florida 1528–1865*. Tuscaloosa: University of Alabama Press, 1989.

Read, William A. *Florida Place-Names of Indian Origin*. Baton Rouge: Louisiana State University Press, 1934.

Revels, Tracy J. *Watery Eden: A History of Wakulla Springs*. Tallahassee: Sentry Press, 2002.

Shofner, Jerrell H. *History of Jefferson County*. Tallahassee: Sentry Press, 1976.

———. *Daniel Ladd: Merchant Prince of Frontier Florida*. Gainesville: University Presses of Florida, 1978.

Simpson, James C. A *Provisional Gazetteer of Florida Place-Names of Indian Derivation*. Tallahassee: Florida Geological Survey, 1956.